Why is Q Always Followed by U?

Word-perfect answers to the most-asked questions about language

Michael Quinion

422

PARTICULAR
BOOKS
an imprint of
PENGUIN BOOKS

PARTICULAR BOOKS
Published by the Penguin Group
Penguin Books Ltd, 80 Strand, London WC2R 0RL, England
Penguin Group (USA) Inc., 375 Hudson Street, New York, New York 10014, USA
Penguin Group (Canada), 90 Eglinton Avenue East, Suite 700, Toronto, Ontario, Canada M4P 2Y3
(a division of Pearson Penguin Canada Inc.)
Penguin Ireland, 25 St Stephen's Green, Dublin 2, Ireland (a division of Penguin Books Ltd)
Penguin Group (Australia), 250 Camberwell Road, Camberwell, Victoria 3124, Australia
(a division of Pearson Australia Group Pty Ltd)
Penguin Books India Pvt Ltd, 11 Community Centre, Panchsheel Park, New Delhi – 110 017, India
Penguin Group (NZ), 67 Apollo Drive, Rosedale, North Shore 0632, New Zealand
(a division of Pearson New Zealand Ltd)
Penguin Books (South Africa) (Pty) Ltd, 24 Sturdee Avenue, Rosebank, Johannesburg 2196, South Africa

Penguin Books Ltd, Registered Offices: 80 Strand, London WC2R 0RL, England
www.penguin.com
First published 2009
1

Copyright © Michael Quinion, 2009

Set in Swift and TheSans
Designed and typeset by Richard Marston
Printed in Great Britain by Clays Ltd, St Ives plc

A CIP catalogue record for this book is available from the British Library

ISBN: 978-1-846-14184-3

Contents

Introduction   vii
Acknowledgements   x

Why is Q Always Followed by U?   1

Introduction

There's no better way of testing your knowledge of any subject than to have people ask you questions about it. There's also no better way of expanding your knowledge than to seek out the answers to such queries.

Over the past ten years, people from all around the world, not all of them by any means with English as a first language, have been asking me about the meaning and history of words in the Questions and Answers section of my online *World Wide Words* newsletter and website (*http://www.worldwidewords.org*). I've been able to answer about 900 of them so far. This book contains revised, corrected, expanded and updated versions of the most popular couple of hundred.

Out of an extraordinarily mixed bag of questions about slang, grammar, vocabulary, word histories and regional usage, I've chosen a selection that mainly refer to words and phrases that you're likely to recognize, no matter which variety of English you're comfortable with. However, I've also included some pieces about quirky phrases (such as *up in Annie's room, behind the clock*) that may no longer be living expressions, or even be recognized by anybody who hasn't been drawing their pension for a while, but which I hope will intrigue you.

Etymology is an uncertain science and we often have to say 'we don't know' to a question about word origins. But we are at a time of huge advances in the resources available to researchers. Searchable digital archives of newspapers and books have transformed the field in the past decade or so, with discoveries being reported almost every week. Not only did many of the entries in this book have to be updated following their first appearance in the *World Wide Words* newsletter as a result of new information, but several even had to be revised during its compilation because researchers had found fresh material that altered our understanding of the provenance of terms. New sources of information are being created all the time, with the British Library newspaper archive becoming available as this book began to be compiled and the announcement of a new wave of newspaper digitization by Google as it was completed.

There was a BBC radio series about archaeology many years ago called *The Changing Past*, a clever title that pointed up the impact of new findings on our understanding of prehistory. The point is just as relevant to etymology and it is a constant delight not only to investigate the stories behind words and phrases and put them within their social and cultural milieu, but also – as a person who has been intrigued with and fascinated by English since a child – to be able at times to provide fresh insight into the way the language has evolved.

One question that comes up regularly – but one that I've not previously answered in any detail – is 'How did you get involved in writing about language?' It's an odd story. Unlike an American author of a previous generation, keen to trumpet his credentials as a man of the people with wide experience of life, I cannot claim to have been a cowboy, roustabout, short-order cook, truck driver or gravedigger. On the other hand, my own progress from youthful budding scientist to semi-doddery old lexicographer must look to an outsider to be at least as random. It hasn't been so much a career, more a series of semi-serendipitous encounters, in which I've leaped from one interesting occupation to another, grabbing opportunities as they drifted past. My first job after leaving university with a degree in science was as a BBC radio studio manager and, later, a radio producer. Since then – among other activities – I've been a freelance creator of

audio-visual programmes for heritage centres, the first curator of
the Museum of Cider in Hereford, a consultant in the heritage-
tourism field and a writer of shareware computer applications.

Getting into lexicography was as coincidental as the rest. I'd
retired from the consultancy in 1991 as the result of a severe
illness. Seeking to cheer myself up, and because of my lifelong
interest in the English language, I bought one of the first copies
of the then recently issued CD-ROM version of the second
edition of the *Oxford English Dictionary*. On consulting it, I realized
that many entries needed updating and that a lot of newer words
were missing (for example, it didn't even have *heritage interpreta-
tion*, the title of my own profession for much of the previous two
decades). So I started sending in examples of new words to the
editors. After a while, one of the senior staff asked me to come
to Oxford. On his desk was the pile of file cards that contained
my recent submissions. 'You do know, Michael,' he queried, with
a slight scholarly hesitation at mentioning the subject, 'that we
pay people to do this?' 'Is that so?' I replied. 'Then you can pay
me for this lot.' And he did. In the sixteen years since, I've sent
in about 160,000 citations to the *OED*, doing my bit to help in the
vast ongoing task of completely revising the whole dictionary.

Starting *World Wide Words* was as much a matter of happen-
stance as the rest. Our son, then 17, had written a splendid
universal spelling checker for Windows and had set up a website
to sell it through. This was in 1996. There was lots of spare space
on the server and it seemed a pity not to make use of it. I started
to write pieces about language and post them online, in the
process becoming a blogger before anybody knew the term.
A newsletter followed and it all just snowballed from there. This
book is one of the results.

I hope you have as much pleasure in reading it as I have had in
writing it.

Acknowledgements

My thanks to everybody who has tested my mettle by asking questions; my apologies to the many hundreds in the past decade who have asked but not been answered, either because there just aren't enough hours in the day or, sadly, because I can't find anything useful to say.

Among research sources, primary acknowledgement must be made to the editors of the *Oxford English Dictionary* – that incomparable repository of knowledge about the way that the English language has evolved over 1,500 years. Though I've contributed to it, my debt to it is far greater than any help of mine can repay. Through a splendid British scheme, my local library gives me free access to the online *Oxford Dictionary of National Biography* to check information about historical figures. Much ill-informed criticism is made of the online world, but for me it has long since proved a wondrous cornucopia of specialist knowledge unrivalled in human history; in particular, dozens of websites run by enthusiastic and knowledgeable organizations and individuals have provided information on many subjects relating to this book.

No doubt, as many readers have down the years, you will be wondering how I found the eclectic mixture of illustrative quotations in this book, some of which have even improved our state of knowledge of the history of words and phrases. I subscribe to several current and historical online newspaper archives and I've made extensive use of free resources, such as those of the Internet Archive, Wikipedia, Making of America, Old Bailey trial transcripts, the British Library Online Newspaper Archive, the Google newspaper archive and Google Books, as well as the archives of many individual newspapers. An important resource has been the digitized collection of books, currently more than 27,000 and increasing every week, that have been prepared by the volunteers of Project Gutenberg, which gives access to much of the standard canon of English literature. The Shakespearean quotations are as they appear in the *RSC Shakespeare*. Bibliographical details have been checked against the online catalogues of the British Library, the Library of Congress and the Australian National Library.

Special thanks go to my commissioning editor at Penguin, Georgina Laycock, an enthusiastic supporter of this work while remaining an objective critic of its execution, to copy editor Lindsay Murray, project editor Ruth Stimson and to Helen Conford; to John Smith, for supplying me with a copy of his article, 'Foxes' Weddings', from which I have borrowed in answering the question about *monkey's wedding*; to Julane Marx of Los Angeles, who has for many years cheerfully added to her full-time job and looking after a family the weekly chore of checking my *World Wide Words* newsletters, particularly for errors concerning American life, and who has read and commented on the text; to the members of the American Dialect Society, whose discussions and investigations into the language of the US have been of considerable help; to the hundreds of knowledgeable readers of the *World Wide Words* news- letter and website – too many to name – who down the years have put me straight when my attempts at explaining some specialist point or arcane matter have gone astray; and of course to my wife, who has coped with a husband forever distracted while he mentally works out the best way to answer some tricky query.

Michael Quinion
Thornbury, South Gloucestershire.
November 2008.

Ahoy!

Q. I have heard that *ahoy* derives from a Czech greeting, apparently popularized by sailors docking in English-speaking ports – from the Czech *ahoj*, meaning 'hello'. Would you like to comment?

A. Wonderful! Another strange etymological story to add to my collection. Your informant, you see, has the matter exactly backwards.

Ahoj, said the same way as *ahoy*, is indeed used informally in Czech, and more widely still, I'm told, in Slovak. Jan Čulík, Senior Lecturer in Czech Studies at the University of Glasgow, tells me that Czech *ahoj* is a modern introduction from English and was borrowed from the sailor's hail, despite the indisputable fact that the Czech Republic is landlocked (the Swiss have a navy, a very small one, but the Czechs don't). A Czech etymological dictionary of 2001 says that it was introduced by hikers, boy scouts, sportsmen and young people; it came into wide use in the 1930s when hiking and scouting became generally widespread, though there are examples on record from as far back as the 1880s, when it was used, for example, as a word of command for the horses pulling sleighs.

Ahoy in English goes back a long way:

> **While he was thus occupied, a voice, still more uncouth than the former, bawled aloud, 'Ho! the house, a-hoy!'**
>
> *The Adventures of Peregrine Pickle*, by Tobias Smollett, 1751. The idea of a person hailing a house as though it were a ship creates a comic image.

It's based on *hoy*, an even older cry that dates from medieval times, a formalized spelling of a natural or inarticulate cry. William Langland was the first person known to have used it, in his poem *Piers Plowman* in the fourteenth century. Down the years it was used when driving pigs or cattle, or when you wanted to attract a person's attention. Its successor is today's uncouth shout of *oy!* In particular – and this is where the maritime connection really does appear – sailors used *hoy!* when hailing another ship. *Ahoy* was a development of this that added force to the cry:

> **I was wakened – indeed, we were all wakened, for I could see even the sentinel shake himself together from where he had fallen against the door-post – by a clear, hearty voice hailing us from the margin of the wood: 'Block house, ahoy!' it cried. 'Here's the doctor.'**
>
> *Treasure Island*, by Robert Louis Stevenson, 1883.

Incidentally, Alexander Graham Bell suggested *ahoy* as the way to answer his new telephone, and operators at his first exchange did just that. This seemed too peremptory for others and *hello* replaced it, a word of the early nineteenth century that was based on shouts such as the hunting-field cry *hollo!*, an exclamation that can be traced back at least as far as Shakespeare's use of it in *Titus Andronicus*.

All-singing, all-dancing

Q. Where does the expression *all-singing, all-dancing* come from? I see it most often applied to some computer wizardry that seems to do everything. I'd guess it's from the theatre – is that right?

A. Though a version was used for stage shows, the phrase itself is from the early days of film.

These days you do usually find that it means something equipped with lots of impressive features or which seems to offer everything you could possibly want, and more, though the superlative can be tinged with sarcasm.

> **Our confidence in James Murdoch's ability to turn BSkyB into an all-singing, all-dancing multi-media stock, offering broadband and telephony alongside pay TV, proved well founded.**
> *Independent*, 1 January 2008.

> **An 'all-singing, all-dancing crimefighting tool' has been revealed with hopes it will be one of the most comprehensive community safety websites in the country.**
> *East Anglian Daily Times*, 5 April 2007.

Variations on the phrase appeared in the days of vaudeville in the US. As an example, the Robison Park Theatre in Fort Wayne, Indiana, advertised several acts around 1907 with the phrase *talking, singing and dancing*. Early attempts at adding sound to film used the same phrase:

> **The talking, singing and dancing pictures, the latest development in the moving picture art, as presented by the Humanovo company, drew another large crowd to the Racine theater last night.**
> *The Racine Daily Journal*, Wisconsin, 2 September 1908. Pay no attention to that man behind the curtain, because he's an actor talking and singing to lip-sync the silent film.

However, the phrase as we know it had to wait for the coming of the version of the talkies that became standard. Several films were promoted as state-of-the-art aural experiences in 1929. The most significant was *Broadway Melody*, famously the first film musical, for which a version of this tagline was used. But it was beaten in the etymological stakes by the slightly earlier *Close Harmony*, advertised in March and April 1929 under several versions of the tagline as *All talking-singing-dancing* and *100% all-talking all-singing*.

The canonical form *all-singing, all-dancing* came along later in the same year. My first sighting is this:

> **'The Gold-Diggers of Broadway.' Warners' all-color, all-singing, all-dancing hit.**
>
> *Syracuse Herald*, 21 October 1929. This film, now almost entirely lost, was only the second *talkie* (as sound films were then known) to have been photographed in Technicolor. It was a lively comedy, with a set of popular songs, including 'Tiptoe Through the Tulips' (best known to most people from Tiny Tim's falsetto version of the 1960s), and lots of lovely showgirls.

The phrase became famous enough, largely through the pressure of early movie promotion, that it entered the language. Oddly perhaps, in view of its country of origin, the expression appears more often in British newspapers than American these days. Perhaps we haven't tired of it yet.

Argy-bargy

Q. A question arose recently during a discussion here in California about the origin of the expression *argy-bargy* (also written *argey-bargey*), meaning a relatively amicable, if somewhat heated, argument. Any ideas?

A. I'm not so sure the term refers to an amicable argument: in my experience (as a spectator, you will understand) *argy-bargies* are often not only heated arguments but also rather bad-tempered ones, amounting to a spat or minor quarrel. But then, the term is mainly a British or Commonwealth one, not that well known in the US, and easily misunderstood out of context.

Argy-bargy was a late nineteenth-century modification of

a Scots phrase, which appeared early in the same century in the form *argle-bargle*. The first part of this older version was a modification of *argue*. The second parts of the two forms, *bargle* and *bargy*, never had any independent existence – they are no more than nonsense rhyming repetitions of the first elements.

An example in the old spelling from later in the century:

Last night ye haggled and argle-bargled like an apple-wife.

Kidnapped, by Robert Louis Stevenson, 1886. An *apple-wife* was a seller of apples from a stall, the female equivalent of a costermonger (who, historically and etymologically, also sold apples, an ancient large ribbed variety called a *costard*). By repute apple-wives were just as argumentative and foul-tongued as their male counterparts.

An early example of the modern form, also as a verb:

Ten minutes at the least did she stand at the door argy-bargying with that man.

Margaret Ogilvy, by J. M. Barrie, 1896. This autobiographical novel, by an author who is most famous for his play *Peter Pan*, takes its title from the maiden name of his mother; it deals with his childhood memories of the death in a skating accident of his 13-year-old brother David in 1867.

Linguists refer to such doublets as *reduplication*. The second part isn't always invented, but can be a real word if one is available that fits in meaning and form. English is fond of the trick and the language is full of such pairs. Some are conventional rhymes (*super-duper*, *hoity-toity*, *namby-pamby*, *mumbo-jumbo*) while others are pairs that modify an internal vowel (*dilly-dally*, *shilly-shally*, *wishy-washy*, *zig-zag*).

Aunt Sally

Q. An obituary of Nathan Pusey, a president of Harvard, contains the following sentence: 'As education is an ever-interesting Aunt Sally, inevitably there are critics of the academic art of money-squeezing.' What does the phrase *Aunt Sally* mean and what is its derivation?

A. An Aunt Sally in its popular sense today is a person or thing that's been set up as an easy target for criticism, abuse or blame, in political circles often to deflect attention from the real issues and waste opponents' time.

> Iraq was set up by the neocons as an Aunt Sally, and its weapons of mass destruction were as much a figment of the imaginations of Messrs Bush and Cheney as they were a figment of Saddam Hussein's.
>
> *New Statesman*, 17 January 2008.

The original Aunt Sally was a game, popular in Britain under that name from the middle of the nineteenth century at fairgrounds and racetracks.

> London, Saturday, March 31st, 1866. Yesterday was Good Friday, which in England is a close holiday. The streets are full, the omnibuses crowded; there are railway excursions, the Crystal Palace is thronged – forty or fifty thousand were there yesterday – and multitudes gather in the parks and play kiss in the ring or Old Aunt Sally. Aunt Sally is a big black doll on a stick, with a pipe in her mouth, and an orange or some toy for a prize, which you win by hitting her with a stick if you are lucky.
>
> *The New York Times*, 16 April 1866. The delay in printing the correspondent's report was because it had to be sent by steamship across the Atlantic; the first fully working cable across the ocean was opened that year but it would have been too expensive for anything except hot news. The writer might have added that the objective was to knock the pipe out of Aunt Sally's

mouth. *Close holiday* is an old term for a public holiday on which businesses *close*; the modern British term *bank holiday* didn't appear in the language until 1871.

From the fairground sense the term moved on, as the result of a moderately obvious process of thought, to become our modern figurative expression. The game itself is still played under that name in pubs in some southern counties of England, notably Oxfordshire, where the Oxford & District Aunt Sally Association was founded before the Second World War. However, the game today instead uses a stubby white skittle, called a dolly, perhaps as the result of greater racial sensitivity.

The *aunt* part of the name may refer to an old black woman, a term employed both by blacks and whites in the USA from the eighteenth century onwards but also known in London; *aunt* could also be applied familiarly to any elderly woman.

The direct influence, according to J. Redding Ware's *Passing English of the Victorian Era* of 1909, may have been an 1820s black-face doll that derived from a low-life character named Black Sal who had been created by Pierce Egan in his series *Life In London* of 1821–8. Ware says that it was probably adopted 'owing to the popularity of that work, precisely as in a later generation many of Dickens's characters were associated with trade advertisements. Very significant of Pierce Egan's popularity, which from 1820 to 1840 was as great as that of Dickens, whose fame threw Egan into obscurity.'

Bail out

Q. How about a discussion of the phrase *bail out*, meaning to escape from some difficult situation? I'm guessing it's spelled that way, rather than *bale out*, but I don't know why. I wonder if it was originally used for leaving an aircraft before landing, or if there is some other origin?

A. It does look from the evidence that the figurative sense – to leave hurriedly, escape an unpleasant situation or abandon a burdensome responsibility – does come from the idea of leaving an aircraft by parachute in an emergency. Americans are pretty certain how to spell it, but Brits much less so.

The early evidence is from the US, in which the term was always spelled *bail*:

> **One or two [parachutists] have said they found the descent exhilarating. However, the average pilot who has to 'bail out' hurriedly from a crippled or burning plane never is able to recall any such sensation.**
>
> *Oakland Tribune*, California, 1 September 1929.

> **He successfully bailed out of an airplane at an elevation of 1,500 feet.**
>
> *The New York Times*, 11 April 1932.

There's little doubt from this early evidence that aviators were thinking that escaping from an aircraft in danger was like bailing water out of a boat, the immediate image being that of throwing the water over the side. Eric Partridge, in *A Dictionary of Forces' Slang*, published in 1948, gave this as the origin. However, seriously muddying the waters, he spelled it *bale*.

The *Oxford English Dictionary* has changed its view on the definitive form. In its Second Edition of 1989 it argued it should be *bale out*, suggesting people may have been influenced in spelling it that way by the image of an escaping airman being like a bale or bundle thrown through the aircraft door. In a recently revised entry online, it goes for *bail out* instead.

The current position is that American English almost always uses *bail out*. British English seems to be divided about 50:50 between that and *bale out*, and it's easy to find examples of *baled out* in the British press:

> **This poor lad had baled out of his plane and was found embedded in the soil, his hand clutching his radio lead instead of the ripcord.**
>
> *Daily Telegraph*, 16 May 2008.

Does the disagreement over the spelling matter? Probably not a lot, since the meaning is always clear from context.

Balls-up

Q. Despite our politically correct times, people seem to casually use the most indecorous expressions every day without considering their effects on those around them. Take *balls-up*, for example. I've assumed it's low slang but, since it is common, perhaps I'm wrong. Where does it in fact come from?

A. Though now widely known in the English-speaking world, this is in origin a British slang term for a bungled or badly carried out task or action, a messed-up or confused situation, or a complete foul-up. It came into the language from First World War services' slang:

> **'What do you make of it, sergeant?' he asked. 'I don' know what to make of it. What the bloody hell do you make of it, yourself?**

After all, that's what matters. I suppose we'll come through all right; we've done it before, so we can do it again. Anyway, it can't be more of a bloody balls-up than some o' the other shows 'ave been.'

The Middle Parts of Fortune, by Frederic Manning, 1929. The novel is set on the Western Front in France during the battles of the Somme in the First World War, which Manning – an Australian – experienced during his service with the King's Shropshire Light Infantry. The text as he wrote it could not be published in his lifetime because of the authentic bad language it contained. *Show* here is services slang for a military engagement, battle or raid.

The obvious implication, as you suggest, is of a testicular association, which is why it is regarded as coarse or low slang, though quite how it might have come about is unclear. As soon as one begins to look into matters more deeply, that origin becomes more unlikely still.

The verbal construction, *ball up* – in much the same sense as in British slang, though not regarded as coarse – turns out to have a long history in the US. Jonathan Lighter has recorded examples in the *Historical Dictionary of American Slang* from the middle of the nineteenth century. The 1856 revised edition of Benjamin Hall's *A Collection of College Words and Customs* records that *ball up* meant to fail a recitation or examination. From no later than the 1880s it implied becoming mixed up or confused in some way. There's a reference to the noun *ball-up* in the US publication *Dialect Notes* in 1900, meaning a confused or muddled situation. It looks highly plausible that *balls-up*, although a British expression, derives from this older American one, perhaps through contact between US and British servicemen in the First World War.

Having said all that, there's no obvious clue from the examples where it might come from. Indeed, Professor Lighter remarks at the beginning of the entry that the term's 'semantic development is obscure', which is academic-speak for 'I haven't a clue, either'. The ball might be of string or yarn that has become snarled up, or perhaps it refers to crumpling a piece of paper into a ball, or conceivably it comes from some incident in college sports. Sylva Clapin, in his *New Dictionary of Americanisms* of 1902, suggested an origin in the *balling up* of a horse in soft, new fallen snow, when a snowball forms within each shoe and stops the horse moving.

You can take your pick from these – there's no more evidence for one than another.

Bells and whistles

Q. For my job – I'm a translator, based in France – I have to read American magazines concerning consumer electronics, home systems, burglar alarms, etc. I very often come across the expression *bells and whistles*, which seems to relate to equipment, accessories or features that are offered to the customer as plusses but are not really indispensable. Is that right? And where does that funny phrase come from?

A. You're right about the meaning, which usually refers to non-essential features added to a piece of technical equipment or a computer program to make it superficially more attractive without enhancing its main function. It has now spread well beyond its American homeland and is familiar, I'd guess, to most English speakers.

> **All in all, the W890i is a standard mobile phone that is worth considering if you are looking for one without bells and whistles.**
>
> *Malaysia Star*, 5 June 2008.

It has widened beyond technical contexts:

> **To get the most out of your super [fund] requires systematic planning to take full advantage of the tax-minimisation opportunities. The more bells and whistles your fund offers the better off you can be.**
>
> *The Age*, Melbourne, 19 June 2005.

The phrase is relatively modern. One of its earlier appearances was in an article in the US magazine *Atlantic* in October 1982, which said it was 'Pentagon slang for extravagant frills'. But I've found that the term is recorded from a couple of decades earlier:

> **A beautiful tri-level in the woods situated on quiet street. This home has many of the plus features: 3 bedrooms, den, family room, 2 baths, 1st floor laundry, patio doors, kitchen with all the bells and whistles, fallout shelter plus many other features.**
>
> A classified advertisement in the *Wisconsin State Journal*, 27 April 1963.

Where it comes from is still a matter of debate. As a literal phrase, it has been around since at least the middle of the nineteenth century, in reference to the noisemakers on streetcars, railway locomotives and steamships. Before modern electronics, there were really only two ways to make a loud warning noise: you either rang a bell or tooted a whistle. US railroad locomotives had both:

> **You look up at an angle of sixty degrees and see sweeping along the edge of a precipice, two-thirds up the rocky height, a train of red-and-yellow railway-cars, drawn by two wood-burning engines, the sound of whose bells and whistles seems like the small diversions of very little children, so diminished are they by the distance.**
>
> *A Day At Dutch Flat*, by Albert F. Webster, in *Appleton's Journal of Literature, Science and Art*, New York, October 1876. Dutch Flat is north-east of Sacramento in Placer County, California. It's a small community these days, but at the time it was a big mining camp for workers extracting gold from one of the richest deposits in the state. The town was actually founded by

I'm told the bells and whistles on locomotives were used for different signalling purposes, so that both were considered necessary, though not strictly essential, parts of its equipment. It may be that the coiners of the modern figurative phrase had this in mind. Indeed, it has been said that the term arose from American model railway societies – to have a layout in which the engines had all their bells and whistles meant that it was fully equipped down to the smallest detail, and thus one up on enthusiasts who didn't have them.

However, it's much more probable the slang sense of the term comes from that extraordinary entertainment machine, the cinema organ, which in the heyday of films would rise out of the pit, bringing with it the organist to entertain during intervals. In an earlier era it enabled the accompaniment to silent films; organs such as the Mighty Wurlitzer augmented their repertoire by sound effects to help the organist, among them car horns, sirens, and bird whistles. These effects were called *toys*, and organs often had *toy counters* with 20 or more noisemakers on them, including various bells and whistles. In the 1950s, decades after the talkies came in, but while theatre organs were still common in big movie houses, these fun features must have been considered no longer essential to their function but mere fripperies, inessential add-ons.

Beyond the pale

Q. I have heard the expression *beyond the pail* from my mother many times as a child, but I don't know what the pail is or what the phrase means.

A. Isn't that where you go when you *kick the bucket*?

I have to tell you that it has nothing to do with containers for carrying water. It's a common misspelling because the word that really belongs in the expression has largely gone out of use except in this one situation. The phrase is properly *beyond the pale*. It means an action that's regarded as outside the limits of acceptable behaviour, one that's objectionable or improper.

> **I look upon you, sir, as a man who has placed himself beyond the pale of society, by his most audacious, disgraceful, and abominable public conduct.**
>
> Mr Pott to Mr Slurk (we never learn their first names) in *The Pickwick Papers* by Charles Dickens, 1837. This is a classic example of the expression but by no means the earliest. That's more than a century older, in 1720, in the third volume of *The Compleat History of the Lives, Robberies, Piracies, and Murders committed by the most notorious rogues*, by a man hiding, perhaps wisely, under the pseudonym of Captain Alexander Smith.

Pale has nothing to do with the adjective for something light in colour except that both come from Latin roots. The one referring to colour originates in the Latin verb *pallere*, to be pale, whilst our one is from *palus*, a stake (also the name of the wooden post that Roman soldiers used to represent an opponent during fighting practice). *Pale* is an old name for a pointed piece of wood driven into the ground and – by an obvious extension – to a barrier made of such stakes, a palisade or fence. *Pole* is from the same source, as are *impale*, *paling* and *palisade*. This meaning has been around in English since the fourteenth century and by the end of that century *pale* had taken on various figurative senses

– a defence, a safeguard, a barrier, an enclosure, or a limit beyond which it was not permissible to go. The idea of an enclosed area still exists in some English dialects.

> **Both Dove-like roved forth beyond the pale**
> **To planted Myrtle-walk.**
>
> *The History of Polindor and Flostella*, by the Elizabethan courtier and author Sir John Harington, written some time before 1612 but published in 1657. This uses *pale* in its literal sense of a boundary or enclosure. In the poem, Ortheris and his beloved risk going beyond the boundary (the pale) of their quiet park lodge with the result that Ortheris is attacked by five armed horsemen. Harington is best remembered now for his *Metamorphosis of Ajax* (this last word being a pun on *a jakes*, meaning a privy) of 1596, a scatological and satirical work that contains the first description of a water closet, more than 200 years before anybody built one.

In particular, the term was used to describe various defended enclosures of territory inside other countries. For example, the English pale in France in the fourteenth century was the territory of Calais, the last English possession in that country. The best-known example is the Russian Pale, between 1791 and the Revolution of 1917, which were specified provinces and districts within which Russian Jews were required to live. Another famous one is the Pale in Ireland, that part of the country over which England had direct jurisdiction – it varied from time to time, but was an area of several counties centred on Dublin. The first mention of the Irish Pale is in a document of 1446–7. Though there was an attempt later in the century to enclose the Pale by a bank and ditch (which was never completed), there never was a literal fence around it. The expression has often been claimed to originate in one or other of these pales, most often the Irish one, but the earliest appearance of 1720 for *beyond the pale* is extremely late if it's linked to the Irish one and much too early for the Russian one.

The earliest relevant figurative sense was of a sphere of

activity or interest, a branch of study or a body of knowledge; we use *field* in much the same way. This first appeared in 1483 in one of the earliest printed books in English, *The Golden Legende*, a translation by William Caxton of a French work. Our figurative sense seems in part to have grown out of this, since those who exist outside such a conceptual pale are not our kind and do not share our values, beliefs or social customs. There may well have been an echo of a literal pale as well, with an implication that civilization stopped at its boundary.

Big cheese

Q. A friend told me the other day, when discussing a new acquaintance, 'He's a big cheese in the rugby world.' What in heaven's name is the origin of this strange term?

A. The *big cheese* is the most influential or important person in a group, though it has often been used in a derogatory way to refer to somebody self-important. These days, it's more than likely to appear as a joking reference to a real cheese, since its slang use is rare and definitely outdated.

There's no shortage of expressions invoking cheese: one may be *cheesed off* (miserable, annoyed, fed up), or something may be *cheesy* (cheap, unpleasant or blatantly inauthentic). These refer to the unhappy habit of ripe cheese making its presence known to anyone within sniffing distance.

But *big cheese* has a quite different origin, based on the only positive slang sense of *cheese* that seems ever to have existed. This was first recorded in London in the nineteenth century, in forms like *he's the cheese*, *it's quite the cheese* or just *the cheese*, with the sense of a thing that was 'good, first-rate in quality, genuine, pleasant or advantageous' as John Camden Hotten defined it in his *Slang Dictionary* in 1859.

Cries Rigmaree, rubbing her hands, 'that will please –
My *"Conjuring cap"* – it's the thing; – it's "the cheese"!'

The Ingoldsby Legends, by R. H. Barham, 1840. The Reverend Richard Barham
wrote the legends partly in verse, partly in prose, under the pretence that
the antiquarian Thomas Ingoldsby of Tappington Everard in Kent was
presenting old documents he had found. The resulting comic and grotesque
retellings of medieval legends and tales of crime, witchcraft and the
supernatural were first published in the magazine *Bentley's Miscellany* from
1837 on. They remained highly popular thoughout the second half of the
century – an edition of 1881 sold 60,000 copies on its first day.

Explanations of its origins were often ingenious rather than
satisfying:

Just the Cheese. This phrase is only some ten or twelve years
old. Its origin was this:–Some desperate witty fellows, by way
of giving a comic turn to the phrase 'C'est une autre chose,'
used to translate it, 'That is another cheese;' and after awhile
these words became 'household words,' and when anything
positive or specific was intended to be pointed out, 'That's the
cheese' became adopted, which is nearly synonymous with
'Just the cheese.'

Notes and Queries, 23 July 1853. The expression is rather older than the
writer's 'ten or twelve years', since the supposed French connection
was floated as its origin in the *London Guide* in 1818. The French phrase
means 'that's another thing'. As it happens, another writer in the
same journal a month earlier had given what we now accept as the
true origin.

Though it seems certain that it had nothing to do with a
literal big cheese, Americans often offer one as its origin.
This was the Mammoth Cheese that was created for
President Thomas Jefferson by the staunchly Republican
citizens of Cheshire, a community in western Massachusetts
that, like its English county namesake, was famous for its
cheese. A Baptist preacher named John Leland conceived
the idea of making a vast cheese from one day's output of
the local cows. It turned out to be more than four feet in

diameter and weighed 1235 pounds (561 kg). It arrived at
the executive mansion (not yet called the White House) on
New Year's Day 1802 and stayed on display for two years; it is
said that slices of it were still being served to guests in 1805.
If you're a fan of the US television series *The West Wing*, you
will remember *Big Block of Cheese Day*, in which White House
staffers met fringe groups that would not otherwise get a
hearing; this refers to a later presentation of an even bigger
cheese to Andrew Jackson in 1837; it's said that he invited
passers-by into the White House to sample it.

Notwithstanding this suggested American connection,
the most probable source is the Persian or Hindi word *chiz*,
meaning a thing.

> **The expression used to be common among Anglo-Indians, e.g.,
> 'My new Arab is the real *chiz*'; 'These cheroots are the real *chiz*,'
> i.e. the real thing. The word may have been an Anglo-Indian
> importation, and it is difficult otherwise to account for it.**
>
> *Hobson-Jobson: The Anglo-Indian Dictionary*, by Sir Henry Yule and Arthur
> C. Burnell, 1886. Sir Henry was primarily a historical geographer of central
> Asia and an expert in medieval travel writing. This huge work was therefore
> something of a sideline, which he completed after Burnell's death in 1882.
> Its unique view of the everyday language of British officers in colonial India
> is so important to scholars that it has proved to be his primary legacy. We
> shall meet the book again in the entry on Blighty.

Another expression with the same meaning that pre-dated
the real chiz was *the real thing*, so it's probable that Anglo-
Indians changed *thing* to *chiz* as a bilingual joke. Once
returnees from India started to use it in Britain, hearers
naturally enough converted the unfamiliar foreign *chiz* into
something more recognizable, and it became *cheese*.

The phrase *big cheese* developed from it in early twentieth-
century America:

> **Roosevelt looks like the big cheese. He stands at the head of
> every preempted party and if the greatest care is not exercised**

> **a vote will be cast for him regardless of whether it is the intention or not.**
>
> *Daily Independent*, Monessen, Pennsylvania, 30 October 1912.

It followed on several other American phrases containing *big* to describe a person of more than common importance, many with animal or vegetable associations – *big bug*, *big potato*, *big fish* and *big toad*, of which the oldest is probably the British English *bigwig* of the eighteenth century (more recent examples are *big shot*, *big enchilada* and *big banana*).

Like the others, *big cheese* was by no means always complimentary and often had derisive undertones, no doubt helped along by the influence of other slang meanings of *cheese*.

Big girl's blouse

Q. Could you possibly shed some light on the origin of the expression *big girl's blouse*? We were having a discussion about it in the office the other day; I checked all my references and couldn't find any information on it.

A. I can tell you what it means and a bit about its history, but tracking it down to its source is impossible in the present state of knowledge. It's a northern English expression that belongs with such obscure gems as the exclamation of surprise *I'll go to the foot of our stairs!* and the deeply dismissive comment, usually uttered by a woman with reference to the uselessness of some male, *he's all mouth and trousers!*

People mean by *big girl's blouse* an ineffectual or effeminate male, a weakling or coward, though it's often used in a bantering or teasing way among friends rather than as an out-and-out insult ('You can't drink Coke in a pub, you big girl's blouse!'; 'Blokes who don't take on dares are big girl's blouses'). It has working-class associations, being more common in downmarket British tabloid newspapers such as the *Sun* and the *Mirror*; it's also a frequent pejorative on the sports pages:

> **The reason [Newcastle United manager Sam] Allardyce had to go was because he wasn't man enough for the Geordie hordes. Wearing a woolly hat and coat in the game against Birmingham when it was only –2 degrees? Pink scarf and sponsored gloves during a defeat to Man City when the thermometer had not touched freezing? Big Sam? Big girl's blouse more like.**
> *Sun*, 14 January 2008.

It seems to have been first used in the 1960s:

> **ELI: Go round talking like that, you'll be hearing from our solicitor.**
> **NELLIE: He *is* our solicitor, you big girl's blouse.**
> *Nearest and Dearest*, Series 2, Episode 1, 1969. This ITV network sitcom starred Jimmy Jewel as Eli Pledge and Hylda Baker as his spinster sister Nellie, who inherit a pickle-bottling factory in Colne, Lancashire. It was rough-and-ready Northern humour, full of innuendo (plus malapropisms from Nellie). This is the earliest example so far known.

It has been suggested that Hylda Baker invented the phrase in her stage act. If she didn't, where *big girl's blouse* came from is likely to remain a mystery. However, as a possible clue, I've been told of a Liverpool variation, 'he's flapping like a big girl's blouse'. This conjures up the twin ideas of a large garment flapping on a washing line and of a man flapping in the sense of panicking. It's plausible as the image from which the current version could have derived.

Other than that, your guess is as good as mine.

Blighty

Q. I am a Brit living in Australia and I've been asked by an ocker where the term *Old Blighty* comes from. I was appalled to realize I had no idea. Can you help please?

A. No worries. *Old Blighty* or *Blighty* is an affectionate way of referring to Britain, still very common among expatriates. It's also a mildly disparaging way by which certain former colonials sometimes refer to the UK:

> That's the conclusion of Her Majesty's government, which acknowledged yesterday that letting pubs stay open past the traditional 11 pm closing has failed to curb old Blighty's notorious binge-drinking problem.
>
> *Boston Herald*, 5 March 2008.

It's a relic of British India:

> Bilayut, Billait. Europe. The word is properly Arabic *Wildyat*, 'a kingdom, a province,' variously used with specific denotation, as the Afghans term their own country often by this name; and in India again it has come to be employed for distant Europe ... The adjective *bilāyatī* or *wilāyatī is* applied specifically to a variety of exotic objects ... most especially *bilāyatī pani*, 'European water', the usual name for soda-water in Anglo-India.
>
> *Hobson-Jobson: The Anglo-Indian Dictionary*, by Sir Henry Yule and Arthur C. Burnell, 1886. The expression *hobson-jobson* was once used by British soldiers in India for any 'native festal excitement', as the authors described it. They explained that it was a corruption of the Muslim exclamation *Yā Hasan! Yā Husayn!* during the Muharram procession; Hasan and Husain were the grandsons of Muhammad who were killed while fighting for the faith.

Blighty was the inevitable British soldier's corruption of it. But it only came into common use as a term for Britain during the First World War in France, about 1915. It then appeared in the titles of many popular wartime songs:

There's a ship that's bound for Blighty, We wish we were in Blighty, and *Take me back to dear old Blighty, put me on the train for London town,* as well as in Wilfred Owen's poems and many other places. Unlike other slangy terms of that conflict, it survived after the war.

In modern Australian usage, *old* has been added to make a sentimental reference to Britain.

Bloke

Q. In addition to calling each other *mate,* us Aussies also refer to *blokes,* as in, 'That Tim is a good bloke, isn't he?' I use the term, but have no idea why, or where it originated! Can you help?

A. This slang term for a male person is originally British, recorded from the early nineteenth century, probably as a variation on the slightly older *gloak* (a *buzzgloak* was a pick-pocket, according to an 1812 glossary of low slang). To start with, *bloke* was the jargon of criminals for a man, usually one of superior status, presumably meaning anybody who wasn't a criminal.

The earliest example I know about is in a virtually illiterate letter by one John Daly, aged 17, read in evidence at his trial for housebreaking at the Old Bailey on 9 April 1829; it appears there once as *blake* and once as *bloke.* (Daly, by the way, was found guilty and sentenced to death.) In 1839, H. Brandon included it in a glossary in his survey *Poverty, Mendacity, and Crime* but spelled it *bloak* and defined it as 'a gentleman'. From the early 1850s onwards it appears in the works of various writers about low life in London, including Henry Mayhew and George Augustus Sala, where it's clearly a straightforward slang term for a man of any class.

It was taken early on to Australia, where it was commonly

used at first to mean the boss or some person of status. That ties in with the one-time lower-deck slang sense in the Royal Navy for the commander of a ship. Americans often think of it as British slang, but it was common in the US in the late nineteenth century and is even now not entirely extinct there. At one time, Americans also used it in the sense of a stupid or worthless person.

The experts aren't altogether sure where it came from. Some, especially in the United States, have suggested it derived from the Celtic word *ploc*, a large, bull-headed person. Others have argued that the 'stupid person' sense may be from the Dutch *blok*, a fool, which is where we get *blockhead* from. This derivation is probably correct, but we're now fairly sure that *bloke* in the broad sense of a man derives either from Romany, the language of the Rom or gypsies, or more probably from Shelta, a secret language used by Irish and Welsh tinkers and some gypsies. It may ultimately derive from Hindi *loke*, a man.

Blow the gaff

Q. I was re-reading one of John Wyndham's science fiction novels last night (*The Kraken Wakes*, as it happens) and came across a character who was said to have *blown the gaff*, clearly a slangy reference to revealing something that others would prefer to keep hidden. It is an extremely odd phrase. I can think of a couple of senses of *gaff*, but neither of them fit. Where does *blow the gaff* come from?

A. That's not so common a slang phrase these days, though it's still about:

> **Tell him to grow up and leave you alone, otherwise you'll blow the gaff on his lecherous behaviour.**
> *Mirror*, 5 January 2006.

Blow the gaff starts to appear early in the nineteenth century as criminal slang. Trying to find an origin isn't easy – a lot of dictionaries don't even try – because the matter is clouded by the fog of ages and the poor state of recording of early slang usage. There are also all sorts of meanings for *gaff* recorded down the centuries – many more than the two you know – which has added to our difficulties.

In the eighteenth century there was another version of the expression, *to blow the gab*, similarly criminal slang meaning to betray a secret or to betray a confederate, in which *gab* comes from the word for conversation or speech (as in *gift of the gab*).

> **I, Crank Cuffin, swear to be**
> **True to this fraternity;**
> **That I will in all obey**
> **Rule and order of the lay.**
> **Never blow the gab or squeak;**
> **Never snitch to bum or beak.**

The Oath of the Canting Crew, taken from *The Life of Bampfylde Moore Carew*, by Robert Goadby, 1749. Carew was born in 1693, the son of the rector of Bickley, near Tiverton, but ran away to join a group of travellers and became known in popular writing as the king of the gypsies. *Crank Cuffin* was a generic slang term for a rogue; *blow*, *squeak* and *snitch* all meant to betray one's associates by becoming an informer; a *bum* was a bailiff, a lowly law-enforcement officer (his name was an abbreviation of *bum-bailiff*, one who was close behind you in pursuit); and a *beak* was a magistrate.

One of the least-known meanings of *gaff* is for a cheating device in gambling. Originally this was a ring worn by card-sharps (Charles Leland describes one in his *Dictionary of Slang, Jargon & Cant* of 1889) with a small hook set in it to grip the cards, so the origin is probably in *gaff* in the sense of a hooked stick for landing large fish, perhaps augmented by some idea of hooking a sucker. It has come to mean any cheating device used by card players.

What may have happened was that *blow the gab* became
the model for a newer phrase, *blow the gaff*, under the influence of the cheating trick sense of *gaff*, where it would at
first have meant exposing the trade secrets of gamblers and
cheats. It's then a short step to extend it to the meaning of
the older phrase – and indeed to supplant it as the older one
went out of fashion.

> One of the French officers, after he was taken prisoner, axed me
> how we had managed to get the gun up there but I wasn't going
> to blow the gaff, so I told him as a great secret, that we got it up
> with a kite; upon which he opened all his eyes, and crying *'Sacre
> bleu!'* walked away, believing all I said was true.

> *Peter Simple,* by Frederick Marryat, 1833. *Axed* here is a dialectal form of
> *asked.*

Boycott

Q. A television program here in the US said recently,
I believe, that *boycott* came from the Revolutionary War and
the boycott of British taxes. Is that right?

A. Wrong country and wrong century, I'm afraid. No one
who organized a boycott in the 1770s or 1780s could have
used the word, because it only appeared in the language in
1880. It's an excellent example of an eponym, a word based
on a proper name, like *wellingtons*, *chauvinism* or the *Ferris
wheel*.

Captain Charles Cunningham Boycott was an Englishman
working in Ireland. In the 1870s he was farming at
Loughmask in County Mayo and serving as a land agent
for an absentee English landlord, Lord Earne. This was the
time of the campaign organized by the Irish Land League for
reform of the system of landholdings. In September 1880,

protesting tenants demanded that Captain Boycott give them a 25 per cent reduction in their rents. He refused and became subject to mob attacks. Charles Stuart Parnell, the President of the Land League, suggested in a speech that the way to force Boycott to give way was for everyone in the locality to refuse to have any dealings with him. Labourers would not work for him, local shops stopped serving him (food had to be brought in from elsewhere for him and his family), and he even had great trouble getting his letters delivered. In the end, his crops were harvested that autumn through the help of fifty volunteers from the north of the country, who worked under the protection of 900 soldiers.

The events aroused so much passion that his name became an instant byword. It was first used – in our modern sense of collective and organized ostracism – in *The Times* of 20 November 1880, even while his crops were still being belatedly harvested; within weeks it was everywhere. It was soon adopted by newspapers throughout Europe, with versions of his name appearing in French, German, Dutch and Russian. By the time of the Captain's death in 1897, it had become a standard part of the English language.

Bringing home the bacon

Q. While looking in *Wikipedia* for something else, I found a page that said *bringing home the bacon* came from a twelfth-century practice that survives only in the English town of Great Dunmow. The church promised a side of bacon (a flitch) to any man who could swear that he and his wife had 'not wisht themselves unmarried again' for a year and a day. Men who 'brought home the bacon' in this way were held in high esteem in their communities. Is this one of those too neat explanations that defy belief?

A. It is. It's also been said that it refers to the old fairground contest of catching the greased pig, whose prize was the pig, so the winner literally brought home the (greasy) bacon. Your story reminded me at once of one of the tales told in that infamous e-mail about life in the 1500s that endlessly circulates online. One version of it claims that 'it was a sign of wealth that a man could *bring home the bacon*.'

That's true today, though usually in a broader sense of supplying material support to one's family or achieving success, but it's hard to assert with a straight face that it was so back in 1500 or 1300. We can't absolutely prove it wasn't around then but its total absence from the historical record before 1906 rather gives a pointer to its being modern.

The first recorded user of the expression was Mrs Gans, mother of Joe. He was a famous boxer at the end of the nineteenth century and the beginning of the twentieth, the first native-born black American to win a world title. That was in 1900, when he was 26. Six years later he fought Oscar 'Battling' Nelson in Goldfield, Nevada. It's virtually a ghost town now but it was a booming community then, the largest in the state. The match has been rated as the greatest lightweight championship bout ever contested, whose fame has endured enough that its centenary was celebrated locally. A report of the fight noted:

> **The following telegrams were read by Announcer Larry Sullivan. Gans received this from his mother: 'Joe, the eyes of the world are on you. Everybody says you ought to win. Peter Jackson will tell me the news and you bring back the bacon.'**
> *Reno Evening Gazette*, 3 September 1906.

Various stories say that after he won the fight (it ended in Gans's favour after forty-two rounds when his opponent hit a low blow and was disqualified) he sent a telegram to his mother in Baltimore: 'Bringing home the bacon'. Other reports claim that what he actually said was that he wasn't only bringing back the bacon but the gravy, too. These are probably later elaborations of what soon became a widely known and popular story.

Was Mrs Gans repeating a saying she already knew and used? Perhaps, even probably. But it isn't recorded anywhere that I can discover before she sent that telegram. And it clearly struck a powerful chord of both originality and relevance with those at the 1906 bout. She repeated the phrase in another telegram at his next match the following January and her words were greeted with laughter and repartee.

Almost immediately – within weeks rather than months – it became common on the sports pages of the newspapers, at first referring to boxing but later also to baseball, football, horse racing and rugby. By 1911 it had started to be used of politics. By the time P. G. Wodehouse used it in *Ukridge* in 1924 ('It may be that my bit will turn out to be just the trifle that brings home the bacon') it had become firmly established in the US.

Both *bring home the bacon* and *bring back the bacon* remain widely known and used, these days often far from American shores:

> **This is how much an hour of your (working) time is worth. Look at all the things you do that could be done just as effectively by someone else for less than $30 an hour – in other words outsource your non-core activities so you can focus all your energy on bringing home the bacon.**
>
> *The Australian*, 12 April 2008.

Brownie points

Q. It is quite common these days to hear of people gaining *brownie points* as reward for some small favour or as a sign of approbation. What is the origin of this phrase?

A. It's originally from the US. A trawl through a database of American newspapers yields a lot of examples from the 1950s, two from 1954 describing it as school slang. I reproduce one of these reports as a quick glance down nostalgia alley for anybody interested in old US slang:

> Miami young people keep their teachers agog with their lingo says Sanford Schnier, of the *Miami Daily News*. He offers these 'cool' expressions: 'Flake out' – Too much study is tiring. 'Browse me on the scene' – Request for information. 'Pull a boo boo' – Make an error. 'Racking up the Brownie points' – Teacher's pet. 'Toe Dancers' – High school sissies. 'Calories' – Plump girls. 'Fluffs' – Fat boys.

> *The Daily News*, Newport, Rhode Island, 15 April 1954.

However, *flake out*, in the sense of being exhausted, is actually American services slang from early in the Second World War. The *Historical Dictionary of American Slang* cites evidence that suggests *Brownie points*, too, was US Army slang from that period, a view backed up by indirect and anecdotal evidence.

The earliest known example to date is this:

> You don't know about brownie points? All my buddies keep score. In fact every married male should know about 'em. It's a way of figuring where you stand with the little woman – favor or disfavor. Started way back in the days of the leprechauns, I suppose, long before there were any doghouses.

> *Los Angeles Times*, 15 March 1951. A different gloss on the meaning.

Several suggestions have been put forward for where it comes from. But it seems most likely that the origin is the obvious one: *Brownie points* is an allusion to the junior branch of the Girl Scouts in the US (Girl Guides in other countries), named by Lady Baden Powell after the elves that do helpful things around the house for small rewards. Linking it to their merit badges, or their good deeds, is a neat idea, to such an extent that even now the phrase almost always appears with an initial capital letter. The phrase was surely a sarcastic, inverted compliment. To earn credit by doing some little task to earn a badge or prize is fine for Brownies but it's childish and embarrassing if an adult does it.

The experts are agreed that the sense was given greater strength and impetus through scatological undertones, being intimately (and I use that word advisedly) associated with the older term *brown-nose*, for a sycophant, toady or *arse-licker*, a person who curries favour to such an extent that his nose seems to be up his superior's backside. *Brownie* by itself is recorded as student slang from 1944 in this sense in the journal *American Speech*, which defined it as 'A person who is always asking and answering questions in class to impress the instructor. Also a person who stays after class to try to insinuate himself into the teacher's good graces.' A teacher's pet or apple polisher, in other words. An earlier issue of the same journal suggested that *brown-nose* itself was pre-war student slang that was carried into the American military by cadets.

Bulldozer

Q. Watching earth-moving near my home the other day, I wondered why the machine that was doing the job was called a *bulldozer*. I can see how it might be like a bull butting, but is that really where it comes from?

A. There is a link. But the story's surprisingly complicated.

The word is definitely American. The earliest sense of *bulldozer* had nothing to do with machinery, but referred to a person inflicting a severe punishment, nominally one applied with a *bullwhip*, also an American term, a big whip with a long heavy lash for driving cattle.

Bulldozer became very widely known during the US presidential election of 1876, which historians suggest may have been the most hard-fought, corrupt and rigged in the history of the Union. All reports say that it came into being as a result of a determined attempt by Democrat supporters in the Southern states to stop blacks from voting Republican:

> In very obstinate cases the brethren were in the habit of administering a *bull's* dose of several hundred lashes on the bare back. When dealing with those that were hard to convert, active members would call out 'give me the whip and let me give him a bull-dose.' From this it became easy to say 'that fellow ought to be bull-dosed, or bull-dozed,' and soon bull-doze, bull-dozing and bull-dozers came to be slang words.
>
> *The Daily Constitution*, 21 November 1876. The paper is reprinting a report from *The New Orleans Times* of 15 November, which records that many journalists have been writing the word wrongly as *bull-dogged*, comments that it was a word coined in Louisiana, and implies that it had been in existence for some months.
>
> 'Bull-dozers' mounted on the best horses in the state scoured the country in squads by night, threatening colored men, and

warning them that if they attempted to vote the republican ticket they would be killed.

Janesville Gazette, Wisconsin, 22 November 1876.

By the early 1880s, the verb *bulldoze* was widely used in the sense of intimidating or coercing by violence, specifically the threat of a flogging. A *bulldozer* could be a bully, an intimidator, or a member of a vigilante mob. It could also refer to a type of gun, presumably seen as a usefully intimidating device.

The next step occurs around the end of the century. We start to get references to *bulldozer* being the name for a powerful machine for bending big pieces of metal.

The unfortunate man proved to be Anton Olson, of the blacksmithing department, who in some unknown way became caught in the machine known commonly as the 'bulldozer,' thereby sustaining severe injuries.

The Daily Gazette, Wisconsin, 23 July 1898. There's no way to tell whether this sense appeared independently or had been borrowed from the earlier ones, but the idea of forceful manipulation or bending something to one's will are common to both.

Our modern sense began to appear around 1910. Various reports mention canal boats fitted with *bulldozers*, blades for breaking up winter ice. Crude mule-powered earth-movers were also fitted with such blades (the problem, it was said, was getting the mules to go backwards ready for the next stroke). As you can imagine, in time *bulldozer*, as the term for the pusher blade at the front of a machine, became extended to the whole machine. But the first cases of *bulldozer* for a powered machine fitted with one appear only at the end of the 1920s and are usually linked with the then new Caterpillar tractors.

It's intriguing that though it might seem our modern figurative sense of the verb *bulldoze*, to force through accept-

ance of some proposal insensitively or ruthless.
the image of the earth-moving machine, the figu.
actually pre-dated the literal one by some 50 years.

Bulls and bears

Q. In Stock Exchange parlance, *bull* and *bear* relate to being
'long' or 'short' of a particular security. I have heard that the
term has its origins in two old English family stockbroking
or banking businesses – the Bulteels and the Barings. The
Bulteels tended toward a more aggressively positive or
bullish view on stocks and shares while the Barings tended
to be more cautious. I should be grateful for your comments.

A. Your explanation of the two terms makes perfect sense to
somebody in the business, but it lacks a bit for the rest of us.
To keep it simple (this being a ritual incantation to prevent
my being nibbled to death by pedants), a *bear* sells shares,
sometimes shares he doesn't own (in the jargon, he is *short*
of the necessary shares), hoping to buy them back at a lower
price in order to make a profit, so he is hoping for a fall in
the market price and he may be considered a pessimist; a
bull buys shares hoping to sell them at a higher price later,
so is essentially an optimist about the way the market is
moving (by analogy, he is said to be *long* because he has some
shares on hand).

The story about the two famous banking families is
widespread, and believed by a lot of people, but there's no
truth in it. Barings was a well-known bank, whose spectacu-
lar demise in 1995 rendered it even more famous than it was
in life. The only bank containing the name Bulteel that I can
find traded as Harris, Bulteel and Co; it was the first bank in
Plymouth, established there in 1773–4 under another name,

was never sufficiently well known to conceivably become the focus for an expression.

In any case, *bull* pre-dates that bank's foundation by more than half a century, being first recorded in 1714. *Bear* is slightly older still:

> A noble gentleman of this city, who has the honour of serving his country as major in the Train-bands, being at that general mart of stock jobbers called Jonathon's, endeavouring to raise himself (as all men of honour ought) to the degree of colonel at least; it happened that he bought the Bear of another officer, who, though not commissioned in the army, yet no less eminently serves the public than the other, in raising the credit of the kingdom, by raising that of the stocks.

> *Tatler*, 7 July 1709. This tongue-in-cheek tale is saying that the major, wanting to buy a promotion, speculated by selling some stock short. When the transaction went wrong, the story goes on, the major described his fellow officer as a *bear-skin man*, among other epithets, and called him out, satisfaction being achieved through a fist-fight, neither man being keen on firearms.

> A *jobber* was a middleman or wholesaler who bought and sold shares. A *train-band* was properly a *trained band*, a company of citizen soldiery, a militia. Many stock transactions at this period took place in coffee houses, which were convenient meeting places; Jonathon's, in Change Alley in the City of London, was the precursor of the London Stock Exchange, much as Lloyd's coffee house later became formalized as Lloyd's of London, the insurance market.

Other early examples described such traders as *bear-skin jobbers*. This expanded form of *bear* gives us the clue we need. There was at the time a proverb, probably borrowed from French *ne vendez pas la peau de l'ours avant de l'avoir tué*, 'don't sell the bear's skin before you've killed him', though the English equivalent refers to catching rather than killing the bear. It had the same sense as 'don't count your chickens before they're hatched' – don't assume your success is assured until it actually happens, don't be over-optimistic.

A *bear-skin jobber* or *bear* sold shares he didn't own, in the hope that their price would fall and that he would be able to 'catch his bear' by buying them more cheaply in the market before he had to deliver them.

The suggestion is that *bull* was invented as an alliterative animal analogy to *bear*, perhaps with a subconscious image of charging forward fearlessly.

Butter no parsnips

Q. Lazing about the other day, I said, *this will butter no parsnips*. But I have no idea of its derivation. Please help.

A. It's interesting you should use the phrase to refer to idleness, since its usual associations are with flattery and honeyed words. The full expression is *fine words butter no parsnips* (or sometimes *soft* or *fair words*), meaning that words alone are useless, especially flattering phrases or extravagant promises, and that you should judge people by what they do rather than by what they say.

As a proverb, it's at least 400 years old:

> **Faire words butter noe parsnips.**
>
> *Parœmiologia Anglo-Latina … or Proverbs English and Latin*, by John Clarke, 1639. Clarke was then headmaster of Lincoln grammar school. One former pupil described him as 'a master very famous for learning and piety', but also remembered him as a conceited and supercilious pedant.

The link between butter and flattery is easy to understand. We have had the verb *to butter up* in the language at least since the early eighteenth century with the meaning of flattering a person lavishly. It and the proverb share the image of fine words being liberally applied to smooth their subject and oil the process of persuasion. Parsnips were featured in the proverb early on because they were common in the

English diet and were usually buttered before being put on the table. There's nothing special about parsnips, however: foreign visitors recoiled in disgust at the English habit of using butter to cook almost everything.

> **Words are but wind that do from men proceed;**
> **None but Chamelions on bare Air can feed;**
> **Great men large hopeful promises may utter;**
> **But words did never Fish or Parsnips butter.**
>
> *Epigrammes, written on purpose to be read: with a Proviso, that they may be understood by the Reader,* by John Taylor, 1651, quoted by Nigel Rees in *Oops, Pardon, Mrs Arden!: An Embarrassment of Domestic Catch Phrases.* John Taylor was a Thames waterman who styled himself as the Water Poet and who made substantial profits from accounts of his well-publicized sponsored travels to exotic destinations.

Taylor's verse shows that other foodstuffs were involved in the saying at that time – indeed there's an example in the *Oxford English Dictionary* from 1645: 'Fair words butter no fish' – and that it's the act of buttering that's the key part of the saying. Our association today solely with parsnips results from the expression's having become fossilized in that one form at some point.

Butter wouldn't melt in his mouth

Q. This is probably desperately simple but perhaps you could please tell me from where the phrase *butter wouldn't melt in his mouth* originates?

A. It's most definitely not simple. It's one of those idioms that are so old their origins are lost in the proverbial mists of time. It refers contemptuously to a person who appears gentle or innocent but isn't as harmless as he looks.

> When a visitor comes in, she smiles and languishes, you'd think
> that butter wouldn't melt in her mouth: and the minute he
> is gone, very likely, she flares up like a little demon, and says
> things fit to send you wild.
>
> *The History of Pendennis*, by William Makepeace Thackeray, 1849.

> At 5 years of age, [he] looks as if butter wouldn't melt in his
> mouth. But he has gained the unenviable distinction of being
> one of the youngest pupils in Britain to be expelled from
> school.
>
> *Daily Mail*, 16 November 2007.

The saying appeared in print first in John Palsgrave's book
about the French language, *Lesclarcissement de la Langue
Françoyse* of 1530, but it's more than likely that he was
borrowing a saying that was already proverbial.

Since putting butter in one's mouth, even straight from
the fridge in these technologically advanced times, is certain to cause it to melt, the saying isn't easy to understand.
It may be tied up with the idea of coolness, of a nonchalant
ease coupled with high self-control that is unaffected by
passion or emotion (a sense of *cool* that goes back at least a
century before the first recorded appearance of the butter
saying). If you are that icily insouciant, the suggestion
seems to be, butter really won't melt in your mouth.

Butterscotch

Q. We do a lot of thinking here at Ben & Jerry's (besides
a lot of eating) and we were suddenly curious about the
origins of the word *butterscotch*. Does it have anything at all
to do with Scotland?

A. It would be neat if it did, but it seems unlikely.
The first part is easy enough because *butterscotch* does

contain butter. The *Collins Dictionary* suggests that the second part may indeed be there because it was first made in Scotland; a Scottish link seems plausible because Keillers of Dundee has made butterscotch commercially. However, there's no written evidence of a Scots link. Some writers have argued that the second part is actually *scorch*, from the manner of its making. Another suggestion was put forward by Charles Earl Funk in *Horsefeathers* in 1958: 'All directions for the preparation of this candy after it is properly cooked close with some such statement as: Pour upon oiled paper or well-buttered pan and when slightly cool *score* with a knife into squares.' He points out that one sense of *scotch* was to score or cut a shallow groove in something. As things stand, you can take your pick between *Scotch*, *scorch* or *score* and nobody can prove you wrong.

The earliest known examples are worth quoting at some length for their period flavour:

> **Well, you know, next morning I put my things in my cart, ready for Nottingham goose-fair: the brandy-balls here, by them-selves – the butter-scotch there – the tuffey in this place – the black-jack in that; then I filled in with cure-all, and hard-bake, and peppermint pincushions: really it was beautiful to look at, I'd done it so nicely.**
>
> *The Boy's Autumn Book*, 1847. Although it was published in New York it quotes a British itinerant seller of sweets. *Tuffey* is toffee; *hard-bake* was also called almond toffee, made from boiled sugar or treacle with blanched almonds; *black-jack* was another treacle-based sweet, but included spices; *cure-all* was presumably some variety of a supposed universal remedy or panacea that would almost certainly also have included treacle (*treacle* was originally the name for a medicinal compound supposed to be a remedy against snake venom, poisons and disease).
>
> **Fisher and Co., Victoria-street, Nottingham, have the honour to announce to the ladies, that Messrs. Hannay and Dietrichsen, Dealers in Patent Medicines and Perfumers to the Royal Family,**

63, Oxford-street, London, have become agents for their
Improved Doncaster Butter-Scotch; celebrated in the North of
England for the immediate relief of coughs, colds, hoarseness,
&c. Taken as a lozenge, and sold in green and gold packages,
stamped and sealed.

The Lady's Newspaper, London, 20 March 1847. This advertisement suggests
by its use of 'improved' that butterscotch was known by that name rather
earlier.

The mention of Doncaster here may be the best pointer we
have to the source. An article published in *The Doncaster
Review* in September 1896 asserts that 'It was on the 11th
of May 1817, that the late Mr. Samuel Parkinson com-
menced the manufacture of butter-scotch' in that town.
Mr Parkinson was claimed to be the first maker of the
sweetmeat. We do not know if he called it that – no records
of the firm survive before 1848 – but it would seem unlikely
considering the lack of any mention before 1847, even in
advertisements.

None of this, however nostalgically evocative, gets us
anywhere near finding out the true history of the word,
though it does strongly suggest that there was nothing at all
Scotch or Scots about it.

By and large

Q. We were talking around the breakfast table on Sunday
morning and my aunt said she had often wondered where
the common expression *by and large* came from. Can you help?

A. With *by and large* the modern landsman means 'in
general; on the whole; everything considered; for the most
part'.

> **By and large, the track record of hiring women directors is no different at any studio, whether the studio is run by a man or a woman.**
>
> *Los Angeles Times*, 20 May 2008.

But it's a nautical expression, from sailing ship days.

> **Taking it 'by and large,' as the sailors say, we had a pleasant ten days' run from New York to the Azores islands – not a fast run, for the distance is only twenty-four hundred miles, but a right pleasant one in the main.**
>
> *The Innocents Abroad; or, The New Pilgrim's Progress*, by Mark Twain, 1869. This was Twain's first bestseller, based on his journeys on the steamship *Quaker City*; it became one of the most successful travel books of the century, selling 80,000 copies in sixteen months. In the tradition of such humorous works – a tradition it helped to create – it poked fun at foreign customs, unhelpful guidebooks, and the inconveniences of travel.

It's easy to get confused when attempting to explain its origins because dictionary editors and writers on word origins (this one included) have a lot of trouble understanding the extremely complicated terminology of sailing-ship operations.

> **We cast off our weather-braces and lifts; we set in the lee-braces, and hauled forward by the weather-bowlings, and hauled them tight, and belayed them, and hauled over the mizen tack to windward, and kept her full and by as near as she would lie.**
>
> *Gulliver's Travels*, by Jonathan Swift, 1726. As condensed a string of nautical terminology as one might find in one sentence anywhere. Don't ask me to explain it. One has to wonder whether Swift, who at the time was dean of St Patrick's Cathedral, Dublin, could have done so at the time.

Imagine a ship at sea. If the wind were blowing from exactly sideways on, it was said to be *on the beam* (the beam being the side of the ship at its widest point, usually by the main-mast). If the wind was blowing from any point nearer the stern, *on the quarter*, the ship was said to be sailing *large*. This comes from the idea of a thing being unrestricted, allowing considerable freedom (as in a fugitive being 'at large'), because ships sailing large were able to maintain their direction of travel anywhere in a wide arc without needing to make continual big changes to the set of the sails.

> **As soon as Desmond stepped on board the grab, the hawser connecting the two vessels was cast off, the mainsail was run up, and the grab, sailing large, stood up the coast.**
>
> *One of Clive's Heroes*, by Herbert Strang, 1906. A *grab* (from an Arabic word meaning a raven) was a large coastal vessel used in Indian waters, drawing very little water and so suitable for inshore work.

Sailing ships were able to make some progress into the wind, that is, with it blowing from forward of the beam. Those with good handling capabilities could get within five or six points of the wind (there are thirty-two compass points in a complete circle). In such cases, the ship was said to be sailing *by the wind*, *by* here having the ancient sense of 'in the region or general direction of, towards'.

> **'But it will serve only when we are sailing by the wind,' I explained. 'When running more freely, with the wind astern, abeam, or on the quarter, it will be necessary for me to steer.'**
>
> *The Sea Wolf*, by Jack London, 1904. The narrator, the literary critic Humphrey Van Weyden, is talking to the poet Maud Brewster, at the point in the story when they have escaped from the sealing schooner *The Ghost* and its ruthless captain, Wolf Larsen.

If the ship were pointed closely into the wind, but with some margin for error in case the wind changed direction slightly, it was said to be *full and by* (sailing by the wind with her sails full of wind, as in the *Gulliver's Travels* quotation above), or *close-hauled*, because the lower corners of the main sails were all drawn as close as possible down to her side to windward.

If the helmsman by mistake turned the ship closer to the direction of the wind than it was capable of sailing, the wind would press the sails back against the masts, stopping the ship dead in the water and perhaps even breaking the masts off; in this case the ship was *taken aback*, the maritime source of another common metaphor.

You will appreciate that a ship could either sail *by* the wind or it could sail *large*, but never both at the same time. The phrase *by and large* in sailors' parlance referred to all possible points of sailing, so it came to mean 'in every possible direction' and therefore 'in all possible circumstances'. You can see how that could have become converted in layman's language into a sense of 'all things being considered'.

C3

Q. In my traversals through Wodehouse I have three or four times encountered the Bertie Woosterism *C3*. From context it obviously means substandard, low-grade, bottom-of-the-barrel, but I haven't found a reference explaining the origin and precise meaning of the term. My guess is that it comes from some sort of government grading or rating system, C3 being the antithesis of A1, analogous to the old US Draft Board designation of 4F.

A. You have the sense and origin exactly right. Here's one of the Wodehousian examples you've surely come across:

> **Anatole, I learned, had retired to his bed with a fit of the vapours, and the meal now before us had been cooked by the kitchen maid – as C3 a performer as ever wielded a skillet.**
> *Right Ho, Jeeves,* by P. G. Wodehouse, 1934.

In the First World War, as a result of conscription under the Military Service Act of January 1916, British recruits were graded from A1 to C3. The latter was the lowest grade, for men who were totally unsuitable for combat training, fit only for clerical and other sedentary jobs (it was discovered that a horrifyingly and scandalously large proportion of men – about 40 per cent of them – fell into this category).

> He was only two hours in the barracks. He was examined. He could tell they knew about him and disliked him. He was put in class C3 – unfit for military service, but conscripted for light non-military duties.
>
> *Kangaroo*, by D. H. Lawrence, 1923.

The C3 classification became a figurative term for somebody of the lowest grade or of grossly inferior status or quality. The system was later simplified, but *C3* caught on as a dismissive epithet and took a long time to vanish again.

> The population, fed on improperly grown food, has to be bolstered up by an expensive system of patent medicines, panel doctors, dispensaries, hospitals, and convalescent homes. A C3 population is being created.
>
> *An Agricultural Testament*, by Sir Albert Howard, 1940. Sir Albert is regarded as one of the key pioneers of modern organic farming, borrowing many techniques from India, which he observed first-hand while running a government research farm at Indore. This book focuses on the loss of soil fertility caused by intensive farming methods and on ways to restore it.

Cack-handed

Q. This is from the *Economist*, so I assume it must be some obscure Briticism: 'And most recently, Mr Pitt has been stunningly cack-handed over the appointment of William Webster as head of the new Public Company Accounting Oversight Board.' What does *cack-handed* mean?

A. It's certainly British. It's only obscure, though, if you're

from somewhere else, since it's a well-known British
informal term for somebody who is inept or clumsy.

> **A decade ago, I acquired an acoustic guitar, and taught myself
> to play. But it requires the endless repetition of monotonous
> exercises, resulting in shredded finger pads and strained eyes
> from squinting at chord patterns. It's tedious enough having to
> listen to your own cack-handed efforts, and many times worse
> for your next-door neighbour as you stumble repeatedly over
> the same passage of Ralph McTell's *Streets of London*.**
>
> *Sunday Herald*, Glasgow, 6 August 2008.

By extension, as I know to my cost, being of the sinistral
variety, it also means somebody left-handed, who does
everything 'backwards' and so looks clumsy or awkward.

It first appeared in the middle of the nineteenth century
in glossaries of various English dialects in the spellings
keck-handed or *cag-handed*. However, it only started to become
at all popular in mainstream British English in the 1960s,
because it required a loosening of people's objections to
using words with obvious sexual or scatological associations. The direct link is with *cack*, another fine old English
term for excrement or dung, with *cachus* (a *cack-house*) being
Old English for a privy. Such words are from Latin *cacare*,
to defecate.

The idea behind *cack-handed* almost certainly derives from
an ancient tradition that has developed among mainly
right-handed peoples that one reserved the left hand for
cleaning oneself after defecating and used the right hand
for all other purposes. At various times this has been known
in many cultures. Some consider it rude even to be given
something using the left hand. So to be left-handed was to
use the *cack hand* or be *cack-handed*.

Can of worms

Q. I have been trying to find the origin of the phrase *open a can of worms*. It was used by a financial expert in commenting on the banking meltdown at the end of September 2008, saying that 'This thing is an unbelievable can of worms.' It's hardly salubrious-sounding, perhaps for that reason appropriate to the situation. Where did this phrase really come from?

A. To open a metaphorical can of worms is to examine some complicated state of affairs, the investigation of which is likely to cause trouble or scandal and which you would much prefer was left alone. It sounds as though it might be a small-scale equivalent of the box or jar that Pandora brought with her as dowry to her husband Epimetheus, which let out all the troubles of the world when she opened it, leaving only hope.

> **The lid is at last being prised off the can of worms containing all the behind-the-scenes goings-on which seem to have characterised the 'reign' of Tony Blair at 10, Downing Street. It is not a pretty sight.**
>
> *Western Daily Press*, 13 May 2008. Just one example from several hundred in newspapers in this one month alone, which I've picked because the writer plays with the idea. The phrase has long since become an overused wordsmith's cliché.

This is the earliest example I've so far found:

> **The question of command for Middle East defense against Soviet aggression is still regarded as 'a can of worms' at General Eisenhower's SHAPE headquarters here.**
>
> *Edwardsville Intelligencer*, Illinois, 26 November 1951.

If you were hoping for some exotic origin, I have to disappoint you. Sad to relate, the original cans of worms were almost certainly real cans with actual worms in them, collected as bait for fishing. Fishermen have told me that the most annoying aspect of opening a literal can of worms is that, being live bait, they crawl out and are a nuisance to put back. It's also easy to see how a non-fishing friend or relative of an angler who opened a can containing a wriggling mass of worms would regard it as something that had better been left unexamined.

Carry the can

Q. I read in a British newspaper that the PM is happy that his successor as Chancellor is more than willing to *carry the can* for the PM's mistakes. There may be a couple of confusing terms in that sentence, especially for your legions of American readers, but the expression *carry the can* piques my curiosity. The journalist's meaning is obvious, but what is the origin of the phrase? I see some bleak public school playing-field, with all the big boys launching themselves at some hapless fourth-former with an empty sausage tin in his hand. Is there anything in this?

A. Nice image, but no, although it's certainly a weird expression. If you *carry the can* for something you're bearing the responsibility for its having gone wrong, frequently with the implication that you're taking the blame for someone else:

> **A judge has questioned why a senior Army officer left his subordinates to carry the can after a brutal punishment session which ended in the death of a soldier.**
> *Daily Mail*, 1 August 2008.

That example is particularly relevant because we're fairly sure the expression derives from services' slang. The first recorded cases are from the Royal Navy in the late 1920s, though Eric Partridge, in his *Dictionary of Slang and*

Unconventional English, says it had been around since the late nineteenth century. In his *Dictionary of Forces' Slang* he suggests that the idiom refers to 'the member of a gang or party who fetches the beer for all and then has the melancholy task of returning the empty'. This was a tedious chore, one moreover that left you open to censure or reprisals if you spilled the beer or dropped the can.

There's an older slang expression that's probably relevant: *to carry the keg*, also as *to carry the cag*. *Cag* and *keg* are variants of the same dialect word, meaning to offend or insult (*cag* or *kag* was also once Royal Navy slang for one of those arguments in which everybody is shouting and no one is listening). *To carry the cag* then was to hold a grudge, or to be easily annoyed or unable to take a joke. There's an obvious pun in the phrase on *keg*, a small cask, being something that you literally might carry, as you would figuratively carry a grudge.

It may be that *carry the can* developed as a joking reference to the older idiom, but then took on a life of its own.

Cash on the nail

Q. You mentioned in your *World Wide Words* newsletter, while reviewing a book on word histories, that the origin of *cash on the nail* given there wasn't correct. Please explain?

A. The origin of *cash on the nail* was there linked to four famous 'nails', bronze pillars with flat tops, like small circular tables, that are set in the pavement outside the Corn Exchange in Bristol. The story says that merchants paid their debts by putting their money on one of these nails. So *pay on the nail* or *cash on the nail* came to mean settling a debt promptly.

> **A couple of days ago, Ashton called on the owner of that property and made an offer. The offer was for cash on the nail.**
>
> *The Case of the Caretaker's Cat,* by Erle Stanley Gardner, 1955, in which Perry Mason investigates Charles Ashton, an irritable caretaker with a shrivelled leg and a Persian cat.

The story is retold in almost every popular book on word history I have on my shelves, as well as in Bristol's tourist literature and on its websites, and is firmly embedded in the minds of a substantial proportion of the British population. Nevertheless, it is untrue. Since extraordinarily robust belief requires equally powerful refutation, I'm going to write about this one in some detail. My apologies if this tells you more than you want to know.

Some history first. The nails were erected in Bristol between about 1550 and 1631. They were originally elsewhere but were moved to their present site after the Corn Exchange was built in the 1740s. Although the story seems to have been captured by Bristol, nails have also been recorded in the stock exchanges in Liverpool and Limerick. The latter dates from 1685:

> **An ample piazza under the Exchange was a thoroughfare: in the centre stood a pillar about four feet high, upon it a circular plate of copper about three feet in diameter; this was called the nail, and upon it was paid the earnest for any commercial bargains made, which was the origin of the saying, 'Paid down upon the nail.'**
>
> *Recollections of the Life of John O'Keeffe, written by himself,* 1826. O'Keeffe was the most produced playwright in London in the last quarter of the eighteenth century; William Hazlitt called him 'the English Molière'. The nail still exists and is now in Limerick Museum.

All this might seem to confirm the truth of the story, though not which nail was the source of the expression. But the linguistic history says otherwise.

The expression *on the nail*, on the spot, at once, without

delay, is first recorded in print in 1596, in a polemical tract by the Elizabethan author and playwright Thomas Nashe. This pre-dates almost all of the known nails. This isn't definitive, because they might have replaced others of earlier date. But the 1826 reference by John O'Keeffe is the first record of the word *nail* for them, an astonishingly late one if they had been the source of *on the nail* by 1596.

Similar expressions were recorded in other languages from even earlier, including German and Dutch. In particular the Anglo-Norman *payer sur le ungle*, to pay immediately and in full, is known from about 1320. *Ungle* is from Latin *unguis*, a finger or toe nail; it's a relative of *ungula*, a hoof or claw, from which we get *ungulate* for a hoofed animal.

The phrase *ad ungulum*, 'on the nail' – to a nicety, to perfection or to the utmost – is in the *Satires* of the Roman poet Horace of 2000 years ago and is based on an even older Greek expression. This may be from the idea of a sculptor having created a carving so perfect that running a fingernail over it couldn't detect any unevenness, or from a joiner testing the accuracy of a joint. This is likely to have been the inspiration for the Anglo-Norman phrase, albeit with a shift in sense from 'to the utmost' to 'completely; in full'.

So the evidence is that *on the nail* is the English version of an old phrase that came into the language via Latin and Anglo-Norman, one that refers to a fingernail rather than brass pillars. It seems certain from the dating that the various nails in the exchanges borrowed their names from the expression, and not the other way round.

Chequered

Q. I have heard the expression *checkered past* for many years but continue to be puzzled about why it should have the meaning it does. What is the origin of it?

A. Somebody with a *chequered past*, which is the British spelling I naturally use as opposed to your American one, or a *chequered history*, has had periods of varied fortune that have probably included actions considered to be discreditable.

> **He joined the church as a fully ordained Baptist minister in 1996 after a chequered past as a gambler.**
> *The Times*, 6 June 2008.

If the game of chess comes to mind, that's a good guess, although it's not the twists of fate experienced by the players that's being referred to, but the board it's played on. The idea behind it is of alternations of good and bad, like the colours of the squares on the board.

Something *chequered* is marked like a chess board, with a geometric pattern in different colours, if not literally arranged in squares. It's pretty much the same word as *checked*, both of which appeared in English in the fifteenth century. The latter was often spelled *chequed* in Britain until about a century ago but has now settled down to the *ck* spelling everywhere. *Chequered* in the literal sense is less common than it once was, although the *chequered flag* that's waved when a racing car passes the winning post continues to be well known.

That usage links us directly with its origin. *Chequered* came out of heraldry – the first known example is in the *Book of St Albans* in 1486, which explains – translated into modern English – that heraldic arms are said to be chequered when they are made in two colours in the manner of a chess

board. The word came from French *escheker*, derived from
late Latin *scaccarium*, a chess board. Our *exchequer* came from
the same source and originally also meant a chess board,
though it came to be connected with finance through a
table covered with a cloth divided into squares on which the
accounts of the revenue were kept using counters.

Chestnut

Q. I found myself using an idiom to a sea of blank faces in
my primary classroom. Where did *old chestnut* originate?

A. I can tentatively give you an answer, one that is described
by the editors of the *Oxford English Dictionary* as 'plausible',
which seems to be about as good as we're going to get.

It is said to go back to an exchange between the characters
in a play:

> ZAVIER: At the dawn of the fourth day's journey, I entered the
> woods of Collares, when suddenly from the thick boughs of a
> cork tree –
>
> PABLO: *(Jumping up)*: A chestnut, Captain, a *chestnut*!
>
> ZAVIER: Bah! You booby, I say, a cork.
>
> PABLO: And I swear, a chestnut – Captain! this is the twenty-
> seventh time I have heard you relate this story, and you
> invariably said, a chestnut, until now.
>
> *The Broken Sword; or, The Torrent of the Valley*, by William Dimond, first
> performed at the Royal Covent Garden Theatre, London, on 7 October 1816.
> It was described on the title page as 'a grand melo-drama: interspersed with
> songs, chorusses, &c'. William Dimond was born in Bath and in 1816 was
> managing theatres in Bath and Bristol. The play was popular, to judge from
> contemporary reports, and was toured and revived in the following decades.

This sounds reasonable enough as the source of the expression, but there are loose ends. *Chestnut*, meaning a joke or
story that has become stale and wearisome through constant

repetition, only starts to appear around 1880. The *Oxford English Dictionary* comments, 'The newspapers of 1886-7 contain numerous circumstantial explanations palpably invented for the purpose', implying that it was then new and that people were as puzzled by it as we are now. Where had it been all that time, if the source was this play? More puzzling still, the British newspapers said it was American.

They were right. It does seem that the word was imported from the US, where Dimond's play had remained as popular for many years as it had in Britain. A newspaper report in that country at the end of the century claimed that the word took on its new sense through the agency of a famous Boston comedian named William Warren, who had often played the part of Pablo:

> He was at a 'stag' dinner when one of the gentlemen present told a story of doubtful age and originality. 'A chestnut,' murmured Mr. Warren, quoting from the play. 'I have heard you tell the tale these 27 times.' The application of the line pleased the rest of the table, and when the party broke up each helped to spread the story and Mr. Warren's commentary.'
>
> *The Daily Herald*, Delphos, Ohio, 23 April 1896, reprinting an article from the *New York Herald*. This event must have occurred, if it ever did, many years earlier, since William Warren died in 1888 and the story noted that the play was 'long forgotten'.

You may take this with as large a pinch of salt as you wish, though the tale was often retold later and a similar story, also attributing it to Warren, is in the current edition of *Brewer's Dictionary of Phrase and Fable*. Even if it wasn't William Warren, it's not hard to see how somebody else familiar with the play could have made the same quip.

As the play remained in the repertory for some decades, and the joke could have been made at any time the play was still known, and as it probably circulated orally for a time before it was first written down, the long gap between the play's first performance and its first recorded use isn't so surprising.

The *old* in *old chestnut* is merely an elaboration for emphasis – another form is *hoary old chestnut* – both of which seem to have come along a good deal later.

Chin wag

Q. A friend of partially Irish ancestry here in Minneapolis, who is a most delightful conversationalist, enjoys a visit to me, which he refers to as having a *chin wag*. I had never heard this term before. What can you tell me about it?

A. On this side of the big pond, it's regarded as unremarkable, though it feels a touch old-fashioned. Stabbing my electronic pin at a collection of newspaper articles, I speared this one:

> He seems to understand that yes, we all enjoy watching football and having a good chin-wag about it, but, at the same time, we've all seen thousands of matches before so let's not get too carried away.
>
> *The Racing Post*, 16 March 2008.

To have a *chin wag* in current usage is to have a gossip or a wide-ranging conversation on some mutually interesting subject. It goes back a long way.

As an example of the byways that searches can take one down, the earliest example that I've found is in the *North Lincoln Sphinx*, a regimental journal prepared by and for the officers and men of the second battalion of the North Lincolnshire Regiment of Foot. The issue for 28 February 1861, prepared while the battalion was based in Grahamstown, South Africa, included some sarcastic 'rules' of whist, whose first item was 'Chinwag is considered rather as an addition to the game, than otherwise, and is allowed.' A footnote said that it was an 'American slang term for excessive talking.'

I wonder if the footnoter was right. All the early examples are British, including this one from *Punch* in 1879: 'I'd just like to have a bit of chin-wag with you on the quiet.' The British slang recorder John Camden Hotten included it in the second edition of his *Dictionary of Modern Slang, Cant and Vulgar Words* in 1873, but intriguingly defined it as 'officious impertinence'. It was more often used in the sense of those facetious whist rules to mean inconsequential talk or idle chatter or to suggest unkindly that some person couldn't stop talking. Wagging one's chin, indeed.

Claptrap

Q. Do you have any idea where the word *claptrap* comes from? I associate it with talking rubbish but I've no idea what a clap is – other than the obvious infectious disease – or why you would build a trap for one.

A. Your *claptrap* is indeed a trap to catch a clap, but it's the sort of clap you make by putting your hands together in appreciation. It was originally a trick of theatrical language to force the audience to applaud:

> **A Clap Trap, a name given to the rant and rhimes that dramatick poets, to please the actors, let them get off with: as much as to say, a trap to catch a clap, by way of applause from the spectators at a play.**
>
> *An Universal Etymological English Dictionary: Comprehending the Derivations of the Generality of Words in the English Tongue, Either Ancient or Modern*, by Nathan Bailey, 1727. 'An Universal', you will note, not 'A Universal'. It was conventional then to treat *U* in writing as a vowel, requiring *an* rather than *a*, even though *universal* was said the same way that we do now.

Such cheap showy sentiment or actorly flourishes, designed to appeal to the unthinking instincts of the audience, were thought unworthy of the serious dramatist or thespian. A writer in *The New-England Magazine* in 1835, fulminating against the star system that was contributing to the decline of the modern drama (how times do change), complained that in order to feed the performance of the lead actor, 'The piece must abound in clap-traps'. Nor was the technique confined to the theatre: an article in *Harper's New Monthly Magazine* in 1855 about a new play said that 'All the clap-traps of the press were employed to draw an audience to the first representation.' And in 1867, back in London, Thomas Wright wrote in *Some Habits and Customs of the Working Classes* that: 'The Waggoner's entertainment, of course, embraced the usual unauthenticated statistics, stock anecdotes, and pieces of clap-trap oratory of the professional teetotal lecturers.'

The word developed from this theatrical technique into a more general term for showy or insincere platitudes or mawkish sentimentality directed at the lowest common denominator of one's audience. From there it was only a short step to the sense of talking nonsense or rubbish, though the older ideas are often still present.

> **The man famous for making more-or-less the same film over and over, brings us another slice of spooky, vaguely supernatural claptrap, as a neurotoxin creates chaos around the world, laying waste to pretty much everyone but Mark Wahlberg and a coterie of friends and well-wishers.**
>
> *Irish Independent*, 9 June 2008. The film being adversely reviewed by Darragh McManus was M. Night Shyamalan's *The Happening*.

Incidentally, some time in the early nineteenth century, 150 years after the word was first recorded, an unsung backstage hero invented a mechanical device, a sort of clapper, that made a noise like that of applause (perhaps to encourage the real thing, though we are not told). Presumably it was similar to a football rattle. This also was called a claptrap. It has led some people into the error of suggesting that this device was the source of the word.

Cleft stick

Q. While reading a news article online I came across the term *cleft stick*. An Internet search turned up several definitions, all of them a variation on 'being stuck in a difficult position'. But, for the life of me, I couldn't find anything that gave a history of it. This is the first time I've ever seen it, and it's such an intriguing term that I'd love to know where it came from, hence I turn to you for help. Any clues?

A. It's mainly a British and Commonwealth expression. It's often rather stronger than just being in a difficult situation – it's one in which you're in a dilemma or bind in which you have no room for manoeuvre and in which any action that you take will be unfavourable to you.

> **Islamabad is caught in the cleft stick between getting into a bloody counter-insurgency war on the side of the unpopular Americans, on the one hand, or surrendering the tribal areas to self-avowed fundamentalists, on the other.**
> *Business Standard*, India, 12 February 2008.

Cleft is now unusual outside a small number of fixed phrases, of which the best known are *cleft palate* and *cleft chin*. It's one of the two past participles of the verb *cleave*, to split or sever, the other being *cloven*, as in animals with cloven hooves. You might know it in Augustus Toplady's hymn of 1775, 'Rock of Ages' ('Rock of Ages cleft for me, let me hide myself in thee.')

The first example in the *Oxford English Dictionary* is dated 1782, in a letter from William Cowper: 'We are squeezed to death, between the two sides of that sort of alternative which is commonly called a cleft stick.' The image is of a stick which has been partially severed along the grain of the wood to make a springy clasp for some object. A thing held in this way is in an unyielding embrace, from which the figurative expression derives.

Things once held in a literal cleft stick included candles (as in *Oliver Twist* by Charles Dickens: 'He bore in his right hand a tallow candle stuck in the end of a cleft stick') and an arrowhead attached to a cleft shaft, but what at once comes to mind for me is a letter or dispatch, a usage intimately connected with nineteenth-century colonial Africa.

> **About the middle of the morning we met a Government runner, a proud youth, young, lithe, with many ornaments and bangles; his red skin glistening; the long blade of his spear, bound around with a red strip to signify his office, slanting across his shoulder; his buffalo hide shield slung from it over his back; the letter he was bearing stuck in a cleft stick and carried proudly before him as a priest carries a cross to the heathen in the pictures.**
>
> *The Land of Footprints*, by Stewart Edward White, 1913. This famous work of travel writing is still in print. It told of the year that White, an American, spent in East Equatorial Africa early in the century. I'm told that the phrase *cleft stick and runner* is known today in South African English ('The parcel took so long to reach to him it would have been quicker to have used a cleft stick and runner').

This is another famous appearance:

> **I should take some cleft sticks with you. I remember Hitchcock – Sir Jocelyn Hitchcock, a man who used to work for me once; smart enough fellow in his way, but *limited*, very little**

historical backing – I remember him saying that in Africa he
always sent his dispatches in a cleft stick. It struck me as a very
useful tip. Take plenty.

Scoop, by Evelyn Waugh, 1938. Lord Copper, the proprietor of the *Daily Beast*,
advises William Boot, the hapless nature writer he has mistakenly engaged
to cover an African revolution. In the shop where he is being fitted out for
his expedition, Waugh neatly illustrates the irregularity of English: "'We can
have some [cleft sticks] cloven for you," she said brightly. "If you will make
your selection I will send them down to our cleaver.'"

Cloud nine

Q. Can you tell me anything about the origin of the
expression *cloud nine* for a very happy person?

A. The phrase *to be on cloud nine*, meaning that one is bliss-
fully happy, started life in the United States and has been
widely known there since the 1950s.

> **Dusty Rhodes of the Giants admitted today he will have to come
> down off cloud nine pretty soon and go to work again.**
>
> *Holland Evening Sentinel*, 20 April 1955. Rhodes was an outfielder for the
> New York Giants, a baseball player about whom it was said that on the
> surface he seemed to be unable to run, hit, throw, or field, but who beat
> you anyway; he's still remembered by aficionados of the game as helping to
> ensure his team's 4–0 victory in the 1954 World Series.

The expression is often said to have been popularized by the
Johnny Dollar radio show of the early 1950s, in which every
time the hero was knocked unconscious he was transported
to *cloud nine*. But there was another show, often listed
alongside it in the schedules:

> **Cloud Nine. Friday. 8:00 p.m. This excitingly new show present-
> ed by the Wm. Wrigley Jr., Co. blends fantasy, music, drama and
> comedy into 30 minutes of imaginative entertainment.**
>
> *Portland Sunday Telegram*, 2 July 1950. Originally produced in Chicago by the

CBS affiliate WBBM, this was the show's network premiere, one of several
that summer sponsored by the chewing-gum manufacturer.

Might this have been the origin? It's certainly the earliest
example of *cloud nine* we have, but it's not the first expression of the type. Others are *cloud eight,* known from Albin
Pollock's glossary *The Underground Speaks* of 1935, in which
it's defined as 'befuddled on account of drinking too much
liquor', and also *cloud seven*:

> **We latched onto an ultimate meetin' where a local crew was
> makin' with the music that liked to rock the roof and everyone
> was havin' a ball. Lots of noises, lots of sounds that put us up on
> cloud seven though we weren't in the States. The drummer was
> beatin' the skins, the pianist was really ticklin' the eighty-eight.
> The sax man was frantic and the horn was the most.**
>
> *Pacific Stars And Stripes*, 20 January 1954. The writer, Private Joe Nevens
> of the US Army, is taking R&R with friends in Tokyo. 'Crush me, Dad, I'm
> stoned.'

Seven and *heaven*, a pair of words that help lyricists by rhyming,
remind us of the Jewish and Islamic *seventh heaven*, the most
exalted level, the place where God dwells over the angels, the
souls of the righteous, and the souls of those yet to be born,
hence the phrase *seventh heaven* as a place or state of supreme
bliss, which dates from the later eighteenth century.

Cloud nine and its variations have always had close
associations with the euphoria that is induced by certain
chemicals, as you can tell from the quotations – alcohol
in its earlier days but more recently cannabis and crack
cocaine. The cloud here is an obvious reference to some
drug-induced dreamy floating sensation.

This link, and the numerical variations, makes deeply
suspect a common explanation of its origin – that it is from
the US Weather Bureau. This organization is said to describe
(or once did describe) clouds by an arithmetic sequence.

Level nine was the highest cumulonimbus, which can reach 30,000 or 40,000 feet and appear as glorious white mountains in the sky. So if you were on *cloud nine* you were at the very peak of existence. I can find no evidence to support this classification's existence.

I suspect that *seven* was chosen in part because of the religious associations and because it's a traditional lucky number and that *cloud* was substituted for *heaven* because of the links with the drug-induced sensation. Today's more usual *nine* may have come to be preferred because it reminds people of other idioms, such as *dressed to the nines* and *the whole nine yards*.

Cock-and-bull story

Q. A really strange movie, *Tristram Shandy: A Cock & Bull Story*, whose title seems to borrow from an incident in Laurence Sterne's book, has sent me unavailingly to the Net for information on the origin of *cock-and-bull story*. All I have been presented with is a tale about two inns in England that's more weird than the movie. Is there any truth in it?

A. Nary a smidgen of a trace of a germ of truth. It's a cock-and-bull story in two senses.

The tale speaks of two inns of these names, which still stand today on High Street in Stony Stratford, Buckinghamshire. This is how it is told in one account:

> I was billeted in a pub called 'The Bull.' This was in a town called Stony Stratford, on the Watling road between London and Birmingham, the oldest road in the British Isles, supposedly. Three doors from The Bull was 'The Cock.' In the old coaching days coaches from London stopped at the Bull, while the ones from Birmingham stopped at the Cock, and the drivers told

their respective stories in their respective Inns. By the time the Birmingham story had been retold in the London crowd and vice versa, you can see why the natives developed the idea of 'a cock and bull' story and this is supposed to be the very origin of the phrase.

Enigma In Many Keys: The Life and Letters of a WWII Intelligence Officer, by Robert E. Button, 2004. Colonel Button of the US Army was seconded to Bletchley Park, where the top-secret decryption of the German Enigma codes was carried out, hence the title.

The story is widely believed in Stony Stratford and is a source of civic pride. Step warily if you ever go there – if you are unwise enough to dispute its truth, any local who ripostes with 'well, tell us where it really comes from then, smart-arse' will leave you in embarrassed confusion, as you won't be able to supply an altogether satisfactory answer.

The experts note a French expression, *coq-à-l'âne*, which appears these days in phrases such as *passer du coq à l'âne*, literally to go from the cock to the ass, but figuratively to jump from one subject to another (in older French, to tell a satirical story or an incoherent one). This meaning is said to have come about through a satirical poem of 1531 by Clément Marot with the title *Epistre du Coq en l'Asne* (the epistle of the cock to the donkey), though the phrase is two centuries older still. *Coq-à-l'âne* was taken into Scots in the early seventeenth century as *cockalane*, a satire or a discon-nected or rambling story.

The suggestion is that some similar story once existed in English, akin to one of Aesop's fables, in which a cock communicated with a bull rather than a donkey. Nobody, however, has been able to discover what it might have been. Another idea is that the French phrase was borrowed in partial translation, with *donkey* changed to *bull* for some reason.

The first sense of the phrase in English, in the seventeenth century, was in much the same sense as *cockalane*, a long, rambling or idle story that may be tedious or misleading. In Sterne's book, *The Life and Opinions of Tristram Shandy, Gentleman*, published 1759–76, the only reference to it is right at the end: 'L..d! said my mother, what is all this story about? – A Cock and a Bull, said Yorick – And one of the best of its kind, I ever heard.' Since the book is a stream-of-consciousness story, rambling and inconsequential, this self-referential summing-up is entirely apt.

It was only at the end of the eighteenth century that the expression came specifically to mean a manufactured tall tale.

Cockles of your heart

Q. Where, pray tell, are the *cockles of your heart*? I even asked a cardiologist, and he didn't know either!

A. It's one of the more lovely idioms in the language, isn't it? Something that warms the cockles of one's heart induces a glow of pleasure, sympathy or affection. It's not surprising that it should be associated with the heart, since that's been assumed to be the seat of the emotions for most of recorded history. It's also linked to the warming effects of strong liquor:

> **Well, come in and taste a drop o' sommat we've got here, that will warm the cockles of your heart as ye wamble homealong.**
>
> In Thomas Hardy's epic drama *The Dynasts* of 1904–8. The speaker is a Wessex rustic, hence the dialect (to *wamble* is to walk with a reeling or staggering gait, which suggests the *sommat*, something, was strong stuff). Hardy had been working on this vast work about the Napoleonic Wars for thirty years (you may judge how vast from the subtitle, 'In three parts, nineteen acts and one hundred and thirty scenes'). You will not be surprised to hear that it has never been performed in full, but then Hardy meant it only 'for mental performance'.

As you say, the problem is to identify these *cockles*. There are many meanings for the word but easily the most likely candidate is the bivalve mollusc, familiar to most British people:

> **In Dublin's fair city,**
> **Where girls are so pretty,**
> **I first set my eyes on sweet Molly Malone,**
> **As she pushed her wheelbarrow**
> **Through streets broad and narrow,**
> **Crying, 'Cockles and mussels, alive, alive oh!'**
>
> A popular song that has achieved the status of an unofficial anthem in Dublin, it's usually attributed to the Scotsman James Yorkston of Edinburgh, whose composition – described as a comic song, though surely one intended to be sung lugubriously with mock pathos, as Molly dies in a later verse – was published in London by Francis Day & Hunter in 1884. A version appeared the year before in *Students' Songs* in Cambridge, Massachusetts. So the song is neither Irish nor traditional and despite widespread belief to the contrary Molly Malone was most definitely fictional.

Cockles are still to be found as a tasty snack, eaten with vinegar, that are associated in many people's memories with the seaside. Their twin shells are ribbed and heart-shaped, which explains why the zoological name of the common British cockle is *Cardium edule*, where *Cardium* is from Greek *kardia*, the heart, and *edule* means edible. Eat your heart out, cockle taster.

Since the ventricles of the heart are similarly ribbed, the obvious conclusion is that they reminded surgeons of the twin shells of the cockle. But – to confirm your failure to find out more from a heart specialist – I can't find an example of *cockle* being applied to the heart outside this expression. Another explanation sometimes heard is that the shape of the cockleshell, suggesting the heart as it so obviously does, gave rise to *cockles of the heart* as an expansion. Some observers of word history, who prefer to speculate along more risqué lines, have noted that in the nineteenth century, the *labia minora* were nicknamed the cockles, implying a different route to pleasure and satisfaction. Sadly for that story, we know that the idiom – appearing first as *rejoice the cockles of one's heart* – is about two centuries older than the low slang term. Another possibility that's been suggested is that the idiom comes from a different sense of the word, in full *cockle-stove*, for a type of heating stove with ribbed projections to radiate the heat better, whose name comes via Dutch from the German *Kachel* for a stove tile. This seems unlikely.

One further explanation is much more probable. In medieval Latin, the ventricles of the heart could be called *cochleae cordis*. *Cochleae* is the plural of *cochlea*, the Latin word for a spiral (the same name is given to the spiral cavity of the inner ear) and *cordis* is an inflected form of *cor*, heart, meaning 'of the heart'.

Those unversed in Latin might have misinterpreted *cochleae* as *cockles*, or it might have been a medical in-joke. Since *cochlea* is also Latin for a snail, if this origin is right we should really be speaking of warming the snails of one's heart, though somehow it doesn't have the same ring.

Cockpit

Q. I can't dream up any relationship between the pit where chickens fight and the place in an F16 fighter where chickens definitely don't fight. Any ideas? Where does the word *cockpit* come from?

A. When you stop and think about it, the term for the pilot's cabin on an aircraft – and other spaces such as the driver's compartment in a racing car or for a helmsman in a yacht – is rather curious, isn't it?

The experts are sure that it does come, as you suggest, from a place where cock fights were held. The word is recorded from the latter part of the sixteenth century, during the reign of the first Elizabeth. It came about because the fighting area for cocks (one of the favourite recreations of the time, together with bull- and bear-baiting) was often thought of as a pit. It was usually a roughly circular enclosure with a barrier around it so that the birds couldn't escape, sometimes fitted up with rows of seats like a tiny theatre so that the spectators could look down on the action. The first recorded mention of the word is in Thomas Churchard's *The Worthiness of Wales* of 1587: 'The mountains stand in roundness such as it a Cock pit were'. Shortly afterwards, a more famous example appears:

> **Can this cockpit hold**
> **The vasty fields of France? Or may we cram**
> **Within this wooden O, the very casques**
> **That did affright the air at Agincourt?**
>
> From the Prologue to *Henry V*, by William Shakespeare, 1600. The chorus laments the inadequacy of a theatre and a limited cast to portray the tumultuous events about to unfold. Shakespeare is using the word – and also *wooden O* – to allude to the round shape and noisy crowd of an Elizabethan theatre, in which the central area in which the groundlings stood was called the pit. The *casques* are the helmets of the troops, though how they affright the air isn't clear.

Nearly a century earlier, Elizabeth I's father, Henry VIII, had bowling alleys, tennis courts and a cockpit built on a site opposite the royal palace of Whitehall. A block of buildings later erected on the site were taken over in the seventeenth century for government offices such as the Treasury and the Privy Council but continued to be referred to by their old function. That explains the entry in Samuel Pepys's *Diary* for 20 February 1659: 'In the evening Simons and I to the Coffee Club, where nothing to do only I heard Mr. Harrington, and my Lord of Dorset and another Lord, talking of getting another place at the Cockpit, and they did believe it would come to something.'

A little later, the term came to be applied to the rear part of the lowest deck, the orlop, of a fighting ship (*orlop* is from Dutch *overloop*, a covering). During a battle it became the station for the ship's surgeon and his mates because it was relatively safe and least subject to disturbance by the movements of the ship. Like all lower-deck spaces, it was confined, crowded and badly lit. During a battle, it was also noisy, stinking and bloody. All this reminded people of a real cockpit, hence the name. On 21 October 1805, Admiral Lord Nelson died in the cockpit of HMS *Victory* during the battle of Trafalgar.

The move to today's sense came through its use for the steering pit or well of a sailing yacht, which also started to be called the cockpit in the nineteenth century. This was presumably borrowed in fun from the older term because it was a small enclosed sunken area in which a *coxswain* was stationed. (To start with, that word was *cockswain*, he being the *swain*, or serving man, who was in charge of a *cock*, a type of ship's boat.) From here, it moved in the early twentieth century to the steering area of an aircraft, and later still to other related senses.

Cock-up

Q. I am not familiar with the term *cock-up* that you used in one of your newsletters, and am interested in both its meaning and its derivation. It's not a phrase that is commonly used here in the United States – indeed, it has connotations that would keep many from using it in a column read by so many subscribers!

A. Oddly, in British English it is not these days a vulgarism, or at least only a very mild one.

> **It was journalism's most spectacular collective cock-up in years – a prime example of the results of 'groupthink'. And it happened on the world's most important story.**
>
> *New Statesman*, 17 January 2008. The writer, Brian Cathcart, is lamenting the way that the press erred so badly in predicting that Barack Obama would easily win the New Hampshire primary that month.

It comes from one of several senses of *cock*, to bend at an angle, as in – for example – cocking a gun, an animal's cocking up its ears, or a man's turning up the brim of his headgear, so producing an old-time naval officer's *cocked hat*.

> **At present a Man may venture to cock up his Hat, and wear a fashionable Wig, without being taken for a Rake or a Fool.**
>
> *The Spectator*, 22 August 1711.

The use of *cock-up* to mean a blunder or error was originally British military slang dating from the 1920s. The penile slang sense of *cock* clearly had a lot to do with its adoption, but this hasn't stopped it being used in respectable publications, and modern British dictionaries mark it merely as informal or colloquial.

Column

Q. Why is there a letter *n* at the end of the word *column*?

A. Or, putting it another way, why is it there but not pronounced?

The source of our word is the Latin *columna*, which had a syllable break between the *m* and *n*, so both letters were pronounced. It was brought into English via French in the fifteenth century, in the earliest examples as *colomne*, in which it kept the Latin syllable break.

However, it went through a lot of changes and different spellings in the following 250 years. William Caxton, the first person to print books with movable type in England, spelled it *colompne* in a work in 1471, taking its form from Old French. Others dropped the ending altogether, leaving a word with roughly the same pronunciation as we use now, but spelled *colum*. It is also recorded with a silent *b* on the end to make it *colomb*.

The spelling settled down to our modern form in the latter part of the seventeenth century:

> **As in a fiery column charioting His godlike presence.**
> *Samson Agonistes*, by John Milton, 1671.

The *n* seems to have been added back by classically educated scholars who wanted to match the spelling of its Latin original, in much the same way that the *b* was added back to *debt*, in medieval times spelled and said *dette*, because the Latin original was *debitum*, 'something owed'. The pronunciation of *column* was unaffected, so the *n* has always been silent (in fact, it's impossible to sound it following the *m* without making an extra syllable of it, as the Romans did). However, it is sounded in compounds like *columnar*.

Come a cropper

Q. I have heard that the phrase *come a cropper* relates to getting a hand crushed in a Cropper printing press in which paper is hand fed, so that any mistiming results in a trapped hand. I have seen a printing press made by Cropper at the Blists Hill Open Air Museum at Ironbridge.

A. We use *come a cropper* now to mean that a person has suffered a bad fall, sometimes figuratively that he has been struck by some serious misfortune. Though getting a hand crushed in a printing press would certainly qualify, it turns out that there's no link between the press and the expression. Henry Cropper made a couple of very well-known manual letterpress machines in the nineteenth century, but the first was only introduced in 1867, about a decade after the expression was first recorded.

Come a cropper actually derives from hunting, where it originally meant a heavy fall from a horse. Its first appearance was in 1858, in a late and undistinguished work, '*Ask Mamma*', by that well-known Victorian writer on hunting, R. S. Surtees, who is much better known for his *Jorrocks' Jaunts and Jollities*. This is an early figurative use:

> When his companion had left him, Nidderdale sat down, thinking of it all. It occurred to him that he would 'be coming a cropper rather,' were he to marry Melmotte's daughter for her money, and then find that she had got none.
>
> *The Way We Live Now*, by Anthony Trollope, 1874.

The earliest easily traceable source of *cropper* is the Old Norse word *kropp* for a swelling or lump on the body. This is closely related to the Old English word for the rounded head or seed body of a plant, from which we get *crop* for the produce of a cultivated plant. In the sense of a bodily lump, it was applied first to the *crop* of a bird but then extended to other bodily protuberances. This is where things get complicated: the same word travelled from a Germanic ancestor through Vulgar Latin and the Old French *croupe* back into English as *croup* for the rump of a horse. From this we also get *crupper*, the strap on a horse's harness that passes back from the saddle under the tail and stops the saddle sliding forward. (The Old French *croupe*, incidentally, also led to *croupier*, the person in charge of a gaming table; a croupier was originally a person standing behind a gambler to give advice and the name was borrowed from Old French *cropier*, a pillion rider or a rider on the *croupe*.)

At the end of the eighteenth century English developed a phrase *neck and crop*, with the sense of completely, totally or altogether.

> **The startish beast took fright, and flop**
> **The mad-brain'd rider tumbled, neck and crop!**
>
> The first known appearance of the phrase, in a poem by Edward Nairne, published in 1793. He was supervisor of customs at Sandwich in Kent, where he was born. Because of his verse he became known as the Sandwich Bard.

Now *neck and crop* is a rather odd expression, and we're not sure how it came to be. It could be that *crop* is a variant of *croup*, suggesting that a horse had collapsed all of a heap, with both head and backside hitting the ground together (one later example does spell the phrase *neck and croup*, though this might be an error). Or perhaps *crop* had its bodily protuberance sense, so the expression might have been an intensified version of *neck*, perhaps linked to an older expression *neck and heels* that's similar to *head over heels*.

Whatever the origin, it's thought that *come a cropper* derives from *neck and crop*, with *cropper* in the role of an agent noun, referring to something done in a *neck-and-crop* manner, and that the phrase developed from there.

Come hell or high water

Q. My wife and I had a discussion a while back after I heard her say 'Come hail or high water'. I politely explained that this was not the correct way to say this, but she argued her point rather intensely. She does make sense when she asks 'What do hell and high water have to do with one another, anyway, aren't hail and high water weather events?' Am I right to persist in arguing that it's *come hell or high water*?

A. We don't do marriage counselling here. Try the Yellow Pages.

But you're right to say that it's *come hell or high water*. The context of many of the earliest examples shows it has nothing directly to do with the weather, nor with any kind of maritime experience. Instead, they strongly point to cattle ranching as the source, in particular the driving of cattle to railheads in the Midwest in the latter part of the nineteenth century.

> **There is an expression still current in the American language: 'In spite of hell and high water.' It is a legacy of the cattle trail, when the cowboys drove their horn-spiked masses of long-horns through high water at every river and continuous hell between, in their unalterable determination to reach the end of the trail which was their goal.**
>
> *The Trampling Herd: The Story of the Cattle Range in America*, by Paul Wellman, 1939.

Further support comes from this story of an old-time cattle-man, Zack Addington, from three decades earlier:

> **He prospered in those palmy days until he became the largest cattle owner in the territory and felt able to take his regular blowout in St Louis, until 1884, when, between the alien land law, drought and rustlers, the 'hell and high water of the cattle-men,' he ... walked out of the Kansas City stock yards a few hundred thousand dollars worse off and no cattle worth putting an iron on, much less pulling grass by hand to feed.**
>
> *Washington Post*, 26 November 1905.

The expression appears in print in the US in the last quarter of the nineteenth century in the *Washington Post*'s form, *hell and high water*. The first example on record is from 1879, but it starts to frequently appear in books and newspapers only from the 1890s. Other variations, including the form you give – which is now standard – came along several decades later.

The phrase can now be used frivolously for problems that are less than serious:

> **'There's only one way of dealing with early mornings,' says John Humphrys of Radio 4's *Today* programme, 'and that's early nights – however good the party you have to leave. I'm in bed at 9pm come hell or high water.'**
>
> *Daily Telegraph*, 4 August 2008.

Compleat and complete

Q. Are *compleat* and *complete* really two separate words, as the *American Heritage Dictionary* seems to say? Or is the former merely an alternate spelling of one meaning of the latter? While *compleat* is said to mean 'quintessential', one meaning of *complete* is closely related as 'skilled; accomplished'.

A. In Britain, *compleat* is regarded by dictionary makers as merely an archaic way to spell *complete*, used nowadays only as a bit of whimsy, and not very often at that. It's rather more common in the US, which is why the *American Heritage Dictionary* – and at least one other US dictionary – has included it as a separate entry. Though hardly in everybody's spelling box, it's not hard to find examples of it in American English:

Professor Mersky was a longtime friend of *The Texas Observer*. He was a generous spirit, a compleat gentleman, and a tireless combatant on behalf of religious and civil liberties.

The Texas Observer, Austin, Texas, 16 May 2008.

Above and behind him a window went up with a rattling bang and he knew what was coming next. 'I hope you rot!' she screamed down at him. The Compleat Bronx Fishwife.

From the revised 1990 edition of *The Stand*, by Stephen King. This incident happens early in this post-apocalyptic novel, which King described as 'an epic fantasy with an American backdrop', before most of the population of the world dies from the superflu bug called Captain Trips.

As the older spelling of *complete*, it died out around the end of the eighteenth century. One of its last appearances was a reference to George III in the US Declaration of Independence: 'He is at this time transporting large armies of foreign mercenaries to compleat the works of death, desolation and tyranny'.

It was reintroduced at the beginning of the twentieth. For this we must blame the continuing popularity of Isaak Walton's *The Compleat Angler*, which combines practical information on fishing with folklore, pastoral songs and ballads. Writing in 1653, he naturally used the older spelling of *complete* and modern editions retain it. Because Isaak Walton's book has stayed so well known, the word in that spelling has been taken as a model for modern book titles, mostly in the USA. The American Psychological Association issued *The Compleat Academic: A Career Guide;* Jake Bernstein wrote *The Compleat Guide to Day Trading Stocks*; there's even *Heart Monitor Training for the Compleat Idiot* by John L. Parker. From its specialized use in book titles, this spelling has escaped into the general written language, though – as I say – it's much more common in the US than in Britain.

I'd argue that there's no real difference in meaning

between the two forms, except that you may feel that *compleat* is pretentious and unnecessary.

Crib

Q. A simple question, but it's bothering me. Where does *crib* come from, in the sense of a cheat's answer sheet or for illicitly copying somebody else's work? It's listed as the same word as the baby's bed, but the connection is beyond me.

A. It is indeed the same word, though a lot lies behind it.

The use of the term for a baby's cot is more common in US English than in British English, where it's mainly reserved for a model of the Nativity of Christ, with a manger as a bed. The verb *to crib* in the sense of plagiarizing or stealing another's schoolwork is mainly British English, though both US and British English know *crib notes*. Both varieties of English share the sense of a barred container or rack for animal fodder, a manger. This is the original, which turns up in English around the year 1000 and which is from an Old German word whose descendants are to be found in modern Dutch and German.

There are other senses of *crib*, especially that of a cabin or hovel (from an extension of the sense of an animal stall), which eventually led to the meaning in the South Island of New Zealand of a small house at the seaside or at a holiday resort; to thieves' slang of the early nineteenth century for a house, shop or public house; to the slightly later US slang usage for a saloon, a low dive or brothel; and to the current US Black English sense of one's room, house or apartment. The baby's bed sense arrived in the seventeenth century as an instance of the barred container idea, others from the same source being a repository for hops during harvest and a wickerwork basket or pannier. A shift from container to contents may explain why it has sometimes meant a light meal or a workman's lunch, though it's also suggested that an eighteenth-century slang sense of the stomach (a repository for food) may be the direct link.

The basket sense was used in particular for one in which a poacher might conceal his catch. The experts guess that this may have led to the thievery sense around the middle of the eighteenth century. They base their view on this example:

> **A brace of birds and a hare, that I cribbed this morning out of a basket of game.**
>
> *The Nabob*, a play by Samuel Foote, 1778. The title borrows a term then only recently introduced into English from Urdu, probably via either Portuguese or Spanish. It originally referred to a Muslim official or governor under the Mogul empire, a *nawab*, but in English came to mean a person of conspicuous wealth or high status, especially one who returned from India to Europe with a fortune, the group that this play savagely satirizes. Foote is the first known user of *nabob* in this sense, in an earlier work of 1760.

The plagiarism sense arrived around the same time, though it seems to have become applied to stealing or illicitly copying another's school work only in the following century.

Crocodile tears

Q. When I used the phrase *crocodile tears* recently I was asked to provide a derivation. My dictionary is not very enlightening; can you help?

A. To weep crocodile tears is to pretend a sorrow that one doesn't in fact feel, to create a hypocritical show of emotion.

> **Inauthentic CEOs downsize their organization, increase their own compensation, and weep crocodile tears for the employees who have lost their jobs.**
>
> *Ethics, the Heart of Leadership*, by Joanne B. Ciulla and James MacGregor Burns, 2004.

The idea comes from the ancient belief that crocodiles weep while luring their prey to its death or devouring it. The story seems to have been taken up by medieval French and English writers and that's where we get it from. The first example known in English is in a travel book of about 1400, *The Voyage and Travail of Sir John Mandeville*. Another is from a deeply misogynistic account about a century later:

> His nature is ever when he would have his prey, to cry and sob like a Christian body, to provoke them to come to him, and then he snatcheth at them; and thereupon came this proverb, that is applied unto women when they weep, lachrymae crocodili, the meaning whereof is, that as the crocodile when he crieth goeth then about most to deceive, so doth a woman most commonly when she weepeth.

In an account of 1565 by John Sparke of the second voyage of John Hawkins to the New World, published in Richard Hakluyt's *The Principal Navigations, Voyages, Traffiques and Discoveries of the English Nation*, 1600. *Lachrymae crocodili* is Latin for crocodile tears.

The story was taken up by Edmund Spenser in *The Fairie Queene* and then by Shakespeare (who put the crack about insincere female tears into the mouth of Othello). Having such authorities on its side made it almost inevitable that the reference would stay in the language.

Quite how the story came into being puzzles zoologists. The experts say that crocodiles can indeed weep – they have tear glands like most other animals – though of course they don't cry in the sense of emitting tears as part of an emotional response. However, there have been observations of caymans and alligators, close relatives of crocodiles, emitting tears while they're eating (a more probable source of the misunderstanding). This probably happens because of the huffing and hissing behaviour that often accompanies feeding. Air forced through the sinuses may force tears in the crocodiles' tear glands to empty into the eye, making it look as though they are weeping.

Cry all the way to the bank

Q. I have noticed that here in Sweden people are now using the English expression *cry all the way to the bank* translated into Swedish. What does the English expression mean?

A. The English phrase means that you're making money undeservedly at the expense of others. It often refers to a sportsman who loses a match, or to a show-business person who gives a poor performance, but who still cynically collects a thumping fee. The expression has become extremely common throughout the English-speaking world in the past decade or so and has become a knee-jerk journalistic cliché. As well as crying, you may sob, smile or laugh your way.

> In all the hoo-ha about rising interest rates and the pain they cause borrowers, one important point has been lost: savers are laughing all the way to the bank.
>
> *The Age*, Melbourne, Australia, 4 March 2008.

The phrase is often credited to that flamboyant and camp American pianist Liberace, he of the candelabra, extraordinary costumes and piano-shaped swimming pool. It became a catchphrase for him and he is often quoted as originating it. The first four examples in the *Oxford English Dictionary* all refer to him, the first being this:

> On the occasion in New York at a concert in Madison Square Garden when he had the greatest reception of his life and the critics slayed him mercilessly, Liberace said: 'The take was terrific but the critics killed me. My brother George cried all the way to the bank.'
>
> *Daily Mirror*, 26 September 1956. Liberace is quoted in closely similar terms in

an article in *The Corpus Christi Caller-Times* of Texas on 23 May 1954. In the form *laughed all the way to the bank*, it's also attributed to him in the *San Mateo Times* of California on 7 November 1953. It has the feel of a story he told to laugh off the interior pain of the stinking reviews he so often got.

This looks pretty conclusive. Sadly, for what survives of Liberace's reputation, he may have borrowed an existing expression:

> **Eddie Walker perhaps is the wealthiest fight manager in the game ... The other night when his man Belloise lost, Eddie had the miseries ... He felt so terrible, he cried all the way to the bank!**
>
> *Waterloo Daily Courier*, Iowa, 3 September 1946. In the following years, this is repeated in various forms and is attributed to other fight managers.

Curate's egg

Q. Could you please give the meaning and derivation of *the curate's egg*? I keep coming across it in books and newspapers but nobody explains it.

A. The phrase *curate's egg* means something that is partly good and partly bad and so not wholly satisfactory:

> **The supporting cast is a curate's egg: Steven Mackintosh is chilling as a predatory weirdo, while Fiennes is miscast.**
>
> In a review in *The Times* on 19 June 2008 of the prison-break film *The Escapist*.

Remarkably, just for once we know exactly where the expression comes from:

> **RIGHT REVEREND HOST: I'm afraid you've got a bad egg, Mr. Jones!**
>
> **THE CURATE: Oh no, My Lord, I assure you! Parts of it are excellent!**
>
> *Punch*, 9 November 1895. This caption is underneath a cartoon with the title *True Humility*, drawn by George du Maurier. A timid curate is overawed

by having breakfast in his bishop's home and desperately attempts to avoid giving offence. One reason why Americans are so often puzzled by the expression is that they don't know that a *curate* is a junior clergyman in Britain, whose lowly status and utter dependence on his bishop for advancement is an important contributor to the joke.

Readers liked this exchange so much that the cartoon led to the catchphrases *good in part, like the curate's egg* and *parts of it are excellent*, along with *curate's egg* itself. The last of these became so over-used that H. W. Fowler referred those searching for it in his *Modern English Usage* in 1926 to the articles on Hackneyed Phrases and Worn-out Humour.

Anyone who uses or hears *curate's egg* will probably have the phrase 'good in parts' spring to mind. However, some modern users of the expression reason, quite logically, that an egg can't be part bad and change the sense accordingly, so completely misunderstanding the point of du Maurier's joke. A guide written for journalists in 2004 correctly described the phrase as a cliché but gave the bad-egg advice, 'If you are tempted to use it, please be aware that it does not mean a bit good and a bit bad – an egg that is good "in parts" is still rotten.' Not in the original cartoon, it didn't, nor in common usage.

Dab hand

Q. I wondered how the phrase *dab hand* originated, meaning someone particularly skilled at a task. Any ideas?

A. This is mainly a British and Commonwealth expression.

> I am a dab hand at ordering a caffè latte, and know not to order a latte in Italy (fools, you will get a glass of milk).
>
> *Daily Telegraph*, 6 February 2008.

The phrase *dab hand* turns up first in the early nineteenth century and is widely recorded in English regional and dialect usage through the century. The first recorded use of *dab* by itself in a related sense is in 1691. It's also in *A New Dictionary of the Terms Ancient and Modern of the Canting Crew* of 1698–9: a *dab* there is 'expert, exquisite in Roguery'. It is also said to have been gaming jargon of the period, indicating a person who was an expert gamester. *Dabster*, an expert, which has mainly been an American word, is from the same source at about the same time. *Dab* has often been reported as school slang, but that may be a later development, as early sightings all had criminal associations.

Nobody is sure where *dab* came from: it may be linked to the Old Dutch *dabben* and German *tappen*. The verb first appears about 1300, when it meant to give somebody a sharp blow; it weakened in sense over time, until in the sixteenth century it arrived at its modern meaning of pressing lightly and repeatedly with something soft (the more recent criminal slang *dabs* for fingerprints seems to derive from this sense, perhaps based on the image of an arrested person giving his fingerprints with an inkpad and paper, though a nod towards *dab hand* might also be there).

It's difficult to see how the idea of expertise grew out of the various senses of *dab* and it's possible that in this sense it's a separate word, perhaps from *adept*, or just possibly from *dapper*.

Darby and Joan

Q. Who were *Darby and Joan*? My dictionary tells me that they were 'a devoted old couple, characters in a poem', but did they actually exist or were they fictional? I'm assuming their devotion was to each other (as opposed to a religion or building model aeroplanes), but does this mean that a Darby and Joan club is about old couples, or merely, as I have always assumed, about old people?

A. In the UK, *Darby and Joan* is still a way to describe an elderly and mutually devoted married couple who live a placid and uneventful life, often in humble circumstances.

> Together with her late husband John, she was a familiar figure around the community centre in Craigyhill. The pair even continued helping with the area's meals-on-wheels service while in their 80s. They were always seen together, referred to fondly by many as 'Darby and Joan'.
>
> *Larne Times*, Northern Ireland, 25 June 2008.

There are many Darby and Joan Clubs, so named, in various parts of the country, social clubs for pensioners, which hold dances and other events. The name is indeed strictly a misnomer, since the clubs are for all pensioners, not only married couples. The term has long been used to evoke an image of companionship in old age. Many modern references are linked to a once-popular song:

> Darby dear we are old and grey,
> Fifty years since our wedding day.
> Shadow and sun for every one,
> as the years roll by.
>
> 'Darby and Joan', words by Frederic Weatherly and music by James Molloy, 1890. As well as being a barrister, Weatherly was a prolific and popular lyricist for more than 50 years, who wrote the words for 'Danny Boy' and 'Roses of Picardy' among many others. It was once usual for wives to refer to their husbands by their surnames, even in private.

But the expression is certainly older than that – it turns up in the middle of the nineteenth century in works by Thackeray, Melville and Trollope. An advertisement in *The Times* on 1 February 1802 announced that a 'comic divertisement' entitled *Darby and Joan; or The Dwarf* was being performed at the Royalty Theatre, London; there was a new dance of the same title, which was 'received with loud and general plaudits' according to the issue of the same newspaper dated 26 May the previous year; in June 1801 the newspaper reported that a ballet of that title was being performed. So by 1800, the phrase was already widespread.

We must go even further back:

> **Old Darby, with Joan by his side,**
> **You've often regarded with wonder:**
> **He's dropsical, she is sore-eyed,**
> **Yet they're never happy asunder.**
>
> *The Joys of Love never forgot. A Song*, an anonymous poem that appeared in the *Gentleman's Magazine* in March 1735.

The *Oxford English Dictionary* describes these verses as 'mediocre' and comments, 'This has usually been considered the source of the names, and various conjectures have been made, both as to the author, and as to the identity of "Darby and Joan", but with no valid results.'

One of the conjectures that's supported by more circumstantial evidence than others is that the author was Henry Woodfall, the eldest of three generations of printers with the same name who worked in London. He was apprenticed to John Darby, a printer who lived in Bartholomew Close with his wife Joan, who was equally active in the business. John Darby died in 1704 aged about 80. The *Oxford Dictionary of National Biography*, in an earlier edition, claimed that Henry Woodfall wrote the ballad to commemorate his late employer and his wife. However, the claim does not appear in the current edition online and the connection seems not so clear-cut as once thought. In any case, the stimulus to publish a eulogistic memorial would have dissipated by 1735, though Henry Woodfall was still alive then.

Leaving aside the question of authorship, it is remarkable that the expression *Darby and Joan* should have remained active in the language for more than 200 years.

Dead cat bounce

Q. I'd never come across the phrase *dead cat bounce* before
the recent dips and dives on the world's stock markets
but then heard it on various media reports three times
in one day. I'd guess it refers to a small improvement in
the market's fortune. Am I correct? And what is its
origin?

A. This bit of gruesome, if graphic, jargon of the financial
world does refer to a temporary recovery from a big drop
in a stock's price, but one that's an illusory sign of improvement and which is short-lived. This early appearance in
print explains the imagery behind it:

> **DeVoe suggests the printing of a bumper sticker reading:
> 'Beware the Dead Cat Bounce.' 'This applies to stocks or
> commodities that have gone into free-fall descent and then
> rallied briefly,' he says. 'If you threw a dead cat off a 50-story
> building, it might bounce when it hit the sidewalk. But don't
> confuse that bounce with renewed life. It is still a dead cat.'**
>
> *San Jose Mercury News*, California, 28 April 1986.

Despite the associations with the US, the earliest known
example appeared in a report in a British newspaper that
had been filed from the Far East:

> **Despite the evidence of buying interest yesterday, they said the
> rise was partly technical and cautioned against concluding that
> the recent falls in the market were at an end. 'This is what we
> call a "dead cat bounce",' one broker said flatly.**
>
> *Financial Times*, 7 December 1985.

The phrase gradually caught on during the 1990s but
became particularly common – for the obvious reasons
associated with the financial turmoil of the time – after
2000. Observers of financial jargon thought that its heyday

was passing, but the economic downturn of 2007 onwards gave it new life:

> **Bank shares were today able to repair some of the damage caused by this week's sell-off. But does this standalone perform-ance mean it is time to call the bottom of the credit crunch, or is this just a Wall Street-inspired dead cat bounce? That was the question brokers were asking themselves today.**
>
> *Evening Standard*, 17 July 2008.

Dear John letter

Q. As a non-native speaker of the English language (I'm Dutch), I wonder where the phrase *dear John letter* comes from. I have always taken it to be a letter in which the recipient is told a love affair is over, but I might be amiss.

A. You have it right. It's conventionally a letter from a woman to a boyfriend or husband saying that all is over between them, usually because the woman has found somebody else.

> **Like many marriages, these partnerships are born of conven-ience and when one partner outgrows the other, or sudden changes in behaviour act as tell-tale signs of disillusion, a Dear John or Dear Jane letter cannot be far away.**
>
> *IT Week*, 29 May 2006. As you might gather from the publication, which focuses on digital technologies, the term is figurative here: the story actually refers to the strains on a vendor partnership between Dell and Intel. *Dear Jane letter* is a more recent form that reflects today's sexual equality.

The expression seems from the evidence to have been invented by Americans during the Second World War. At this time, thousands of US servicemen were stationed overseas for long periods; many of their wives and sweethearts left at home found that absence didn't make the heart grow fonder. The unhappy news was necessarily communicated in a letter.

> **'Dear John,' the letter began. 'I have found someone else whom I think the world of. I think the only way out is for us to get a divorce,' it said. They usually began like that, those letters that told of infidelity on the part of the wives of servicemen ... The men called them 'Dear Johns'.**
>
> *The Democrat and Chronicle*, Rochester, NY, 17 August 1945.

Why *Dear John*? That isn't entirely clear but a couple of pointers give a plausible basis for it. *John* was a common generic name for a man at this period (think also of terms like *John Doe* for an unknown party to a legal action). Such letters were necessarily written in a formal way, since any note of affection would obviously have been out of place. So a serviceman getting a letter from his wife or girlfriend that started stiffly with 'Dear ... ' knew at once that a particular kind of bad news had arrived.

A second pointer may be an American radio programme, at first called *Dear John*, broadcast between 1933 and 1944, starring the former silent-film actress Irene Rich. Drama episodes were framed by a letter from the gossipy lead character to her never-identified romantic interest that began with these words. It's conceivable this played a part in the genesis of the term.

Derby

Q. This one has been worrying me for a long while – ever since I was asked and didn't know the answer. So why do we call a game between two local sides a *Derby*? I presume it has nothing to do with the name of the horse race which was named after Lord Derby.

A. Actually, it does. That race, first run in 1780, was named after Edward Stanley, 12th Earl of Derby (its proper name is the *Derby Stakes*, universally abbreviated). Legend has it that the race was nearly named the *Bunbury Stakes*, because Lord Derby and another racing enthusiast, Sir Charles Bunbury, tossed a coin to determine which of them was to have it named after him. Sir Charles's consolation prize was to have his horse win the first Derby.

It soon became established as the high point of the racing season as part of the meeting at Epsom in Surrey in early June. Benjamin Disraeli once famously described it as 'the Blue Ribbon of the Turf'. *Derby day*, the day of the race – always a Wednesday until very recently – became a hugely popular event:

> **It is the one great London holiday, which in variety, in cheer-fulness, and in cordial good fellowship of all classes of the community, beats hollow, in my opinion, even the merriest of our Bank holidays.**
>
> *London Up to Date*, by George Augustus Sala, 1895. This work, published in the year of Sala's death, was – as he admitted in his preface – 'so many detached essays describing scenes and characters which did not find a place in *Twice Round the Clock*', his earlier and better-known work about London, published in 1859.

It became so important that other classic races were named after it, such as the Kentucky Derby, though Americans understandably say the word the way it's spelled rather than the British *darby*. At about the time Sala was writing, the word was moving into more general use to describe any highly popular and well-attended event. In particular, it came to be applied to a fixture between two local sides, first called a *local Derby* and then often abbreviated. It has become widely known and extremely common:

**The Auckland Blues adapted best to experimental new rules to
end a run of home defeats against the Waikato Chiefs with a
32–14 win in the Super 14 local derby yesterday.**

Taipei Times, Taiwan, 17 February 2008.

Dogsbody

Q. In browsing your biographical details on the *World Wide
Words* site from here in New York I notice that you served
as *dogsbody* at one time in your career. What a great word!
Where does it come from?

A. A *dogsbody* is a lowly person who gets all the dirty jobs,
like emptying the ashtrays or putting new toner in the
photocopier. Anything menial, disagreeable or boring
somehow makes it into the job description. Americans
might prefer *gofer* instead.

> **I'm Lieutenant Marc Vitrac, US ASF, and one of the Ranger squad
> here, which means specimen-collector, liaison with the locals,
> and general dogsbody.**
>
> *The Sky People*, by S. M. Stirling, 2006. New arrivals are being introduced
> to Venus, which in this alternate universe has been made habitable by
> an alien species of Great Ones; in the sequel, *In the Courts of the Crimson
> Kings*, we find they have also terraformed Mars, now inhabited by a race of
> beings with more than a passing resemblance to those created by Edgar Rice
> Burroughs.

The word is probably a product of that great melting-pot
and fount of culture, the Royal Navy. Sailors at the time
of Nelson were just about the worst-fed people around,
living as they did on a monotonous diet that included such
culinary awfulnesses as boiled salt beef and ship's biscuits
(which after weeks at sea had to be rapped on the table to
persuade the weevils to leave before you could eat them).
One of their staple foodstuffs was dried peas boiled in a bag.

The official name for this concoction was *pease pudding* (*pease* being the old form of the vegetable's name that was later wrongly presumed to be a plural and changed to *pea*) but the jolly Jack Tars called it *dog's body*. We don't know why. Perhaps it came from the shape and look of the bag after it had been boiled.

In the early part of the twentieth century, the same word began to be applied to midshipmen, who got unloaded on to them all the nasty jobs that more senior officers wanted to dodge. Presumably the term was borrowed from the sailor's foodstuff, though we can't be sure about that, since there's no link in meaning or any evidence how it got from the one to the other.

Anyway, the word seems to have escaped the Royal Navy in the early 1930s to become a more general term in the civilian world for the person in a group who got stuck with all the rough jobs. And so it has remained.

Doolally tap

Q. What is the origin of *doolally tap*? I used to hear the phrase as a youngster in London fifty years ago and used in the context of someone being rather peculiar mentally.

A. This is an excellent illustration of the reach of the English language. The expression is certainly a British one – though now not so often heard in that form – but to find its origins we must travel to India.

In 1861, the British Army established a military base and sanatorium at Deolali, about 100 miles north-east of Bombay (it is still an important Indian military centre today). One of its functions was to act as a transit camp for soldiers who had finished their tours of duty ('time-expired', in the jargon of the time) and were waiting for a troop ship to take them back to Britain. Ships left Bombay only between November and March, so a soldier ending his tour outside those dates might have a long wait. It was often dispiriting:

> The time-expired men at Deolalie had no arms or equipment; they showed kit now and again and occasionally went on a route march, but time hung heavily on their hands and in some cases men who had been exemplary soldiers got into serious trouble and were awarded terms of imprisonment before they were sent home. Others contracted venereal disease and had to go to hospital. The well-known saying among soldiers when speaking of a man who does queer things, 'Oh, he's got the Doolally tap,' originated, I think, in the peculiar way men behaved owing to the boredom of that camp.
>
> *Old Soldier Sahib*, by Frank Richards, 1936. This described his service in India and Burma in the years 1902–12. It followed his earlier book of 1933, *Old Soldiers Never Die*, a memoir of a private soldier in the Great War. *The Times* said of this book, 'He has the double gift of conjuring up sights, sounds, and smells and of slipping in pungent anecdotes to illustrate and enliven his narrative.'

To say someone was *doolally tap* meant he was mad, or at least very eccentric. The first bit is obviously the result of the standard British soldier's way of hacking foreign place names into something that sounded at least vaguely English. The second part is from a Persian or Urdu word *tap*, a malarial fever (which is ultimately from Sanskrit *tapa*, heat or torment). So the whole expression might be loosely translated as 'camp fever'.

We're not sure when the term entered soldier's jargon. The earliest example I know of is in a glossary forming part of the book *Rhymes of the Rookies* by W. E. Christian, published in 1917.

The full expression, though it's still heard from time to time, must have already been falling out of common use when you heard it, since most reference books imply that by the 1940s it had already been shortened to *doolally*. That's the way most people have learned it, meaning that somebody's behaviour goes well beyond the merely odd. You still come across it, though not one speaker in a hundred can connect it to a place in India.

> **'And what's wrong with me saying Cirencester?' Danny asked politely. 'Nothing, given the right context,' said the voice smoothly. 'In a conversation about Cotswold towns, nothing could be more natural. In the present case, though, a less charitable man than myself might take it as proof that you've finally gone completely doolally.'**
>
> *Flying Dutch*, Tom Holt, 1991. Concerning Julius Vanderdecker, the immortal captain known as The Flying Dutchman, who took out an insurance policy around 1588 with the House of Fugger (a real business, by the way), which is now worth more than enough to buy up the whole world. Danny is Danny Bennett, a journalist who finds conspiracy involving the Milk Marketing Board at every turn.

Dreaded lurgi

Q. Do you know the etymology of the phrase *dreaded lurgy*? I know it's related to illness and the Cambridge online dictionary says it's 'a humorous way of speaking of any illness which is not very serious but is easily caught'.

A. This is the immediate origin:

> **Lurgi is the most dreadful malady known to mankind. In six weeks it could swamp the whole of the British Isles.**
>
> *The Goon Show*, Series 5, Programme 7, broadcast 9 November 1954. This anarchic and surreal radio comedy series starred Peter Sellers, Harry Secombe and Spike Milligan. Spike also wrote most of the scripts. There was no epidemic – it was a fraud perpetrated by those arch-criminals, Count Jim 'Thighs' Moriarty and the Honourable Hercules Grytpype-Thynne, trading as Messrs Goosey and Bawkes, a barely disguised reference to the music publisher and instrument maker Boosey and Hawkes. They

put it about that nobody who played a brass-band instrument had ever
been known to catch lurgi; this resulted in their disposing profitably of vast
amounts of merchandise.

The Goons were then highly popular and the episode resulted
in the phrase *dreaded lurgi* becoming a school playground
term for some horrid infection that you had supposedly
contracted, especially one you had as a result of being dirty
or smelly or just not like the other kids. It has survived to the
present day, though it's now almost invariably spelled *lurgy*
and is most common in Australia and New Zealand:

> **The team are struck down by the dreaded lurgy while on the
> trail of a murderous gang who are killing witnesses in a high-
> profile court case.**
>
> From the television guide in the *New Zealand Herald*, 3 May 2008.

However, all Americans seem to be inoculated against it at
birth, since it's virtually unknown to them (but then, they
never experienced the Goons phenomenon and instead have
cooties; these are literally body lice, from a Malay word, but
figuratively a cootie is an imaginary germ that only infects
people you don't like).

OK, so much for the background. Where did this word
lurgi or *lurgy* come from? There are several theories bandied
about. One school of thought holds that Milligan invented it
out of the air. It might, say others, be *allergy* with the beginning cut off; it's an ingenious idea, though English doesn't
usually lose a stressed initial vowel and *lurgi* is said with a
hard *g*, to rhyme with *Fergie*, so that the soft *g* in *allergy* tells
against it. The most plausible suggestion is that it's from
the Lurgi gasification process, which was developed by the
company of that name in Germany in the 1930s to get gas
from low-grade coal and which Milligan came across during
his military service in the Second World War.

Intriguingly, there was once a dialect term that might

have played a part in its genesis. The *English Dialect Dictionary* notes *lurgy* or *lurgie* from northern England, meaning idle or lazy. This may well be linked with *fever-largie*, *fever-lurden* or *fever-lurgan*, a sarcastic dialect term for a supposed disease of idleness; this was recorded as still current in some places at the time the dictionary was compiled at the end of the nineteenth century (I mean the term was still being used, but presumably the malady was lingering on as well).

> **The coolie, drawn from his native village reluctant, like a periwinkle from its shell, is never a good starter, and when he finds himself at the end of a tow-rope or bowed beneath half a hundredweight of the sahib's trinkets, with a three-thousand-feet pass to attain in front of him, he is extremely apt to burst into tears – idle tears – or be overcome by a fit of that fell disease – 'the lurgies'. Lest my reader should not be acquainted with this illness, at least under that name, here is the diagnosis of the lurgies as given by a very ordinary seaman to the ship's doctor. 'Well, sir, I eats well, and I sleeps well; but when I've got a job of work to do – Lor' bless you, sir! I breaks out all over of a tremble!'**
>
> *A Holiday in the Happy Valley with Pen and Pencil*, by Major T. R. Swinburne, 1907. The valley is in Kashmir; his work remains a significant record of early tourism in that region and is still in print.

Spike Milligan and the Goons would have been tickled by the idea of an epidemic outbreak of idleness.

Dribs and drabs

Q. I overheard someone recently saying money was arriving *in dribs and drabs*. What is the origin of that phrase? Is it to do with art or painting?

A. Neither of those things, as it happens. However, *dribs and drabs* – scattered or sporadic amounts of something – contains some interesting etymological archaeology.

Drib is known from some English, Irish and Scottish dialects of no later than the eighteenth century and meant an inconsiderable quantity or a drop. It's most probably a variant form of *drip* or *drop*. It was taken by emigrants to the US and at one time was fairly common there. The *English Dialect Dictionary* quotes this:

> **We are sending such regiments and dribs from here and Baltimore as we can spare to Harper's Ferry, supplying their places, in some sort, by calling in Militia from the adjacent States.**
>
> A letter written to Major General George Brinton McClellan by US president Abraham Lincoln on 25 May 1862. McClellan was then commanding, if that's the right word, the Army of the Potomac in the Civil War.

The experts are undecided whether the second half is an invented rhyming echo of the first, as in reduplicated compounds like *helter-skelter*, *see-saw* and *hurly-burly*, or if *drab* is a real word in its own right. *Drab* certainly existed as a dialect term that could mean much the same as *drib*, though it was used in particular for a minor debt or a small sum of money. The first example in the *Oxford English Dictionary* is this:

> **Drab, a small debt. 'He's gain away for good, and he's left some drabs.'**
>
> *The Dialect of Craven, in the West Riding of the County of York*, by W. Carr, 1828. In standard English, 'He has gone away for ever and he's left some debts.' The *English Dialect Dictionary* also quotes this entry and notes that the word is recorded only from Yorkshire and Cheshire.

The *Oxford English Dictionary* is fairly sure that it isn't the same word as the one that describes a dirty and untidy woman, which may either be from Gaelic *drabag* or Irish *drabog*, a dirty woman, a slattern, though it might be linked to the old Low German *drabbe*, dirt or mire. Nor is it the word for something drearily dull – this began by referring to undyed cloth and comes from French.

The limited distribution of *drab* suggests that the word in the phrase is indeed a mere variation on *drib* for the sake of a neat and bouncy phrase.

Duct tape

Q. Is that universal sticky tape stuff that everyone has in their toolkit called *duct tape* or *duck tape*? I've read and heard it both ways but can't work out which is correct.

A. It's possible to make a case that either is right. The story behind the stuff is confusing enough to require some sorting out. Bear with me while I trace the evidence and the contrary opinions.

Let's first dispose of one possible confusion. Examples of *duck tape* are recorded from as far back as the beginning of the twentieth century, which might suggest it's the older form. But that's misleading. This duck tape isn't the sticky-backed stuff but plain fabric cotton tape made from the material called *duck*. It's been called that for four centuries; its name is from the Middle Dutch *doek*, linen or linen cloth; only later was it manufactured using cotton. It was a lighter and finer material than canvas, often used for seamen's trousers and sometimes for sails on small craft. *Duck tape* was widely used at one time for the vertical binding tapes of venetian blinds.

There's nothing in any records of usage in historic databases or in the entries for both terms in the *Oxford English Dictionary* that suggests what the original name of the adhesive-backed material might have been. Various accounts have appeared on web pages and in a column by William Safire in *The New York Times* in March 2003. All tell the same story (so much so that they arouse unworthy suspicions).

The original material was developed, it is said, by the Permacel division of Johnson & Johnson in 1942 for the US Army as a waterproof sealing tape for ammunition boxes. The tape proved immensely versatile and was used for all sorts of repair purposes on military equipment. These facts come from Johnson & Johnson's historians, so ought to be accurate. But the story goes on to say that because the fabric backing was made from cotton duck and perhaps because it repelled moisture 'like water off a duck's back', soldiers started to call it *duck tape*. However, there's no known relevant use of *duck tape* in any document of the Second World War that anyone investigating the matter has looked at. A column by Jan Freeman in the *Boston Globe* in March 2003, partly in response to Safire's, implies that the story about the name *duck tape* might have been a folk etymology passed on in good faith by employees of Johnson & Johnson. Otherwise, we have no idea what Permacel – or the US Army – called the material.

Some time after the war, it is said, engineers began to use the tape to seal the joints in air-conditioning ducts. This tape was manufactured in the same way, though to match the ducting it was coloured silver rather than the green of the Army version. Because of this use, it became known informally as *duct tape*. There are examples of that name in newspaper advertisements dating from the mid 1960s, though the earliest ones don't make clear what the material is. One in *The News* of Frederick, Maryland, dated 17 November 1966, is the first I've found that describes a product like the modern one – a plastic 'self-adhering' tape, in rolls 2 inches wide and 30 feet long.

Duck tape is a trademark of Henkel Consumer Adhesives,

dating from 1982, who sell it under that name in several countries. John Kahl, the CEO of the firm, was reported by Jan Freeman in the same article as saying that his father chose the name after noticing that *duct tape* sounded like *duck tape* when customers asked for it. (The collision of the two *t*s in the middle of *duct tape* causes the first one to be lost by a process called elision.) The term *duct tape* has never been trademarked, though several compound terms that include it have – it looks as though it had become generic before anybody thought of registering it. Apart from a one-off instance in the *Oxford English Dictionary* of *duck tape* from 1971 (which looks like a case of the *duct–duck* elision), I can't find *duck tape* in the adhesive sense until the 1980s.

The evidence strongly suggests that the original name among non-military users post-war was *duct tape*, given to it informally by heating engineers, and that the *duck tape* version is elision in rapid or casual speech, later capitalized on by a manufacturer. But, as things stand, nobody knows for sure.

Dude

Q. I was taken aback to read the following in Jerome K. Jerome's book *Three Men in a Boat*, which was published in 1889: 'Maidenhead itself is too snobby to be pleasant. It is the haunt of the river swell and his overdressed female companion. It is the town of showy hotels, patronised chiefly by dudes and ballet girls.' Just how long have *dudes* been with us?

A. Many people have first come across references to dudes in connection with *dude ranches*, where American urbanites could experience a sanitized version of Western life, and it is often assumed that this is the source of the term. However, *dude ranch* is relatively recent, with the first known examples being from 1921. The *Oxford English Dictionary*'s first example of *dude* is from 1883, though we now know it had been around for a few years before that in the sense of an effete man. It's definitely an Americanism. So how could it be casually used in a British book as early as 1889 with no hint that it was other than a native word?

The cause was an extraordinary craze or fashion identified by that name:

> It is d-u-d-e or d-o-o-d, the spelling not having been distinctly settled yet. Nobody knows where the word came from, but it has sprung into popularity within the past two weeks, and everybody is using it ... The word 'dude' is a valuable addition to the slang of the day.
>
> *Brooklyn Eagle*, 25 February 1883.

A detailed description of the *dude* appeared the following month and was widely syndicated:

> A dude is a young man, not over twenty-five, who may be seen on Fifth Avenue between the hours of three and six, and may be recognized by the following distinguished marks and signs. He is dressed in clothes which are not calculated to attract much attention, because they are fashionable without being ostentatious. It is, in fact, only to the close observer that the completeness and care of the costume of the dude reveals itself. His trousers are very tight; his shirt-collar, which must be clerical in cut, encircles his neck so as to suggest that a sudden motion of the head in any direction will cause pain; he wears a tall black hat, pointed shoes, and a cane (not a 'stick'), which should, we believe, properly have a silver handle, is carried by him under his right arm, (projecting forward at an acute angle, somewhat in the manner that a sword is carried by a general at a review, but with a civilian mildness that never suggests a military origin for the custom). When the dude takes off his hat, or when he

is seen in the evening at the theatre, it appears that he parts his hair in the middle and 'bangs' it. There is believed to be a difference of opinion among dudes as to whether they ought to wear white gaiters.

New York Evening Post, 10 March 1883.

The article noted that dudes, unlike the mashers of the time and the dandies, fops and swells of earlier generations, set out to give an impression of protest against fashionable folly and of being instead serious-minded young men with missions in life: 'A high-spirited, hilarious dude would be a contradiction in terms.' But dudes were also widely reported as being vapid, with no ideas or conversation.

The *Brooklyn Eagle* fleshed out this portrait by noting that a dude was as a rule a rich man's son, was effeminate, aped the English, had as 'his badge of office the paper cigarette and a bell-crown English opera hat', was noted for his love of actresses (to the extent of carrying on scandalous 'affairs') but with no knowledge of the theatre.

In June, the *Daily Northwestern* reported that dudes had taken to wearing corsets, 'in order to more fully develop and expose the beauties of the human form divine'. The *Richwood Gazette* of Ohio argued in July that the dude was useful 'as an example of how big a fool can be made in the semblance of a man'; the *Prince Albert Times* of Saskatchewan noted the same month that 'The dude is one of those creatures which are perfectly harmless and are a necessary evil to civilization.' *The New York Times* reported that a city man staying in a hotel in Long Branch, New Jersey, had been 'grieved in his spirit' by being called a dude and asked in its headline whether the word should be considered defamatory. The *Manitoba Daily Free Press* reported the story, 'bearing evident marks of reportorial invention', that a dude was seen being chased up Fifth Avenue, by a cat.

You will note that *dude* was most definitely a term of ridicule. The geographical spread of the references shows that the whole of North America was variously intrigued and disgusted by the spread of the dude phenomenon in the cities of the East Coast. The *Atlanta Constitution* wrote in June, 'So great a success the dude has had here in the United States, most every newspaper in the country has written editorials on him and brought him before the public in such manner as to create comment, if not surprise.' News of him crossed the Atlantic very quickly. In fact, the *Oxford English Dictionary*'s first example of the word is in the *Graphic*, a popular illustrated paper of London. Its report in March 1883 reads as if it were cribbed from the *New York Evening Post*: 'The one object for which the dude exists is to tone down the eccentricities of fashion ... The silent, subfusc, subdued "dude" hands down the traditions of good form.'

Dude became widely known in the UK and it isn't surprising that Jerome K. Jerome came across the term, as he was at the time an actor in London. Indeed, some US newspapers stated at the time that the term had been brought to New York from the London music halls and that this was the reason for the pronounced Anglophile streak in the fashion. But, so far as I know, nobody has found British examples that pre-date the US ones.

That leaves us without any direct leads to the source of *dude*. Earlier examples are on record – the *Historical Dictionary of American Slang* takes it back to 1877 and there's at least one instance of it as a personal name or nickname a year or two earlier still as well as a Dude Club that was mentioned in a newspaper from Dubuque in 1877. But it is clear from the 1883 articles that these had made no impression on the American public. We may leave aside the theory of Daniel Cassidy in his book *How the Irish Invented Slang*, that it is from the Irish word *dúd* for a foolish-looking fellow or dolt, since he provides no evidence and none is known. But it has been plausibly linked by etymologists to the much older *duds* for clothes, which could especially refer to ragged or tattered ones or even to rags, with *dudman* being an old term for a scarecrow (hence, at the end of the nineteenth century, *dud* meaning something useless). We may guess that *dude* was a sarcastic way to describe the understated but foppish dress of these fashionable young men. Another possibility is that it is linked to the old song 'Yankee Doodle Dandy'; an 1830 poem refers to *Yankee Doodle Dandies*, a pretty obvious reference, and the middle word might well have been extracted and shortened.

Dude has softened and changed in the century since. It can now refer to a man who is no more than stylish or fastidious; in Black American speech in particular it often means simply 'chap', 'guy' or 'fellow'. The Coen brothers film *The Big Lebowski* of 1998 did much to make *dude* more widely known, since Jeffrey Lebowski refers to himself as *The Dude*. As an aside on the way language develops, two women governors of US states – Sarah Palin in Alaska and Kathleen Sebelius in Kansas – have husbands who are known not as *first gentlemen*, which would be the male equivalent of the common term *first lady*, but as *first dudes*.

Eavesdropper

Q. Settle an argument, please. Can you tell us where *eavesdrop* and *eavesdropper* originate?

A. It began in Anglo-Saxon England, when the word was *yfesdrype*, related to an Old Norse word of similar sense, which in modern English would be *eavesdrip*. People later turned it into *eavesdrop* for no good reason anybody can work out.

One meaning was the area around a building that was liable to be wetted by water pouring off the projecting eaves of the roof above (gutters hadn't been invented yet). The word also referred to an old custom in English law by which a landowner was prevented from building within two feet of his boundary, for fear that the water cascading off his eaves might cause problems for his neighbour. This was considered a sufficiently important issue that a special legal term was invented in connection with it: *stillicide*. If a householder were to let rain fall from his eaves on to the land of a neighbour, he first needed the neighbour's permission, called a *servitude*.

By the latter part of the fifteenth century, the word *eavesdropper* had been invented for somebody who stood within this strip of ground, close to the walls of a building, in order to listen surreptitiously to the conversations within. This was initially also a legal term:

> **Eavesdroppers are such as stand under walls or windows by day or night to hear news and to carry them to others, to make strife and debate among their neighbours: these are evil members in the commonwealth, and therefore are to be punished.**
>
> *Les termes de la ley; or Certain difficult and obscure words and terms of the common laws and statutes of this realm now in use, expounded and explained,* by John Rastell, first compiled in 1527. I've modernized the spelling. John Rastell was a lawyer, printer and member of Parliament, among other accomplishments, who married Sir Thomas More's sister, Elizabeth.

The verb *to eavesdrop* in the same sense came along about a century later.

Elephant in the room

Q. I keep coming across the expression *elephant in the room* in newspapers and wondered if you could shed any light on where the phrase comes from.

A. The expression is American in origin, though it has been around in the UK since about 2000 and has become extremely common in the press and broadcast media since 2004, becoming a fashionable journalistic cliché. The American phrase started life as *the elephant in the living room* but it has generally been shortened to your form, though the longer version can still be found in the US.

It refers to a problem or issue that everyone ignores or avoids mentioning, because it's politically or socially embarrassing, though in truth it's too big to ignore:

> **For much of the day Zimbabwe was the elephant in the room, a crisis the summit strenuously avoided discussing.**
> *Sky News*, 1 July 2008.

An early example is the title of a well-known American book of 1984 by Marion H. Typpo and Jill M. Hastings, *An Elephant in the Living Room: A Leader's Guide for Helping Children of Alcoholics*.

Two earlier examples are not in our current sense but are obviously its precursors. A piece in the *Winnipeg Free Press* in October 1976 said, 'What is big and unfamiliar is mistrusted. Anyone would feel uncomfortable with an elephant in the living room, no matter how friendly it might be.' There's another from *The New York Times* of June 1959: 'Financing schools has become a problem about equal to having an elephant in the living room. It's so big you just can't ignore it.'

The idea seems to have been around for quite some time before it became common or took on its modern sense, most probably being reinvented from time to time by writers seeking a vigorous image.

Faffing

Q. Whilst talking with one of my colleagues recently she expressed a great deal of amusement at the term *faff*, as in *faffing about*, where the meaning is to be doing something without any real purpose and often in an effort to avoid doing something else. I often accuse my children of *faffing around*, especially in the mornings when they ought to be getting ready for school but will do pretty much anything to avoid it. Is my definition of *faff* correct, and where did the term come from in the first place?

A. You're correct with your definition. It's originally British, informal but not rude, and moderately common, especially – as you say – in the form *to faff about* or *faff around*.

> **Let us all hope our blessed British climate smiles upon us: hope for just enough rainy days to make it all grow well, enough sunny ones in which to enjoy faffing about and plenty of gorgeous balmy evenings so we can knock back a few outdoor bevvies with friends.**
> *Daily Telegraph*, 4 January 2008.

> **A new report says that we waste three hours faffing around, doing nothing in particular, pootling, dawdling, pottering, hanging about.**
> *Guardian*, 13 August 2008.

It can be used as a politer alternative to another four-letter word beginning with *f* (which, I suspect, is why your colleague was amused) but has no link with it. It starts to appear as a dialect word in Scotland and northern England

at the end of the eighteenth century, as a description of the
wind blowing in puffs or small gusts.

> **As when a person blows chaff away from corn held in his hands,
> or the wind when it causes brief puffs of smoke to return down
> the chimney.**
>
> *A Glossary of the Cleveland Dialect*, by the Rev. J. C. Atkinson, 1868. John
> Atkinson was an antiquary and amateur archaeologist based for most of
> his adult life in the North Yorkshire village of Danby, from where he also
> wrote books on folklore and ornithology, as well as several for children.
> He's best remembered for his 1891 book, *Forty Years in a Moorland Parish*.
> He had enough energy left over to be married three times and sire 13
> children.

Faff may have been imitative of the sound of gusty wind, or
it may be a variation on *maffle*, a more widely distributed
dialect term in Scotland and England that means to stutter
or stammer or to waste time or procrastinate; this might
be from the old Dutch regional word *maffelen*, meaning
to move the jaws. There's also *faffle*, another dialect word,
which has very similar senses and geographical distribution, and which might have influenced the sense.

The word started to move into the wider language around
the end of the nineteenth century in its modern sense,
though it didn't much appear in print until the 1980s.

Fair cop

Q. In one of the *Monty Python* movies, as a woman falsely
accused of being a witch is being carted off to her destiny
she says under her breath, *that's a fair cop!* Is this the
common British slang for being arrested?

A. *It's a fair cop* was what the essentially good-natured thief
with a typically British sense of fair play was once supposed
to say as his collar was fingered by the fuzz, meaning that

the arrest was reasonable and he really had done what he was accused of doing. You will appreciate that this was an entirely fictitious and romanticized view of the relationship between criminals and the police, despite late nineteenth-century newspaper reports:

> **'It's a fair cop,' said the thief.**
>
> *The Daily News*, 24 October 1891.

It's a well-understood British and Commonwealth expression, though it has been used so often in second-rate detective stories and police television series down the decades that it has long since ceased to be possible to use it seriously and the *Monty Python* team was playing on its hackneyed status.

> **Thank you to David Brayford who wrote in, 'prepare to blush, Louise', listing the grammatical errors in [my book] *A Novel in a Year*. It's a fair cop. Anyone who has the nerve to write a how-to-write book deserves to be corrected, after all.**
>
> *Daily Telegraph*, 21 September 2007. Louise Doughty has suffered a version of McKean's Law, named after its inventor, Erin McKean, the editor of the *Oxford American Dictionary*: 'Any correction of the speech or writing of others will contain at least one grammatical, spelling, or typographical error.'

Cop here comes from the same root as *cop* for a policeman. This may be from the slang verb *cop*, meaning to seize, originally *cap*, a dialect term of northern England that by the early nineteenth century was known throughout the country. This can be traced back through French *caper* to Latin *capere*, to seize or take, from which we also get our *capture*. So a *cop* in this sense was a seizure or capture.

Fair dinkum

Q. I'm looking for the origins of the Australian slang phrase *fair dinkum*, which I'm told originates from Chinese. It means *real*, and is used to allay any potential disbelief about some claim the speaker is making. Apparently, Chinese gold miners in the nineteenth century would tell others of any discoveries of gold using the phrase *din gum* meaning 'real gold' in Chinese.

A. People are particularly intrigued by *dinkum* because it's a totemic Australianism that seems to have no connection with any other word in the language. *Fair dinkum* means something that's reliable or genuine, fair and square or on the level.

> **If the government is fair dinkum about the binge drinking issue they must increase the tax on cask wine and they must increase the tax on beer, or alternatively bring the tax back on alcoholic beverage drinks.**
>
> *The Age*, Melbourne, 15 May 2008.

Yours is an excellent story, full of oriental charm. It's been told before:

> **Jim Kable believes that 'dinkum' may come from the Cantonese expression 'din kum', meaning 'real gold'. It would have come, he says, from Chinese workers during the gold rush.**
>
> *Sydney Morning Herald*, 9 February 1984.

It *is* possible to generate a Cantonese phrase *ding kam*, 'top gold', but there's no evidence at all that any Chinese ever used it, whether in the goldfields or anywhere else. It's just another example of folk etymology – a well-meaning attempt to make plain the puzzling and explain the inexplicable.

Most dictionaries published outside Australia and New Zealand are unhelpful about where *dinkum* comes from, just saying 'origin unknown'. But it seems highly probable that – like a lot of Australian expressions – it's from English dialect. Almost the only place in which it's recorded is in Joseph Wright's *English Dialect Dictionary* of 1896–1905 in which he notes *dinkum* is used in Derbyshire and Lincolnshire in the sense of a fair or due share of work. A correspondent told him that *fair dinkum* existed in north Lincolnshire, used in the same way that people might exclaim *fair dos!* as a request for fair dealing. But there's no clue where *dinkum* comes from, and dictionaries are cautious because it is not well recorded.

It turns up first in Australian writing in 1888 in *Robbery Under Arms* by Rolf Boldrewood, in which it had the sense of work or exertion: 'It took us an hour's hard dinkum to get near the peak'. Early on it could also mean something honest, reliable or genuine, though this is actually first recorded in New Zealand, in 1905. *Fair dinkum* is recorded from 1890 in the sense of fair play, and soon after for something reliable or genuine. The related *dinkum oil* for an accurate report came out of soldiers' slang in the First World War.

> **Woggo? He's all right. We get the dinkum oil off him. He knows all the jockeys and trainers and everything.**
>
> *Here's Luck*, by Lennie Lower, 1930. Lower was once considered Australia's funniest writer. This was his one novel, a classic of Australian humour that observed life in the eastern suburbs of Sydney and which has never gone out of print.

For me, being about as far from Australia as it's possible to get on this planet, *dinkum* first brings to mind Robert Heinlein's *The Moon is a Harsh Mistress*, dated 1956, about a future penal colony on the moon in which everyone speaks a weird patois containing elements of Australian, American and Russian slang. The sentient computer at the centre of the story is described as 'a fair dinkum thinkum'.

Fair to middling

Q. Here in Dallas, Texas, I have often heard the phrase *fair to Midland* in response to the inquiry 'How are you doing?' Any ideas on the origins of this phrase?

A. *Fair to Midland* is a Texas joke, a play on *fair to middling*, in reference to the city called Midland in the state.

Fair to middling is a phrase now not as much heard as it once was. It was formerly common in Britain and Commonwealth countries as well as North America, but is best known now in the last of these areas. It refers to something that's merely moderate to average in quality, at times written the way people often say it, as *fair to middlin'*. All the early examples that I can find in literary works – from authors like Mark Twain, Louisa May Alcott and Artemus Ward – suggest it became common on the east coast of the US from the 1860s on.

> **The night was intensely cold, in-doors as well as out; the house [theatre] was thin; the playing from fair to middling; yet I was in raptures from first to last.**
>
> *Recollections of a Busy Life*, by Horace Greeley, 1868. Greeley was a famous journalist and social reformer of the mid nineteenth century, a key supporter of the abolition of slavery. He established the *New York Tribune* in 1841 and edited it for the next thirty years.

But occasional examples turn up from earlier in the century:

> ***Dinner on the Plains.* – On Tuesday last, there was dinner at the country seat of J. C. Jones, Esq., in honor of the officers of the Peacock and Enterprise. The viands were – 'from fair to middling' – (we wish we could say more).**
>
> *New Bedford Mercury*, 21 April 1837, reporting an event that took place in Honolulu the previous September (these were more leisurely times).

The phrase is undoubtedly American. But *middling* turns out to have been used as far back as the previous century for an intermediate grade of various kinds of goods, both in Britain and the US – there are references to middling grades of flour or meal, pins, and the like. This developed in the US early in the nineteenth century into a fuller form:

> **J. Haskell has just received 4 cases prime HATS, new style – also 4 cases imitation HATS, at $2, 'from fair to middling'.**
>
> An advertisement in the *Eastern Argus* of Maine for 23 March 1824. I can find no clue as to the nature of an imitation hat.

> **We venture to assert that a moderate advance was realized on all kinds of Beef, and we quote prime market Beef at $5 per cwt.; from fair to middling 3½ to $4, and thin qualities less.**
>
> *Connecticut Courant*, 3 November 1829.

Despite these and other examples that connect the expression with a variety of commodities, American newspapers and journals later in the century link it with one trade in particular:

> **Every man is said to have his price, and I had long known that if you were not particular about quality one of the cheapest articles in the London man-market was a detective. Ours was 'from fair to middling,' in cotton-brokers' phrase, and we purchased his services for two guineas.**
>
> *Harper's New Monthly Magazine*, New York, September 1867.

Fair and *middling*, it turns out, were terms in the cotton business for specific grades – the sequence ran from the best quality (*fine*), through *good*, *fair*, *middling* and *ordinary* to the least good (*inferior*). The expression *from fair to middling* was a reference to a range of intermediate qualities – it was common to quote indicative prices, for example, for *fair to middling grade* or *fair to middling quality*.

Because the cotton trade was so important to the US at this period, it was widely known and used, to the extent that it escaped into the wider language. It was brought to

Britain on the back of the cotton imports that fuelled much of Lancashire's prosperity at the time.

For Pete's sake

Q. I was wondering if you can shed any light on the set phrase *for Pete's sake*. A very interesting explanation was given on a TV show, which attributed it to Michelangelo requesting funds for St Peter's.

A. That's a classic example of a ridiculous invented origin that we needn't spend much time refuting, even if we assume it was meant seriously, which I somehow doubt. Michelangelo spoke a dialect of Italian, so how did it get into English? And the expression isn't recorded before about 1900, so *for Pete's sake* where has it been in all the centuries in between?

In this case, there's an etymological vacuum that the speaker was trying to fill. There's no very obvious origin, though we're not totally without ideas. One clue is that another version of the exclamation is *for the love of Pete*, which seems to be about the same age. In turn that reminds us of *for the love of Mike*, which is also contemporary. This last expression seems to have been a euphemistic cry to replace *for the love of God*, which is known from the early eighteenth century as an irritated exclamation. Another well-known cry, *for pity's sake*, seems likely to have been a strong influence on the choice of *Pete*.

As a result, at some point around 1900, Pete joined Mike as the person to invoke when you were impatient, annoyed, frustrated or disappointed in someone or something, both men being stand-ins for the God that it would be blasphemous to mention.

From pillar to post

Q. Please shed light on the origin and meaning of *from pillar to post*. I'm rather puzzled about it, because I recently came across the version *from pile to pillar*.

A. That's an interesting variation, showing how little the idiom is now understood. A lot of people are unsure even of the meaning, which is to be forced to go from one place to another in an unceremonious or fruitless search for assistance.

> **His grouse is that for the past one month he and other members of his team have been moving from pillar to post, but all their efforts have failed thanks to a simple error in handling computerised records.**
>
> *Calcutta Telegraph*, 25 December 2007.

There are two main theories about its origin among the experts.

The one that most dictionaries rather cautiously subscribe to sounds less than credible. It's said that it derives from the ancient game now called real tennis (court tennis in the USA) to distinguish it from its upstart successor, lawn tennis. The game was played by personages of high status in rather complex indoor courts based on the medieval cloisters in which it first evolved; it is supposed that the pillars and posts were parts of the court. There were gallery posts in real tennis courts but I can't find evidence that they were ever described as pillars.

A second suggestion that has been widely put forward argues that the full form was originally *from whipping-post to pillory*. The suggestion is that a criminal being punished in medieval times would first be tied to a post to be whipped and then put in a pillory for public spectacle, amusement and further punishment. In support of this idea the original version of our idiom was the inverted *from post to pillar*. If that origin were true, you'd expect to get at least some examples of *from post to pillory*; it does appear in John Ray's *A Compleat Collection of English Proverbs* of 1737 but that's two centuries after *from pillar to post* is first recorded and there are no known examples of the *pillory* form before Ray. In favour of it is the first appearance of the expression:

> **Thus from post to pillar was he made to dance.**
> **And at the last he went forward to penance.**
>
> *The Assembly of the Gods*, often said to have been composed by John Lydgate around 1420. I've modernized the spelling. The character Freewill, having enlisted in the army of Vice and been captured on its defeat by Virtue, is passed successively to Conscience, Humility, Confession, Contrition and Satisfaction.

The *Oxford English Dictionary* notes, however, that the idiom usually appeared early on as *tossed from post to pillar*, which rather suggests some sort of game and not the punishment. It also argues that it was the near rhyme of *post* with *tossed* that caused the medieval idiom to invert to our modern *pillar to post*.

As so often happens at the end of an etymological enquiry, we're now much better informed but no wiser.

Gander

Q. Where does the phrase *take a gander at*, meaning to have a look at something, come from? I heard it used on radio recently for the first time in years, and both parties in the telephone conversation (one of whom was in America) knew what was meant without a moment's hesitation.

A. *To take a gander* is as weird a formation as one might encounter anywhere. What can a male goose possibly have to do with looking at something?

SEAGOON: 'Good evening. Do you mind if I take a gander around the shop?'

CRUN: 'No, as long as it's housetrained.'

'1985', a popular and successful parody of George Orwell's *Nineteen Eighty-Four* that Spike Milligan and Eric Sykes wrote for an episode of the *Goon Show* broadcast on 4 January 1955. The stimulus for it was the controversial BBC Television screening the previous autumn of Nigel Kneale's adaptation of Orwell's book.

A quick, er, gander at the word's history is illuminating. It seems the verb *to gander* in this sense is actually American in origin, something I find more than a little surprising, because it sounds English to me. Further delving, however, shows that the roots of the expression are indeed from this side of the pond. A work of 1887, *The Folk-Speech of South Cheshire*, says, 'Gonder, to stretch the neck like a gander, to stand at gaze'. The next known example is from the *Cincinnati Enquirer* of 9 May 1903: 'Gander, to stretch or rubber your neck'.

There's your source. Think of a gaggle of farmyard geese, wandering about in their typically aimless way, poking their noses in everywhere and twisting their necks to stare at anything that might be interesting. Geese are the archetypal rubberneckers. It's likely that *gander* became the term because *goose* had already been borrowed; this was taken from the way that the birds were known to put their beaks embarrassingly – and sometimes painfully – into one's more private places.

The form you quote, *to take a gander*, is recorded from the USA around 1914; here, *gander* is a noun in the sense of an inquisitive look. In the century since, that form has become much more common while the verb has lost ground.

Gas and gaiters

Q. In the P. G. Wodehouse novel *Joy in the Morning*, Bertie Wooster uses the expression, *everything is once more gas and gaiters*. Could you enlighten us on the origin and relevance of the expression and its terms?

A. It's a delightfully typical Wodehousian expression, which he employs more than once:

> **She cries 'Oh, Freddie darling!' and flings herself into his arms, and all is gas and gaiters again.**
>
> *Ice in the Bedroom*, by P. G. Wodehouse, 1961. In which Freddie Wigeon is conned by trickster Thomas 'Soapy' Molloy into buying junk oil stocks. The setting is Valley Fields, the London suburb that's a thinly disguised Dulwich, where Wodehouse went to school. Stolen jewellery (the punning *ice* of the title) also features.

But the original is this:

> **'Aha!' cried the old gentleman, folding his hands, and squeezing them with great force against each other. 'I see her now; I see her now! My love, my life, my bride, my peerless beauty. She is come at last – at last – and all is gas and gaiters!'**
>
> *Nicholas Nickleby*, by Charles Dickens, 1839. A mad old gentleman who has been paying his addresses to Mrs Nickleby arrives precipitously down the chimney of an upstairs chamber dressed only in his underwear. Miss La Creevy comes into the room and the man mistakes her for Mrs Nickleby. The mad gentleman had immediately before this called for 'bottled lightning, a clean tumbler, and a corkscrew', for 'a thunder sandwich' and for 'a fricassee of boot-tops and goldfish sauce'. 'All gas and gaiters' was clearly designed by Dickens to be another incomprehensible utterance of similar kind.

Despite its being nonsense (or perhaps because it was), *all is gas and gaiters* became a well-known interjection. The sense – as you will realize – is of a most satisfactory state of affairs. This is what Wodehouse meant by it, in common with other writers of his time.

He shook his head. 'What I want to say – what I have been wanting for the past twenty-four hours to say to every man, woman, and child I met – is "Mabel and I are betrothed, and all is gas and gaiters."

Trent's Last Case, by E. C. Bentley, 1913, published in the US as *The Woman in Black*. Bentley was irritated by the infallibility of Sherlock Holmes in Conan Doyle's stories and conceived this book as an antidote, in effect a send-up of the genre, in which the convincing solution worked out by his gentleman sleuth Philip Trent was proved wrong in the end.

But another sense grew up in the twentieth century in which *gaiters* was a metaphor for senior clergy – such as bishops and archbishops – because of their traditional dress that included those garments, and *gas* alluded to their supposedly meaningless eloquence. So *all gas and gaiters* can mean mere verbiage or pompous nonsense.

A BBC television and radio programme in the late 1960s had the title *All Gas and Gaiters*, about the goings-on at a cathedral, starring Robertson Hare and Derek Nimmo, for which an alternative title was suggested by a wag at the time: 'fun with the clergy'. This brought the phrase back into usage for a while.

Get one's goat

Q. I was in a bookstore looking to spend some of the gift certificates I got when I retired from teaching and came across a priced-down book on word histories. I looked it over and came to the expression *get someone's goat*. According to the book, it used to be known that putting a goat in the stall of a horse would quieten the horse and make it more docile, but if someone wanted to irritate another person, he would steal the goat, creating trouble in the home of its owner. This explanation struck me as being in the same class of etymology as *Ship High in Transit*, *Port Out Starboard Home* and

For Unlawful Carnal Knowledge. Please put the author right
and me out of my misery.

A. It's a perplexing expression. *To get somebody's goat* means
you're annoying or irritating them. It's first recorded from
the US in the early twentieth century, but is now known
wherever English is spoken.

> **The bit that has really got my goat is that that Minister chose to
> attack their integrity.**
>
> *Hawke's Bay Today*, Hastings, New Zealand, 23 February 2008.

The earliest known reference to it is in a book, *Life in Sing
Sing*, of 1904, in which *goat* is glossed as prison slang meaning anger. Examples begin to appear in US newspapers in
the following years:

> **The crowd simply got his goat, to which many far more
> seasoned players than Knight have succumbed, not only here,
> but in nearly every city in both big league circuits.**
>
> *Philadelphia Inquirer*, 6 October 1907.

In 1910, Jack London included it in a letter: 'Honestly,
I believe I've got Samuels' *goat*! He's afraid to come back',
and later used it in several of his books. The saying became
common in the next decade and reached the UK no later
than 1916, when it featured in *Punch*.

The most common story to explain the phrase – the one
on which your book provides a muddled variation – was
promoted by H. L. Mencken and relates to horse racing in
North America. It was said to have been common practice to
put a goat in a stall with a skittish thoroughbred racehorse
to help calm it. Enterprising villains capitalized on this by
gambling on the horse to lose and then stealing the goat.
I agree that a substantial desire to suspend one's disbelief is
needed to accept this story at face value.

Other people have tried to identify it in some way with

scapegoat, have seen it as a variant form of *goad*, have linked it with an old French phrase *prendre la chèvre* (literally, 'to take the goat', but idiomatically to offend somebody), and suggested that the tendency of irritable billy goats to butt people could have associated the animals with anger in people's minds. But evidence is lacking for all of them.

Gibus

Q. What the heck does *gibus* mean? I read it in a Lord Peter Wimsey mystery. From context it might be an article of clothing, a type of hat perhaps, but I find no mention of it in any of my dictionaries.

A. That's not surprising. It's one of those words that have gone out of the language because the things they refer to are now not used, though *gibus* is still to be found in several British dictionaries.

Was this what you came across?

> **A quarter of an hour late, Mr Bredon emerged from his seclusion. As she had expected, he was in evening dress and looking, she thought, very much the gentleman. She obliged by working the lift for him. Mr Bredon, the ever-polite, expanded and assumed his gibus during the descent, apparently for the express purpose of taking it off to her when he emerged.**
>
> *Murder Must Advertise*, by Dorothy L. Sayers, 1933. Mr Bredon is, of course, Lord Peter Wimsey in disguise.

The unknowing reader will be puzzled what the object was and how it might be expanded while in a lift. You're spot on with your guess. It's a type of hat. More precisely, it's a species of top hat, whose crown can be folded down flat with the brim by means of an ingenious arrangement of rods and springs. The general name for them is *opera hats* or *crush hats*. Some writers identify the gibus with the *chapeau bras*, one designed to be carried under the arm, but the gibus was never used like that.

The *gibus*, often with an initial capital letter, was named after the Frenchman Antoine Gibus, who invented it while based in London; it was also known in French as a *chapeau claque*, from the noise it made when it opened. There is disagreement about dates, because he's not well recorded – some references say Gibus created it in 1823, others 1812; my *Petit Robert* dictionary gives 1834 for the first use of the hat's name in French, which may also have been the date at which it was patented in that country.

Such hats became popular. Top hats at the time were very tall and they were cumbersome to carry; theatre cloakrooms could overflow with the hats of a whole audience. You could instead fold a gibus down and slip it under your seat.

The word often turns up in English works of the nineteenth and early twentieth centuries. By the time that Dorothy L. Sayers was writing, it was going out of style, as H. G. Wells noted in a minor work of 1929, *The Autocracy of Mr Parham* ('His Gibus hat, a trifle old-fashioned in these slovenly times'). If you ever saw the film *Top Hat*, you may remember that Fred Astaire popped open a collapsible top hat as part of a routine. That was of the Gibus type.

So far as I know, its first appearance in English is this:

> **Ask little Tom Prig, who is there in all his glory, knows everybody, has a story about every one; and, as he trips home to his lodgings in Jermyn Street, with his gibus-hat and his little glazed pumps, thinks he is the fashionablest young fellow in town, and that he really has passed a night of exquisite enjoyment.**
>
> *A Book of Snobs*, by William Makepeace Thackeray, 1848. It had originally been published anonymously in *Punch* between March 1846 and February 1847 as a series of articles with the title *The Snobs of England. By One of Themselves*, not altogether a false statement.

Gobsmacked

Q. There's a word that I keep hearing here in the US that I've not encountered before: *gobsmacked*. In print and on radio, it's heard used as a colourful word to connote being flabbergasted or absolutely astounded. It feels British. Is that right?

A. It is. *Gobsmacked* is one of a set that includes *gobstruck* and the verb *gobsmack* formed from the adjective. It combines *gob*, mouth, and *smacked*. It is indeed much stronger than merely being surprised: it's used for something that leaves you totally speechless, or otherwise stops you dead in your tracks. It may suggest the rather theatrical gesture of clapping a hand over the mouth as a way to show extreme surprise, or it may be based on the idea that something is as unexpected as suddenly being hit in the face.

> **'No,' said Alf, clicking his fingers, 'we do have a player we can field!' 'Who?' He pointed at me. 'Thursday!' I was gobsmacked. I hadn't played for over eight years.**
>
> *Something Rotten*, by Jasper fforde, 2004, in which Thursday Next saves the day in the Swindon superhoop final of the World Croquet League, thereby defeating the machinations of the dastardly Goliath Corporation.

> **I popped into the local Marks & Spencer the other evening to buy something. The girls on the check-out were completely gobsmacked when I just turned up with my basket.**
>
> *Guardian*, 17 May 2008. Cherie Blair relishes her new-found freedom from the constraints of being a prime minister's wife, while being chuffed with her continuing celebrity.

It comes from northern dialect, most probably popularized through television programmes set in Liverpool or Manchester, where it was common long before it was written down. One of its earliest appearances in print was in Jeffrey Miller's *Street Talk – The Language of Coronation Street* of 1986, which was created to help those North American viewers who were addicted to this Manchester soap, and who probably, but with luck only temporarily, believed that everyone in England went around saying *blimey O'Reilly*, *ecky thump*, and *same to you with knobs on!*

It's an obvious derivation of an existing term, since *gob*, originally from Scotland and the north of England, has been a dialect and slang term for the mouth for 400 years (often in insulting phrases like *shut your gob!* to tell somebody to be quiet). It possibly goes back to a Scottish Gaelic word meaning a beak or a mouth, which has also bequeathed us the verb *gob*, meaning to spit. Another form is *gab*, from which we get *gift of the gab*.

The phrase came out of the working-class slang of football terraces (it appeared in print first in the *Guardian* in February 1985 in a report of an encounter with the famous footballer Sir Stanley Matthews, in which it was implied that it was even then 40 years old). It was taken up shortly afterwards by the broadsheet newspapers (such as *The Times*, *The Sunday Times* and the *Independent* as well as the *Guardian*) and various politicians, who used it to display their demotic credentials. It has since travelled to such countries as the US and Australia. William Safire commented in *The New York Times* in 2004 that 'the locution is sweeping the English world'.

Green-ink letter

Q. Although the meaning is quite clear to us and examples of use are readily available on the web, so far we have not been able to locate the expression in any dictionary, let alone discover how it came about! Why *green-ink letter*?

A. I knew immediately what you mean by a *green-ink letter*, or one written by a member of the *green-ink brigade*, the form which is more common. They are terms largely restricted to Britain, though I've come across a couple of isolated references in American publications.

They refer to a particular kind of letter writer, who may variously claim he or she is the victim of injustice, or who composes long and vehement complaints against a person or organization, or who believes that a numerical calculation based on the name of the prime minister shows him to be an agent of the devil, or who puts forward a thesis which, if adopted, will inevitably lead to world peace.

> Now it is quite impossible to prove to the people who write to me in green ink, complaining that the Pope and the Queen Mother are putting thought-rays into their heads from outer space, that His Holiness and Her Majesty are doing no such thing.
>
> Bernard Levin, writing in *The Times*, 20 January 1987.

In most cases, the expression is figurative, the key characteristic being the eccentricity or disturbed reasoning of the individuals, not their actual use of green ink. Or indeed their writing of letters:

> Sipping coffee in the House of Lords, [Lord] Lawson bristles at the charge that his book is nothing more than an upmarket green ink letter from an ill-informed retiree.
>
> *Guardian*, 3 May 2008. The book was *An Appeal to Reason: A Cool Look at Global Warming*, in which Nigel Lawson, a former Chancellor of the

I'm sure that the term arose in journalism, though – like you – I can find no information about exactly when. I've asked several senior journalists of my acquaintance about it. They all know the expression. Some claim to remember receiving letters of the type in their younger days, while others deny literal green-ink letters ever existed. But they all think the phrases were coined relatively recently to reflect journalistic experience or folklore.

An earlier reference, less direct, is from Kingsley Amis's *Lucky Jim* (1953). The hero gets letters from a person purporting to be an editor of a learned journal, 'ill-written in green ink'. The implication is that green ink is a sign of mental instability (the writer turns out to be an academic thief).

In the civil service and certain of the more bureaucratic professions, the use of green ink was once restricted to senior staff, so that juniors receiving a note written or annotated in green ink would know immediately that it was to be given priority. Green ink has also been used for proofing, because it shows up better against black text. It may be that deranged writers of green-ink letters used green because they thought that their letters would command more immediate attention or they would stand out from other correspondence. The suggestion that at one time all senior civil servants were thought to be deranged is one we may discount.

The term can hardly refer to the emotion mentioned in an article that appeared in several US newspapers in 1970 (here from the *Modesto Bee* of California): 'If a girl writes you a letter in green ink, young fellow, do not treat it lightly. It is supposed to convey eternal love.'

Grog

Q. My twin brother recently brought back from an arduous medical congress on Grenada a splendid bottle of rum, which bore an equally splendid story that the origin of the name of the daily ration of *grog* served to British seamen was to be found in that island, and was derived from the brand with which the casks were marked, namely GROG, or *Georgius Rex Old Grenada*. The George in question is said to be George III. Does this story hold any water?

A. No. Nor rum either. However, the real story sounds even less likely, though the experts are pretty much convinced it is true.

Parts of the bottle's tale are correct, though. The ration of rum mixed with water that was once served to sailors on board British warships was indeed called *grog*. And the rum did come from the West Indies – the custom of serving it instead of other strong spirits such as brandy began in 1687, following the British capture of Jamaica.

In 1740, Vice Admiral Edward Vernon was commanding officer of the British naval forces in the West Indies during the conflict with Spain that was weirdly named the War of Jenkins' Ear, after Robert Jenkins; he claimed that in 1731 he had had an ear sliced off during an encounter with the Spanish *guarda costa* in the Caribbean (it was believed by some at the time that Jenkins' ear was intact and hidden beneath his wig). Vernon was so concerned about the bad effects of the rum ration that he issued an order that in future it was to be served diluted:

> **To Captains of the Squadron! Whereas the Pernicious Custom of the Seamen drinking their Allowance of Rum in Drams, and often at once, is attended by many fatal Effects to their Morals as well as their Health, the daily allowance of half a pint a**

man is to be mixed with a quart of water, to be mixed in one
Scuttled Butt kept for that purpose, and to be done upon Deck,
and in the presence of the Lieutenant of the Watch, who is to
see that the men are not defrauded of their allowance of Rum.

Order to Captains No 349, issued on board HMS *Burford* at Port Royal,
Jamaica in August 1740. The usual allowance in the following century was
a pint of rum a day, served in two halves, at 12 noon and 6 pm; it became
known as *three-water grog*, because of the ratio of one part rum to three
parts water. *Scuttled butt*, by the way, is the origin of *scuttlebutt*, meaning
gossip (see p. 258).

One may presume the tars were not best pleased by this,
not least considering the foul stuff notionally called water
that was usually available on board ship (the Admiral said
graciously later in his order that men might, if they had the
money, buy sugar or limes to make the water more palat-
able to them).

The men, as was their custom, had already given Vernon
a nickname. His was *Old Grogram*, shortened to *Old Grog*,
because on deck in rough weather he wore a cloak made
of a coarse fabric called grogram, a mixture of silk with
mohair or wool, often stiffened with gum. (Its name is from
French *gros grain*, coarse grain.) So it was a short step to
naming the diluted drink *grog*.

Until recently, no contemporary example of *grog* has been
found, which suggests that the story ought to be dismissed
as no more than another folk tale about word origins.
However, Stephen Gorenson of Duke University has turned
up this:

The next Day, we met a Spanish Sloop from Cadiz, going into
the Havaana, who told us of the Peace: I cursed him for coming
in our Way, for we should have gone and taken all the Galleons
else and been as rich as Princes. I am sure we deserved it, for we
lived at Short Allowance all the Cruize, and but two Quarts of
Water a Day, to make it hold out in Hopes of meeting them (but

short Allowance of Grog was worst of all) and now we have brought this Prize here, we are told she will be given up to the Spaniards again, so we have fought them for nothing.

In an article headed *An exact Account of the late Action fought between Admiral Knowles and the Spanish Admiral, taken from the Jamaica Gazette*, which was reprinted in the *Whitehall Evening Post or London Intelligencer* of 31 January 1749. *The Havaana* is the way Havana was described at the time. Admiral Charles Knowles was then commanding the *Cornwall*. With two other ships, he had unavailingly engaged the Spanish treasure fleet off Cuba on 1 October 1748, for which he was court-martialled in December 1749 and sentenced to be reprimanded. He later became governor of Jamaica, causing great disturbances when he insisted on moving the capital from Spanish Town to Kingston. In November 1747, he had been responsible for what became known as the Knowles Riot as a result of his over-eager empressment of men in Boston for his depleted ship. One writer noted sourly that you could tell where Knowles was at any moment by checking where riots erupted.

Within the Royal Navy it was certainly believed to be the origin, to judge from this:

**The sacred robe which Vernon wore
Was drenched within the same;
And hence his virtues guard our shore,
And Grog derives its name.**

Lines written by Dr Thomas Trotter, the surgeon of HMS *Berwick*, on board ship in early August 1781.

The term was broadened by landlubbers who were ill-conversant with naval customs to mean any strong drink, though in Australia and New Zealand it can also mean beer. *Groggy*, a word first recorded in the West Indies in 1770, came from *grog* to mean a person overcome by strong liquor; later its meaning expanded to include anybody who was unsteady and dazed for any reason.

Grub

Q. What is the origin of the term *grub* for food?

A. You might not like to know that it's the same word as the one we use for caterpillars or other insect larvae, though you will be relieved to hear that it has nothing to do with actually eating them.

> **Then there's all that lovely grub you can line your stomach with – no wonder this is such a popular port of call, for both discerning drinkers and eaters (I can particularly recommend the home-made curries of the day).**
>
> *Liverpool Echo*, 16 November 2006. *Lovely grub* is a catchphrase from the Second World War, still to be heard.

The source is an old Germanic word meaning to dig, which is also the source of *grave*. The verb *to grub* came first in English, around 1300, and meant just what it still does: to break up the surface of the ground or to clear the ground of roots and stumps. Derived from it is our adjective *grubby* for somebody or something dirty and the Australian *grub* for a person who is unclean or who has messy habits.

The connection with food is the idea of animals foraging. In their wild state, for example, pigs *grub* for edible roots and the like. The larval sense comes from this, because grubs often feed in leaf litter or around roots. The slang sense of human food appears around the middle of the seventeenth century and is also linked to the figurative idea of grubbing in the ground for something to eat. The two ideas were neatly combined in the US mining slang term *grub-stake*, for food and equipment provided to a prospector. *Grub* has remained slangy – at best informal – ever since.

Grub, by the way, has had several other slang senses that have not survived, such as that for a dwarfish, mean, slovenly sort of person, or someone of small abilities who can survive only by the most menial sort of work. *Grub Street* was a development:

> **GRUBSTREET, originally the name of a street in Moorfields in London, much inhabited by writers of small histories, dictionaries, and temporary poems; whence any mean production is called *Grubstreet*.**
>
> *A General Dictionary of the English Language*, by Samuel Johnson, 1755. The street was possibly named after a man named Grubbe. Despite Johnson's implication, it was officially renamed Milton Street only in 1830. *Grub Street*, as we now write it, had become a collective term (always more a state of mind than a physical location) for such drudges and their products by the beginning of the eighteenth century – hence the short-lived sense of *grub* in that century for an impoverished author or needy scribbler.

Gruntled

Q. I have, for some time, been fascinated by *disgruntled*. How may you be disgruntled if you are not already gruntled? I do not know how to be *gruntled* and I've not been able to find the word in the dictionaries I've examined. Any thoughts about them?

A. Any mention of *gruntled* is likely to bring this to mind:

> **He spoke with a certain what-is-it in his voice, and I could see that, if not actually disgruntled, he was far from being gruntled.**
>
> *The Code of the Woosters*, by P. G. Wodehouse, 1938. In which we meet the magistrate Sir Watkyn Bassett and the fascist would-be dictator Roderick Spode, by whom Wodehouse is guying Sir Oswald Mosley; Spode's organization was the Black Shorts, because all the shirts had been taken ('Footer bags, you mean?' said Bertie Wooster. 'How perfectly foul.') There is much complicated comedy involving sundered lovers, a leather-covered notebook and a cow-creamer. The code of the Woosters, it transpires, amounts to 'never let a pal down'.

If you're the opposite of disgruntled, the implication is that you're pleased, satisfied and contented. Wodehouse invented this sense and has been quoted or flatteringly imitated many times since, almost always humorously:

> **Our Terry does seem to have had something of a sense of humour failure about the whole exercise this year; he was worryingly less than gruntled, for a start, by Dustin's reference to the disputed territory of his scalp; Wogan has never conceded that he wears a wig.**
>
> *Daily Mail*, 27 May 2008.

The assumption behind it is that putting *dis-* on the front of a word makes it negative in meaning in some way, as in *disappear*, *discontent*, *disconnect*, *dishonest*, and dozens of others. Adding *dis-* is an active way of making new words – it has been used in recent decades to create *disinformation*, *disambiguate* and many others. So if you take the *dis-* off, people assume, you turn the word positive in sense.

Sometimes, however – very rarely and only in old words – *dis-* is what the grammarians call an intensifier: it makes an existing sense stronger. For example, the unusual word *disannul* was used in the sense 'to make null and void, bring to nothing, abolish' and *dissever* means 'to divide, separate, disjoin'. A third example is our *disgruntled*, a state of being that's more than merely gruntled.

Time to introduce a second grammatical term: *frequentative*. This is an ancient trick of word formation, now obsolete, in which an ending created a verb to suggest some action is often repeated. The one most often used was *-le*. So *crackle* is the frequentative of *crack*, *gamble* of *game* (in the wagering sense) and *sparkle* of *spark*. Most examples are so old that they're based on verbs that no longer exist, at least in the sense in which they were used when the ending was attached to them; others are disguised by changes in spelling.

Gruntle is the frequentative of *grunt*. The first sense of *gruntle* was of a repeated grunt, especially the conversational noise that pigs make in company.

> **After this his speech went quite away, and he could speak no more than a Swine or a Bear. Therefore, like one of them, he would gruntle and make an ugly noise, according as he was offended, or pleased, or would have any thing done.**
>
> *The Life and Death of Mr Badman*, by John Bunyan, 1680. He intended this work to be a companion to the first part of *Pilgrim's Progress*, in which instead he would show the travel of an allegorical person, personified as Mr Badman, from this world to Hell.

Gruntle appeared in the fifteenth century; by the end of the next century it had begun to be used to mean grumbling or complaining. I think of it as old-retainer mumble, the noise that someone fed up with their condition will make under their breath all the time.

If we put the intensifier and the frequentative together in one word, *disgruntled* has its current meaning. Taking the intensifier off ought not to turn it into a word for a pleasant emotion, despite Wodehouse and his modern imitators.

Gussied up

Q. I am moved to inquire if you might know of the origin of the phrase *gussied up*. I recall hearing it used by my Nebraska grandmother in the 1940s in reference to the way a woman looked when she had obviously given extra time and attention to her appearance, including special, or dressy, clothing and make-up. When female family members were getting ready to attend a special occasion and had donned finery not normally worn on a day-to-day basis, she would say 'My, aren't you all gussied up!'

A. As you say, something that's been *gussied up* has been made more attractive. However, the phrase is often used for something that's been done over in a showy or gimmicky way, so it's often far from complimentary. The British equivalent in this case would be *tarted up*.

> **'He's gussied up more than a twenty-dollar whore,' Anytime said.**
>
> *Holmes on the Range*, by Steve Hockensmith, 2006. Gustav 'Old Red' Amlingmeyer, a cowboy of 1893, comes across the Sherlock Holmes story *The Red-Headed League* and decides to apply the precepts of the great detective.

The expression is definitely American. This is the first example I've found:

> **The young Shipping Clerk used to fly to his Kennel and get himself all Gussied up and then edge into the Parlor and turn the Music for Miss Livingstone, who looked to him like Lily Langtry and sounded like Adelina Patti.**
>
> *Out of Class B into the King Row*, a short story by George Ade, included in his collection *Knocking the Neighbors*, 1912. It was first published in syndicated form in US newspapers on 17 March that year. It was one of a long-running series called *Fables in Slang*, which weren't written so much in slang as in the colloquial vernacular of the time. George Ade was a famous humorist who specialized in gentle satires that often featured the little man or the experiences of the country boy in the city. The capitalization of nouns, weird to our modern eyes, is presumably intended to imitate the standard usage of earlier generations.

Suggestions about its origin include a connection with *gusset*, a piece of fabric sewn into a garment to strengthen or enlarge a part of it, which might have indicated that it was more fancy than usual. Until recently, *gussied up* was thought to date from the early 1950s, so some years ago I proposed a link with the American tennis player 'Gorgeous Gussie' Moran, who is best remembered for appearing at Wimbledon in 1949 wearing frilly panties, which caused considerable interest and controversy. As I have since found

the George Ade 1912 quotation, I have refuted myself, a
disconcerting experience.

Both the *Oxford English Dictionary* and *The Historical
Dictionary of American Slang* point to an earlier use of *Gussie*
(or *Gussy*) as a term for an effeminate or weak person, which
came into being in the US at the end of the nineteenth
century. It was used in Australia from about the same period
to describe a male homosexual. It looks as though any male
who took care with his appearance or who wore something
more dressy than the norm was suspected of unnatural
inclinations, was called a *gussie* and was said to be *gussied
up*. It is noteworthy that the three early examples I've found
– down to the 1930s – refer to men, not women.

Early on, *Gussie* was usually written with an initial capital
letter, which suggests it comes from the proper name
Augustus. This name is one that many authors have linked
to an effete or weak-willed man – think of P. G. Wodehouse's
Gussie Fink-Nottle, who wasn't gay but otherwise fitted the
stereotype.

We don't need to look any further for the origin, I'd argue.

Gyp

Q. My father-in-law often referred to something painful as
giving me gyp. This does not seem to correlate with the other
meaning of 'cheat'. Any suggestions?

A. *Give someone gyp* is a moderately common expression,
mainly restricted to the UK and Commonwealth:

> **The world's greatest golfer took the title despite a knee injury
> which was giving him considerable gyp throughout.**
> *Daily Telegraph*, 17 June 2008. The golfer with the superlative is Tiger Woods.

My gut feeling is that it's now mostly used by older people, though it does also appear in the broader sense of something that's a nuisance or annoyance, a figurative pain:

> **Being stuck in heavy traffic behind a car with its driver holding a cellphone in one hand and steering with the other, or similar in an oncoming car, is enough to give anyone the gyp.**
> *Rotorua Review*, New Zealand, 20 June 2008.

This sense of pain is connected with a Yorkshire or Lakeland English dialect word, variously spelled *gip* or *jip*, that almost always appeared in the form 'to give somebody or something jip'. It could mean to give a person or an object a sound thrashing (one example is of a man giving a carpet a beating with a stick in each hand), or generally to treat roughly or to cause pain, perhaps as a punishment.

We're not certain where it comes from, but the *English Dialect Dictionary* gives one sense of the word as 'to arouse to greater exertions by means of some sudden, unexpected action'. That fits with the suggestion in the *Oxford English Dictionary* that it's a contracted form of *gee-up*, a conventionalized version of the cry one utters to get a horse to move. Since the cry has often been accompanied by mild physical hurt, either with a whip or by digging one's heels into the horse's flanks, it's easy to see how an association with pain arose.

The other meaning you give, to cheat, has no connection. It's a derogatory term that arose in the US and which is sometimes said to be from *gypsy*. Gypsies were once thought to be from Egypt, though they actually have their origin in north-western India and arrived in Europe via Constantinople and the Balkans in the fifteenth century. The verb only began to appear in print near the end of the nineteenth century and took some time to become well known (it's not in the 1913 edition of the *Webster Unabridged Dictionary*, for example). Most people who use *gyp* in this

sense probably don't associate it with *gypsy*, although some
US dictionaries and newspaper style guides warn against
using *gyp* as a verb because it may be considered to be a
racial epithet.

There are several other senses of the word in various
spellings, including the old dialect one of *gip* in the
Shetland Islands and in Whitby in Yorkshire for gutting a
fish. A college servant at the universities of Cambridge and
Durham is a *gyp*; this word is also sometimes said to be from
gypsy, though it may equally well come from the obsolete
gippo, a menial kitchen servant; this once meant a man's
short tunic, from the obsolete French *jupeau* which – like
the modern French *jupe* for a skirt – derives ultimately from
Arabic. There's also *gyppy*, as in *gyppy tummy*, a term for diar-
rhoea. This does have the same origin as *gypsy* – a mangled
version of *Egyptian*. *Gyppy tummy* is noted by Eric Partridge
as Second World War services slang for the ailment suffered
by British forces in the North African campaign, and it was
a phrase common in Britain after the war. It seems certain
that *gyppy* was influenced in its creation by the pain sense
of *gyp*, but also built on *gyppy* or *gippy*, a slang term for an
Egyptian that can be traced back to Lord Kitchener's army in
Egypt in the 1880s.

Hackneyed

Q. A friend was kind enough to refer to a poem I'd written as
hackneyed. Before I take any action, it would be good to know
the origin and exact meaning of the word!

A. Remonstration would be justified, though I would not
advise physical violence.

Let us consider the geography of London. Hackney is
now the name of an area embedded within the metropolis,

north-east of the City. But if we take a large step back in time, say to the year 1300, Hackney was then a small village that lay on the west side of the River Lea but separated from it by a large area of marshland, which was to be commemorated about 550 years later by a music-hall song whose refrain went: 'With a ladder and some glasses / You could see the Hackney Marshes, / If it wasn't for the houses in between.'

The countryside around Hackney was pleasant, open, good-quality grassland, which became famous for the horses bred and pastured there. These were riding horses, 'ambling horses', as opposed to war horses (*destriers*) or draught horses. Hence *hackney* became the usual term for a horse of this type, bred for strength and endurance rather than looks. It's now the standard name, adopted in the eighteenth century, for a breed of gentle and elegant horses that are mostly bred for harness work.

Because riding horses were often made available for hire, the word also came to refer, about the end of the fourteenth century, to any horse that was intended to be hired out. Later still, the emphasis shifted from 'horse' to 'hire': it came to be used for any passenger vehicle that was similarly available, especially the *hackney coach* or *hackney carriage* (even *hackney-boat*, by which Joseph Addison translated a Dutch term in 1711) and sometimes even more widely, as in *hackney-woman* or *hackney-jade*, a prostitute (no doubt with a knowing reference to *ride*). *Hackney carriage* became the usual term for a vehicle that plied for hire – London's black taxis, and those in other cities, are still formally referred to in legislation by that title.

Horses of the *hackney* type were often worked heavily, in the nature of things hired out to all and sundry. So the word evolved in parallel with the previous sense to refer figuratively to a person who was overused to the point of drudgery:

> At the office all the morning, where comes a damned
> summons to attend the Committee of Miscarriages to-day,
> which makes me mad, that I should by my place become the
> hackney of this Office, in perpetual trouble and vexation, that
> need it least.
>
> *Diary*, Samuel Pepys, 11 February 1668. Pepys was then Secretary to the Navy
> Board and was continually being called to account over the mismanagement
> of the recent war with the Dutch, in which De Ruyter's ships sailed up
> the River Medway and burned a number of English warships in Chatham
> Dockyard. In another entry four years earlier, Pepys used *hackney* in the
> sense of a carriage for hire.

Hackney was abbreviated about the start of the eighteenth
century to *hack*, as in *hack work*; it was applied in particular to
literary drudges who dashed off poor-quality writing to order;
hence its modern application to journalists, who wear the
title as a self-deprecatory badge of membership and honour.

> Some years ago I came up with the idea of IQ points for journal-
> ists – no, not the usual measure of abstract intelligence, which
> let's face it was always going to be a bit of a non-starter when
> applied to such alcohol-addled, trivia-obsessed types as us
> hacks.
>
> Julie Burchill, in *The Times*, 30 July 2005.

Hackney horses were also widely available and commonly
seen, to the extent that they became commonplace and
unremarkable. So yet another sense evolved – for something
used so frequently and indiscriminately as to have lost its
freshness and interest, hence something stale, unoriginal
or trite. The adjective *hackneyed* communicated this idea
from about the middle of the eighteenth century on.

By the way, it was thought at one time that this whole set
of words derived from the French *haquenée*, an ambling horse.
The first edition of the *Oxford English Dictionary* considered
this to be so, but modern French etymologists are sure that
the French term was borrowed from the English place name

around 1360, so great was the reputation of Hackney's horses at the time.

Hairbrained

Q. I was reading an article by Lewis Lapham, editor of *Harper's Magazine*, in which he used the term *hairbrained*. I'd always assumed it was *harebrained*. Which is it, and how did it come about?

A. It would be easy to say the right answer is *harebrained*, because that's the first form recorded and the reference is clearly to the apparently stupidly senseless behaviour of hares in the mating season (they're not so different from humans, I note from long observation, but don't let me side-track myself). Approach the term through *mad March hares* and you will get the idea.

> **One of my friends came up with this harebrained scheme to ride through all the counties in England in a few days and I told him it was ridiculous.**
>
> *Pocklington Post*, North Yorkshire, 23 May 2008.

So is *hairbrained* wrong? A search through newspaper archives shows that many journalists don't agree: *harebrained* is only about twice as common as *hairbrained* in one database I searched, with thousands of examples of each. And even a quick look at the historical evidence gives one pause. The first example in the *Oxford English Dictionary* is dated 1548, and that has *hare*. But the second is from 1581, spelled *hair*. The editor who compiled the *Oxford English Dictionary*'s entry seems to have deliberately alternated examples in the two forms, since there's roughly one of each cited from every century since.

The reason for this, at least in early years, was that *hair* was another way to spell *hare*. This spelling was preserved in Scotland into the eighteenth century. As a result, it's hard to tell when people began to mistakenly write *hairbrained* instead of *harebrained*, in the belief that it referred to somebody who had a brain made of hair, or perhaps the size of a hair. When Sir Walter Scott used it in *The Monastery* in 1820 ('If hairbrained courage, and an outrageous spirit of gallantry, can make good his pretensions to the high lineage he claims, these qualities have never been denied him'), he was perpetuating the Scots spelling, not making an error.

The current status of *hairbrained* is disputed: some style guides say that it should not be used, as does the Fourth Edition of the *American Heritage Dictionary*: 'While hairbrained continues to be used and confused, it should be avoided in favor of harebrained which has been established as the correct spelling.' *Garner's Modern American Usage* dismisses it as a 'common blunder'. The Third Edition of *Fowler's Modern English Usage* describes it as an erroneous form 'which is still occasionally found' (rather more often than that, Dr Burchfield, as my research shows). Other guides disagree, a case in point being *Merriam-Webster's Dictionary of English Usage* which says of *hairbrained*, 'Our opinion based on the evidence is that it is established'.

At the very least, it's an error of such antiquity that the patina of age has softened the hard edges of disfavour. My own feeling, however, is that it's better to stick to *harebrained*; at least you have the original animal associations on your side with which to fight off critics.

Hairy at the heel

Q. I'm a fan of Agatha Christie, and I have seen her use the phrase *hairy at the heel* several times. It sounds so terribly English, yet I'm unsure what it means, or its derivation. Any reflections would be welcome.

A. One example from her books is this:

> **The Colonel delivered himself of the opinion that Godfrey Burrows was slightly hairy at the heel, a pronouncement which baffled Poirot completely.**
>
> *Murder in the Mews*, by Agatha Christie, 1937, a story about Ms Christie's Belgian detective Hercule Poirot. His little grey cells are understandably perplexed by this curious English idiom; his bafflement is a state he shares, I suspect, with most readers.

Walter James Macqueen-Pope made its meaning clearer in *Back Numbers* in 1954, in which he described someone as 'a cad, a bounder, an outsider, hairy at the heel'. Putting it simply, such a person was ill-bred, not one of us.

You're right to say it's characteristically English, but it was a term more of clubland, the upper middle classes and the landed gentry than of people at large. It placed the speaker as much as the person being spoken about:

> **I can't say I ever liked him, and I've once or twice had a row with him, for he used to bring his pals to shoot over Dalquharter and he didn't quite play the game by me. But I know dashed little about him, for I've been a lot away. Bit hairy about the heels, of course. A great figure at local race-meetin's, and used to toady old Carforth and the huntin' crowd. He has a pretty big reputation as a sharp lawyer and some of the thick-headed lairds swear by him, but Quentin never could stick him. It's quite likely he's been gettin' into Queer Street, for he was always speculatin' in horse flesh, and I fancy he plunged a bit on the Turf.**
>
> *Huntingtower*, by John Buchan, 1922. This extract sets the linguistic and social background beautifully. For the story behind *Queer Street*, see p. 24.

The reference to horse racing is spot on, because the term came out of bloodstock breeding. It used to be said that it was a sign of poor breeding if a horse had too much hair about the fetlocks. It didn't take much to shift the saying, figuratively, to humans. Of course, it applied only to thoroughbred racehorses and to humans who aspired to belong to society's equivalent: heavy working horses such as shires have very hairy heels, but then they're common as muck.

The expression was rather variable, also appearing as *hairy in the fetlocks*, *hairy round the heels*, *hairy-heeled*, even at times simply *hairy*, though it doesn't seem to be connected to any of the many other senses of that word. Dating-wise, its heyday was of the late nineteenth century to the middle of the twentieth. You can still find it on occasion, but it's outmoded, a term solely of elderly upper-class men remembering their youth.

Hang fire

Q. Can you tell me the origin of the expression *to hang fire*? I came across it in a racing newspaper the other day, 'That one can hang fire a bit under pressure, however, so the temptation to back him at longer odds should be resisted.' It seems rather odd.

A. It's a pleasure to report that, unlike so many expressions, this one is well understood.

It dates from a time when firearms were loaded and primed using a gunpowder charge poured from a flask, which was then ignited by a spark from a flint striking against an iron plate. Gunpowder was notoriously unreliable, partly because it varied a great deal in quality, but also because the slightest damp stopped it igniting properly.

When this happened, the powder in the firearm smouldered instead of exploding and was said to *hang fire*.

> **It was a very curious kind of gun ... sometimes it would hang fire, and then seem to recollect itself, and go off, maybe, just when you were going to take it down from your shoulder.**
>
> *Boy Life; stories and readings selected from the works of William Dean Howells, and arranged for supplementary reading in elementary schools*, edited by Percival Chubb, 1909.

This was highly dangerous, as you may imagine, because the remainder of the powder might explode at any time, perhaps while its owner was trying to clean the gun out and reload it. So *to hang fire* became an expression for some event that was slow in acting or of a person hesitating, usually with the inference that a matter of some importance was involved.

This expression should not be confused with the closely related *flash in the pan* for an ineffective effort or outburst. This referred to gunpowder that burned fiercely but ineffectually in the touch hole of a gun, without igniting the main charge. The result was a flash and some smoke, but the gun didn't fire, and the ball didn't actually go anywhere.

Happy as Larry

Q. Who is Larry and why is he happy?

A. It's a neat question, but readers may need some background before I can address it.

The phrase *happy as Larry* seems to have originated in Australia and New Zealand:

> **We would be as happy as Larry if it were not for the rats.**
>
> *Adventuring in Maoriland in the Seventies*, by George Llewellyn Meredith. Though published only in 1935, his anecdotes and observations were written in the 1870s and this sentence is probably dated 1875.

Now that the adventure was drawing to an end, I found a peace of mind that all the old fogies on the river couldn't disturb. I was as happy as Larry.

Such is life: being extracts from the diary of Tom Collins, by Joseph Furphy, writing as Tom Collins, published in 1903 in severely abridged form from a manuscript of 1220 pages that had been in existence since about 1897. The author called himself 'half bushman and half bookworm' and described the book as 'offensively Australian'.

Australian (and New Zealand) English is fond of fanciful similes and outrageous phrases. *Happy as Larry* belongs with *happy as a pig in shit* and *happy as a flea at a dog show*, all meaning extremely happy, as opposed to obscurely fantastic descriptions of the opposite emotion, such as *happy as a boxing kangaroo in fog time*, *happy as a bastard on father's day* and *happy as a sick eel on a sandspit*.

We could add *happy as an etymologist with an unknown origin* to this second set, because nobody knows the source of *happy as Larry* for certain. It might include the name of the nineteenth-century Australian boxer Larry Foley (1847–1917), though why he was especially happy nobody now seems able to say. Was he naturally gifted with a sunny disposition, or did he just win a lot of contests?

Another suggestion is that it comes from English dialect *larrie*, joking, jesting, a practical joke. A further possible link is with the Australian and New Zealand term *larrikin* for a street rowdy or young urban hooligan, recorded from the late 1860s but known especially in both countries from the 1880s onwards in reference to a specific subculture. Like other groups before and since, the larrikins had their own dress style, in their case very neat and rather severe, rather like the dudes in the US a little later. Their name may have come from another English dialect word, *larrikin*, for a mischievous youth, once known in Warwickshire and Worcestershire. Either of these could afterwards have

been reinforced through a supposed connection with
Larry Foley.

The expression is now known outside Australia and New
Zealand:

> **He pointed out that an official in the Commons refreshment
> department, guilty of such 'embezzlement', would have been
> summarily dismissed. MPs who have been subject to the
> committee's 'punishments' take their 15 minutes of pain and go
> around the House 'as happy as Larry', as Mr Field put it.**
>
> *The Sunday Times*, 3 February 2008.

Have one's guts for garters

Q. I mentioned to a work colleague here in the United
States that my sister back in Britain would *have my guts for
garters* if I didn't send her a card, but she didn't understand.
Any ideas on the origins of this saying, sadly falling into
disuse, it would seem?

A. Somehow I don't think this one is going to go away
soon, at least not to judge by its track record. This exagger-
ated threat may not be meant literally these days, merely
implying that the speaker will take some unspecified but
severe reprisal for unacceptable behaviour, but when it
first appeared, around the end of the sixteenth century, it
sounded horribly literal:

> **I'll make garters of thy guts, thou villain.**
>
> *The Scottish History of James the Fourth*, by Robert Greene, *c.* 1590. Greene,
> a novelist and playwright, is best known today for having written the first
> contemporary reference to Shakespeare, as an 'upstart Crow, beautified
> with our feathers', though he also may have worked on the *Henry VI* plays
> or *Titus Andronicus*.

There were other expressions around this time, such as *our guts should be about our ears*, as well as the still-common *to hate somebody's guts*. *Guts for garters* dropped out of literature after the eighteenth century, perhaps in deference to higher standards of decorum, though it never vanished from the spoken language, being kept alive in part by hard-shouting NCOs in the services. That the expression has persisted surely owes a lot to the alliteration of *guts* and *garters*.

It has risen somewhat in the social scale in recent times to become a macho phrase among some middle managers and to become noticeable, if not exactly common, in newspapers and books.

> **I was absolutely gutted, but I was actually more worried about what Gemma would say. I thought she would have my guts for garters but she didn't have a go at me at all.**
>
> *Salford Advertiser*, 26 June 2008. The speaker lost the disk containing the couple's recent wedding photos.

The fact that modern British men rarely wear garters, and that when they do they tend to call them sock suspenders, has not affected the popularity of the phrase one jot.

Heath Robinson

Q. In my office someone said they had a *Heath Robinson* solution to a problem, to the complete confusion of the international members of the team. Can you tell me who was Heath Robinson, and was everything he did makeshift and temporary?

A. A device or solution that's *Heath Robinson* in nature is neither of these things but instead is simultaneously absurdly ingenious and impracticable:

> It is true that the existing EU rulebook, the Nice treaty, is
> enough to keep things going, though there is a real danger that
> its Heath Robinson machinery and complex procedures will
> collapse under the sheer strain of an enlarged union.
>
> *Guardian*, 30 May 2005.

William Heath Robinson was a gifted illustrator of the
first half of the twentieth century. But his enduring fame,
and the reason why his name entered the language early
in his lifetime, was a result of the other side of his work
– comic drawings. The typical Heath Robinson creation was
a machine for carrying out some whimsical purpose, such
as training cat burglars, or stretching spaghetti, or putting
square pegs into round holes. His meticulously conceived
and magnificently executed mechanisms were miracles of
ineffective ingenuity. Every participant was intent on serious purposes while managing some aspect of an absurdly
over-complicated construction of magnets, pulley wheels
and conveyor belts, all linked and controlled by lengths of
knotted string. Every part of his daft machines exhibited
evidence of regular use over a long period, often amateur-
ishly patched or repaired.

His name became slang as long ago as the early years
of the First World War, as a result of a series of newspaper
cartoons in which he mocked the enemy (such as harness-
ing the German Army to a goose to teach it to goose-step,
or an attempt by the Germans to make the British troops
cry by whittling onions under cover of night, a sarcastic
reference to chemical warfare). The *Oxford Dictionary of
National Biography* remarks of these cartoons: 'The Germans
(wearing the uniforms of the Franco-Prussian War) invented
"frightful" means of teasing, discomfiting or embarrassing
our troops who (looking scarcely less ridiculous) confounded
them.' Their fame quickly spread:

W Heath Robinson, the British cartoonist, keeps up his extraordinary jests upon the German methods of conducting war. Mr. Robinson is undoubtedly one of the oddest geniuses of our day. His infinite capacity for imagining grotesque details and combining them in a pleasing and artistic picture gives him a unique position. When, however, he draws inspiration from the peculiar forms of warfare by which the Germans are slaughtering his fellow countrymen, his calmness takes one's breath away. Perhaps the strangest thing about it is that the English highly appreciate Mr. Robinson's cartoons in the *London Sketch*, and laugh heartily at 'the ridiculous methods employed by the scientific barbarians to kill them,' as one Briton has expressed it.

The San Antonio Light, Texas, 3 October 1915.

In the US, the equivalent is a *Rube Goldberg device*, a term taken from the strip-cartoon creations of Reuben Goldberg that illustrated some unnecessarily complicated though ingenious procedure for carrying out a simple task:

Charles Jackson is accused by the state with using a Rube Goldberg device to break Leslie Betterton's leg, in a complaint on file here today. Jackson is formally charged with assault by automobile. This is how Betterton's leg was broken, according to the complaint: Jackson's cement truck and another truck sideswiped; Jackson's truck struck a car, caromed into another car which was parked, and the latter was pushed into the automobile in which Betterton was sitting.

The San Antonio Light, Texas, 19 December 1937.

His nibs

Q. Do you have any idea of the origin of the term *his nibs*? I use it as a facetious way of referring to the 'man of the house', or sometimes even to my infant grandson, and I was wondering where it came from. I'm English, although I reside in the US, and my American-raised daughter questioned the use of the expression, which she didn't know.

A. It's a mock title used to refer to a self-important man, especially one in authority.

> **Stollen only became enriched with butter in 1647, when the Pope got involved (it took a letter to his nibs from Duke Albrecht to get permission to include butter in the recipe during what was then a time of fasting).**
> *Observer*, 9 March 2007.

It's modelled after the pattern of references to the British aristocracy, such as *his lordship*. It's first recorded in print about 1820, but is presumably older. Most sources say something like 'origin obscure', a fair description. Several closely similar words have been around at various times – *nab*, *knap*, *neb* and *nob* (plus *knob*), as well as *nib*. It seems the vowel was highly fluid and that all the words may in fact be connected, though the evidence is unclear. Bear with me while I particularize.

There's some evidence that *nibs* is a variant form of *nabs* (*his nabs* is a slightly older variant form of *his nibs*) and that both may have an origin in the ancient Germanic word *neb* that meant a beak or nose, or more generally, the protruding bit of anything (*nib* for the business end of a pen is from the same root). A *knap* – by far the oldest of the set – was the summit of a hill or a sudden steep rise; another sense of *nab* at one time was a promontory or a steep hill. *Knob* was a slang term for the head in the eighteenth century. *Nib* itself was once used as a slang term for a gentleman, as was *nob*, another old slang word that's still to be heard, which may be just a variation on *knob*.

Perhaps the idea behind it is that those supposed social superiors may have been so elevated in self-importance that they had their noses in the air or were stuck up?

Hobson's choice

Q. I have long been puzzled by the expression *Hobson's choice*. Was there ever a real Hobson involved?

A. There was indeed a real Mr Hobson, who has bequeathed us this expression meaning a choice that is no choice at all.

> **Buyers get a choice of three doors or five, and Hobson's choice of a three-cylinder 989cc petrol engine.**
> *Aberdeen Press & Journal*, 30 July 2003.

Thomas Hobson was the proprietor of an extremely prosperous carrier's business that ran between Cambridge and London, which he took over when his father of the same name died in 1568. One edition of the *Oxford Dictionary of National Biography* says that he 'conducted the business with extraordinary success, and amassed a handsome fortune'. He continued to travel to London in person until shortly before his death in 1631, aged about 86. John Milton wrote two poems about him shortly after his death, in one of which he said that he died of enforced idleness, having been prevented from travelling because of an outbreak of plague: 'And surely Death could never have prevailed, / Had not his weekly course of carriage failed.'

However, it wasn't his carrier's firm that gave rise to the term, but his other business of hiring out horses. Many of his customers were undergraduates; these young men often treated his horses very badly, driving them too hard and wearing them out. He kept telling them that they'd get to London just as quickly if they didn't push mounts so hard, but that had no effect. So, to give his horses some time to recover, he instituted a rota. The most recently returned horse was put at the back of the stable queue, and customers had to take the next one available at the front, which was therefore the most rested. There were no exceptions to the rule: if the customer didn't like the horse he was offered, he could take his custom elsewhere. So Hobson's choice was no choice at all.

> **When a Man came for a Horse, he was led into the Stable, where there was great Choice, but he obliged him to take the Horse which stood next to the Stable-Door; so that every Customer was alike well served according to his Chance, and every Horse ridden with the same Justice: From whence it became a Proverb, when what ought to be your Election was forced upon you, to say, 'Hobson's Choice'.**
>
> Richard Steele, in *The Spectator*, 10 October 1712. Steele is using *election* here in the sense of 'choice'. Note the eighteenth-century preference for capitalizing nouns, which we've come across before and which makes prose of the period look a little like modern German.

Some people today use it to mean a poor set of choices, none of which they like. This is an understandable extension of the original sense, but it would be nice to keep it reined in to the original idea of 'no choice at all', if only to commemorate the late Mr Hobson.

Hoodwink

Q. I know what *to hoodwink* means, but cannot imagine
how it came about. There seems no connection between its
meaning and the individual words it is made up from. But
then, I'm Dutch, so what do I know?

A. If asked, most native English speakers would be confused
by this one.

The original sense of *hoodwink* was to prevent somebody
seeing by covering their head with a hood. Our main sense
now is a figurative one derived from it, to deceive or trick
(as we might also say, *pull the wool over someone's eyes*), which
appeared in the early seventeenth century.

> **A photograph of the grinning couple, taken in Panama, surfaced
> four years after he disappeared. They had hoodwinked police
> and insurance companies.**
>
> *Daily Record*, Glasgow, 24 July 2008. This refers to the notorious case of the
> canoe couple, in which the husband faked his death in a staged accident;
> both were jailed in 2008.

There's no problem with the first part – a hood is just a hood
– but *wink* here isn't in the sense we use now of closing and
opening one eye quickly as a signal of some sort. When it
first appeared, in Old English in the form *wincian*, it meant
to close both eyes for some reason, or to blink, or to close
the eyes in sleep (hence *forty winks*).

A hoodwink was usually an opaque hood that covered the
whole head. It deprived somebody of the power of sight as
though they had closed their eyes. Hoodwinks were used to
cover the heads of prisoners.

> **But my escort gave the password, each of the guards questioned
> me separately, and we exchanged recognition signals. I got
> the impression that they were a little disappointed that they
> couldn't let me have it; they seemed awfully eager. When they**

were satisfied, a hoodwink was slipped over my head and I was led away.

If this Goes On—, by Robert Heinlein, 1940, an SF short story that tells of a theocratic US society, ruled by a prophet, that began in 2012 with the election of a backwoods preacher named Nehemiah Scudder to be US president, after which elections ceased.

Incidentally, when we say that somebody winks at some offence, meaning that they connive at it, we're also using a relic of the same sense. And long before *wink* became a flicker of one eyelid it meant a significant glance. If you find something written before the nineteenth century that says one person winked at another, a glance is what's meant – both indicate that the person is sending a message, but the method is slightly different.

Hullabaloo

Q. I am an English teacher and we had a poser today – where does the word *hullaballoo* come from? No one in our staffroom could give the answer – can you solve the mystery?

A. The sound is evocative of the uproar, noisy confusion, fuss or commotion to which it refers:

> **Jack had a good strong voice, but it was almost drowned out by the hullabaloo in the theatre. Such howls, such cheers!**
>
> *Life Mask,* by Emma Donoghue, 2005, a novel set in the eighteenth century, a fictionalized account of a supposed triangular relationship between the Earl of Derby, an actress and a widowed sculptress.

The usual spelling now is *hullabaloo,* but it has been written in so many ways down the years that that has to be considered arbitrary. This is its first known appearance:

I would there was a blister on this plaguy tongue of mine for making such a hollo-ballo, that I do.

The Adventures of Sir Launcelot Greaves, by Tobias Smollett, 1762.

Several explanations have been made for where it comes from. Some dictionaries just say it's a rendering of a semi-inarticulate cry. But the *Oxford English Dictionary* suggests it might come from a call of the hunting field, variously said and written – among other ways – as *halloo*, *hullo*, *hilloa* and *hollo*. The first in this set turns up in *view-halloo* (first recorded in the spelling *view-hollow* at the end of the eight-eenth century), the shout of a huntsman on seeing a fox break cover. All of these are related to our modern greeting *hello*, which first appeared in the US near the beginning of the nineteenth century.

A French connection is also plausible since that language has the closely similar *hurluberlu* for a person who is scatter-brained or behaves in a bizarre manner. François Rabelais used it first, in 1564, as the name of an imaginary saint, two centuries before the first appearance of *hullabaloo* in English. Unfortunately, French etymologists are no more sure of the genesis of *hurluberlu* than English ones are of *hullabaloo*. One suggestion is that it was borrowed from the even older English *hurly-burly*, with the closely similar senses of strife, uproar or tumult, known from about 1530.

> **FIRST WITCH: When shall we three meet again?**
> **In thunder, lightning, or in rain?**
> **SECOND WITCH: When the hurly-burly's done.**
> **When the battle's lost, and won.**

Macbeth, Act 1, Scene 1, by William Shakespeare, 1606.

Hurly-burly is a contracted form of *hurling and burling*, where a *hurling* is an even older term for a commotion or disturbance, based on the verb *hurl*. *Burling* never existed on its own – it's no more than a rhyming variation on the first word for emphasis and rhythm, as happened also in *namby-pamby*, *itsy-bitsy* and lots of other reduplicated terms.

The image of a word ping-ponging across the Channel, changing its form as it travels, may seem bizarre, but there's nothing intrinsically idiotic about it. The worst one can say of it is that it may not be true.

Ivy League

Q. It has been my understanding that *Ivy League* referred to a sporting competition held long ago between four US colleges, so *ivy* was formed by saying the Roman numerals *IV*. I'm now told that the *ivy* is that which actually grows on the walls of these ancient universities. I took this *ivy* explanation as being folk etymology. Would you know which is correct?

A. There has been much confusion, but the creeper is undoubtedly meant.

The *Morris Dictionary of Word and Phrase Origins* of 1962 gave more details of the supposed origin from the Roman numerals than did other works, calling it 'a plausible theory'. It quoted a letter from a Columbia graduate who said that it refers to a nineteenth-century athletic competition between Harvard, Yale, Columbia and Princeton. Though a meeting did take place in 1873 between four colleges (though not those four) to try to fix the rules of college football, only three attended and no formal link was established.

However, *Ivy League* did start as a sporting term:

> **The so-called 'Ivy league' which is in the process of formation stage among a group of the older eastern universities now seems to have welcomed Brown into the fold and automatically assumed the proportions of a 'big eight.'**
>
> *San Antonio Light*, Texas, 7 February 1935. The eight colleges were Brown,

Columbia, Princeton, Yale, Cornell, Dartmouth, Harvard and the University of Pennsylvania.

Teams from the Military Academy at West Point and the Naval Academy joined later but dropped out again in 1940. Ever since then, the league has been made up of the original eight college teams, a group that became official in 1954. You can attach the numbers ten or eight to the group, but not four.

The earliest form of the phrase was a little different:

> The fates which govern [football] play among the ivy colleges and academic boiler-factories alike seem to be going around the circuit.
>
> Stanley Woodward, in the *New York Herald Tribune*, 16 October 1933.

It has been argued that *ivy league* was formed from this by another sports writer connected with the same paper, Caswell Adams. Charles Earle Funk, in *Heavens To Betsy! and Other Curious Sayings* (1955), reprints a letter from Adams in which he recalls, a little vaguely, that he coined the phrase 'in the mid-thirties', but says Woodward borrowed it, crediting him. However, no supporting evidence is known to exist and Adams's claim to its invention remains unproved.

These days the sporting associations are only a small part of the concept that we understand by the term *Ivy League*. For many, it has become a disparaging term for long-established eastern US universities that exhibit academic excellence, selectivity in admissions, and a reputation for social elitism. Their great age is integral to the term, since there's no doubt that it is the ivy on the college walls that led Stanley Woodward to create the term *ivy college* in 1933. But he was surely borrowing an association that had long been made between ivy and ancient institutions of learning:

> He had his ticket and a sleeper reservation – it was fifteen
> hours' journey back to the old ivy-covered halls which had
> grown dear in his memory.
>
> *Red and Black*, by Grace Smith Richmond, 1919.

Jesus H. Christ

Q. On a British internet discussion group, the question came
up – why do people say *Jesus H. Christ*? It never seems to be
any other letter. It sounds American, but what does it stand
for and where did it originate? *Holy* seems to be a strong
candidate, or could it be from 'Hallowed be Thy (middle)
name'?

A. Some consider it blasphemous, but it's a relatively mild
oath in the US that indicates exasperation with some mal-
functioning piece of equipment or frustrating situation. It's
familiar to most of us here in the UK through the influence
of American films and books, though we don't use it much.

> Don't you know anything, woman? Jesus is the new cool word.
> Anytime you want to swear, you can say Jesus. Or Jesus Christ.
> Or if you're really pissed off you can say Jesus H. Christ.
>
> *Hollow Be Thy Name*, by Tom Reilly, 2002. Mr Reilly is Irish, born in Drogheda.

Various ingenious theories have been suggested for the *H*,
but the one that's most plausible is linked to the Greek
monogram for Jesus, *IHS* or *IHC*. These forms are extremely
ancient: the *Oxford English Dictionary* records the first examples in England from about the year 600 for the first and 900
for the second. They're generated from the first two letters
plus the last letter of His name in Greek (the letters iota, eta,
and sigma; in the second version, the C is a Byzantine Greek
form of sigma). The H is the capital letter form of eta, but
as knowledge of Greek wasn't common, churchgoers were

puzzled by it, thought it was the Latin letter H and came to believe in their ignorance that it must be the Saviour's middle initial. Since medieval times the monogram has also been expanded into Latin phrases, such as *Iesus Hominum Salvator*, Jesus Saviour of Men, *In Hoc Signo (vinces)*, in this sign (thou shalt conquer), and *In Hac Salus*, in this (cross) is salvation.

The oath does indeed seem to be American, first recorded at the end of the nineteenth century.

> **Jesus H. Christ, will you lay there all day?**
>
> 1892. Recorded in *Folk Songs of North America*, by Alan Lomax, 1960.

Mark Twain wrote in his *Autobiography* about an incident during his time as a printer's apprentice on the *Courier* in Hannibal around 1847. With another apprentice, he set in type a sixteen-page sermon by a visiting evangelist, the founder of the Disciples of Christ, Alexander Campbell, but accidentally left out two words. To avoid having to reset the type, the words *Jesus Christ* were abbreviated to *JC*. Campbell insisted that the name should appear in full, which gave the two apprentices a lot of work. It appeared in the reset text as *Jesus H. Christ*, a joke that Twain insisted was due to his fellow apprentice. The implication is that the form was known even then.

Its long survival must have a lot to do with its cadence, and the way that an especially strong stress can be placed on the H. You might also think of it as an example of emphatic infixing that loosely fits the model of words like *abso-bloody-lutely* or *tribu-bloody-lation*.

Joe Soap

Q. *Who do you think I am – Joe Soap?* My dear old mother used to use this expression occasionally. We migrated to Australia from the UK in 1951 and I've never heard it used by Australians. What is its origin and is it still in use in the UK?

A. It remains only moderately common. But the meaning has shifted since your mother learned it. She was clearly using the expression to refer to a stupid or naive person, one who could be easily put upon or deceived. That was the original slang sense; these days it usually refers to an ordinary person:

> **Ms Ash, who was already quite wealthy, was able to sue the health service, where the average Joe Soap is not.**
> *Sunday Mercury*, Birmingham, 27 January 2008.

The earliest example in the *Oxford English Dictionary* is from a 1943 British book, *Service Slang*, by John Hunt and Alan Pringle: 'Joe Soap, the "dumb" or not so intelligent members of the forces. The men who are "over-willing" and therefore the usual "stooges".' It's also in the caption below an illustration in Cyril Jackson's *It's a Piece of Cake – RAF Slang Made Easy*, also from 1943: 'The Erk. A.C.2 Joe Soap, who carries the can for one and all.' A services origin is further supported by this:

> **Farther along the road to Enna I saw many captured German vehicles. German divisional and regimental signs had been painted out and flaring red Canadian maple leaves painted on sides and fenders. On one captured truck was painted in huge letters 'Smith's Transport.' Another had the sign 'Joe Soap and Company.'**
> *Lethbridge Herald*, Alberta, Canada, 30 July 1943.

The implication of the other examples is that the Canadian soldiers borrowed the term from British ones. However, the opposite route is just about possible.

The usual view is that the second part is rhyming slang for *dope*, a stupid person, which started life as local English dialect (it's first recorded in Cumberland in 1851). The first part is the short form of Joseph, widely used in compounds to refer to an ordinary person, more often in the US than the UK – *Joe Bloggs, Joe Blow, Joe Sixpack, Joe Average, Joe Citizen, plain Joe, ordinary Joe, Joe Doakes, Joe Public* – there are lots of examples.

It was first noted as a generic term, in a different sense:

> **Joe, an imaginary person, nobody, as Who do those things belong to? Joe.**
>
> *The Swell's Night Guide to the Great Metropolis*, by 'The Lord Chief Baron', 1846. The author's real name was Renton Nicholson. He is best remembered for running a series of enormously popular mock trials called the Judge and Jury Society at the Garrick's Head and Town Hotel in Covent Garden, London. Judges, lawyers, peers and members of Parliament visited the trials and even took part.

Jolly hockey-sticks

Q. My colleagues and I here in Australia are puzzled as to the origins of the phrase *jolly hockey-sticks*, used, it seems, to describe old-school-tie-type high jinks or behaviour. Can you elucidate how this phrase began?

A. It's not especially surprising that you're puzzled, since you are half a world away from the British girls' schools that provoked this parodic phrase, and in attitudes even further, if that were possible.

> **Indeed, with her throaty, upper-crust voice and manifest pluck when the going gets rough, there's more than a hint of the**

jolly hockey sticks about her, like one of PG Wodehouse's more amiable aunts.

Daily Telegraph, 21 March 2007. The actress in question is Joanna Lumley.

It's gently dismissive of the hearty, games-playing, unscholastic tone of many girls' public schools (which, confusingly for Americans, in British parlance mean fee-charging private schools), in which the game of hockey has long been a favourite sport. Such schools for girls were late on the scene compared with their counterparts for the male of the species. Early examples, in the middle nineteenth century, were set up in deliberate imitation of public schools like Winchester and Eton. By the early years of the twentieth century, there were enough in existence for a new genre of writing to evolve, of which the most celebrated early exponent was Angela Brazil. She and her successors and imitators did much to further this energetic, adventurous, sporting image.

A BBC radio comedy programme from 1950 was called *Educating Archie* and featured the ventriloquist Peter Brough and his dummy Archie Andrews. Yes, a ventriloquist on radio, one of the stranger ideas in broadcasting history, though there was an American precedent in the entertainer Edgar Bergen. Though the show, even viewed in rose-tinted retrospect, was moderately dreadful, it was also extremely popular, in part because its producer was a genius at spotting up-and-coming new performers. The list of Archie's tutors and supporting cast reads like a *Who's Who* of British talent from the fifties – Harry Secombe, Hattie Jacques, Benny Hill, Sid James, Max Bygraves, Tony Hancock, Alfred Marks, Dick Emery, Robert Moreton, Bernard Miles and Julie Andrews, among others.

One of Archie's tutors was Beryl Reid, who played the part of a ghastly schoolgirl named Monica, a parody of the sporty public-school type. She invented the phrase *jolly hockey-sticks!*

on the show because, as she said once, 'I know what sort of thing my characters should say!' Her phrase struck a chord and it has passed into the language.

Katy bar the door

Q. I recently heard the phrase *Katie bar the door* while drinking coffee with older gentlemen. It was said in this context: 'She came in mad as hell and it was Katie bar the door when she found him kissing another girl.' Then I also heard it used in the film *Dodgeball*. I know what it means, but where did it come from?

A. Various sources have been put forward. However, the more one investigates, the further away a simple answer seems to get, which is so often the case in the etymologist's life.

Katy bar the door! (also as *Katy bar the gate!* and more often these days spelled *Katie*) is an American exclamation, at one time more often heard in the South than elsewhere, but now appearing quite often, especially in sports reports. It often means – as your example shows – that trouble is coming and that it would be wise to take prudent precautions or keep a watch out:

> Mark my words, if Dallas wins Saturday in Seattle, which by the way I predict they will, all ... will be talking about how genius Bill is and how he must stay and on and on and on. If they don't, katy bar the door, because this is going to get U-G-L-Y.
> *Fort Worth Star-Telegram*, 5 January 2007.

> There were not many opportunities at auction. Therefore, when decent auctions did pop up, it was pretty much 'Katie bar the door!' in terms of sale prices. Up, up and away!
> *Implement & Tractor Magazine*, 1 March 2008.

In that form, it's from the late nineteenth century. It's in a poem, *When Lide Married Him*, by James Whitcomb Riley, published in the collection *Riley Love Lyrics* in 1894. A young lady marries a known drunkard against family advice and forcibly reforms him. The first stanza ends with the line: 'When Lide married *him*, it wuz "*Katy, bar the door!*"'

One possible source is a traditional Scots ballad from medieval times, usually entitled *Get Up and Bar the Door*, which is still widely known and sung. But no version I've found mentions a person called Katy, although it's just possible that 'get up' was later converted to 'Katie'.

Others have pointed to a different tale, also from Scotland, involving one Catherine Douglas. King James I of Scotland, a cultured and firm ruler, was seen by some of his countrymen as a tyrant. Under attack by his enemies while staying at the Dominican chapter house in Perth on 20 February 1437, he was holed up in a room whose door had the usual metal staples for a wooden bar, but whose bar had been taken away. The legend has it that Catherine Douglas, one of the queen's ladies-in-waiting, tried heroically to save James I by barring the door with her naked arm. Her attempt failed, her arm being broken in the process, and the King was murdered, but she was thereafter known as Catherine Barlass.

> Like iron felt my arm, as through
> The staple I made it pass: –
> Alack! it was flesh and bone – no more!
> 'Twas Catherine Douglas sprang to the door,
> But I fell back Kate Barlass.

The King's Tragedy, by Dante Gabriel Rossetti, 1881. The nearest that Rossetti comes to the conventional expression in the poem is 'Catherine, keep the door!'

In this poem's favour as a source is that the first known example of *Katy, bar the door!* is from only seven years after it was published. Though it was popular, both in Britain and the USA, it's hard to see why the expression should have appeared first in the USA rather than Britain. It's probable that it merely acted as a stimulus to some existing expression that we have no record of.

Kettle of fish

Q. A very common turn of phrase, in Melbourne anyway, is someone referring to a separate case or situation to one being discussed as a *different kettle of fish*. It would make more sense to me if it were *pot*, *frying pan* or *basket*. I keep picturing someone trying to force a fish into a kettle presumably to boil it, or maybe add an unusual flavour to someone's tea. Do you have any information on its history or derivation?

A. Its origins are, alas, mysterious.

These days, especially in Britain and in Commonwealth countries, we think of a kettle solely as a container in which to boil water to make tea. In the eighteenth century, though, a kettle was any large vessel for boiling stuff in. For example, *a kettle of hats* was a trade term for a number of hats all dyed at the same time in a dye kettle.

There are actually two common idioms based around the phrase *kettle of fish*. The first is an exclamation; it has appeared in a variety of forms, such as *a pretty kettle of fish*, *a fine kettle of fish* or *a nice kettle of fish*, meaning that some awkward state of affairs has arisen or that some situation has been thrown into muddle or confusion. It dates from the early eighteenth century and in its various forms has long been common.

When a person has perplexed his affairs in general, or any particular business, he is said to have made a fine kettle of fish of it.

Lexicon Balatronicum, A Dictionary of Buckish Slang, University Wit and Pickpocket Eloquence, the 1811 enlarged version of *A Dictionary of the Vulgar Tongue*, by Captain Francis Grose. One of the contributors was named on the title page as Hell-fire Dick of Cambridge, which suggests a detailed acquaintance with the subject matter.

There's an end to the Clock trade now, and a pretty kettle of fish I've made of it, haven't I? I shall never hear the last on it.

The Clockmaker; or, The Sayings and Doings of Samuel Slick, of Slickville, by Thomas Chandler Haliburton, 1837. Sam Slick was a Yankee pedlar, who took advantage of the gullible locals in Nova Scotia, Haliburton's home area. The book is an early collection of dialect humour and is a valuable source for word historians because it contains many expressions not previously recorded in North America.

The other idiom is the one you quote – *that's a different kettle of fish* or *that's another kettle of fish* – which means 'That's a different matter from the one previously mentioned'. This is early twentieth century in date and seems to be derived from the earlier one.

Warner was thinking how the Pueblo-type Indians were a different kettle of fish from the Sioux and the Blackfeet, who lived in tents, and would as soon, or even sooner, kill a white man as look at him.

A Life, by Wright Morris, 1973, a sequel to his *Fire Sermon* of two years earlier. It recounts the last hours of the lonely figure of Floyd Warner, aged 82, who is murdered for his watch in the empty spaces of Nebraska.

Nobody is sure where the expression comes from, but we do know that the phrase *a kettle of fish* was originally a literal term. There was, it transpires, a custom in the eighteenth century by which folk on the border of Scotland with England would hold picnics (though that term was not then known) on the banks of the river Tweed:

> It is customary for the gentlemen who live near the Tweed to entertain their neighbours and friends with a Fete Champetre, which they call giving 'a kettle of fish'. Tents or marquees are pitched near the flowery banks of the river, on some grassy plain; a fire is kindled, and live salmon thrown into boiling kettles. The fish, thus prepared, is very firm, and accounted a most delicious food.
>
> *A Tour in England and Scotland in 1785*, by Thomas Newte, 1788. Newte's real name was William Thomson; he was a Scottish lawyer who wrote prodigiously under several pen names, including Sergeant Donald Macleod and Andrew Swinton.

Later writers confirmed that the tradition continued well into the following century:

> A custom prevails in these parts of holding what may be described as a salmon-picnic. 'The Kettle', as the party or club is technically called, appoint a day, and come together at some part of the river agreed on, provided with the elements of a feast. The fish already bespoken are kept alive in the river till the last moment, and are then transferred to the kettle and boiled, and eaten with the adjuncts; and sports and pastimes end the holiday.
>
> *Northumberland, and the Border*, by Walter White, 1859, one of a series of travel books based on the walks he took during holidays from his post as assistant secretary of the Royal Society.

What puzzles scholars is how this literal reference became an idiom – assuming, of course, that the phrase comes from the custom, which isn't altogether certain, though nobody has come up with a plausible alternative. The idiom would seem to be sarcastic – that the messy situation being referred to is far from that of the firm appearance of the salmon boiling in their kettle. Or might it have something to do with being in figurative hot water? We can only guess, a most unsatisfactory state of affairs.

Lieutenant

Q. Members of my wife's online quilt workshop were discussing the different pronunciations of *lieutenant*. Can you add to or clear up the confusion?

A. I'd rather not add to it, if you don't mind. There's been more than enough head-scratching down the years about why Americans say the word as *ljutenant* or *lootenant* while British and Commonwealth people prefer *leftenant*.

Like other military words (*army*, *captain*, *corporal*, *sergeant* and *soldier*), *lieutenant* came into English from Old French after the Norman Conquest. It's from *lieu*, meaning 'place' (ultimately from Latin *locus*), plus *tenant*, holding. A lieutenant is a place-holder, a person who at need fulfils the role of a more senior one or who functions as his deputy. He acts – one might say – *in lieu of* another, where *in lieu of* now means 'instead' but could equally be construed as 'in the place of'. *Lieutenant* is closely related in origin and meaning to *locum tenens* for a person who stands in temporarily for someone else of the same profession, such as a cleric or doctor.

On etymological grounds the pronunciation ought to be *lieu*, which suggests that Americans are saying it 'correctly'. Historical evidence, on the other hand, shows that we English early on adopted the way of saying the word which is still our standard one, that this was taken by emigrants to the North American colonies and that it was only in the nineteenth century that it slowly changed to its modern pronunciation there.

Why English settled on *leftenant* isn't at all clear. Some writers have suggested that early readers began by misreading *u* as *v*. This sounds plausible: in fourteenth-century English, when *lieutenant* first appeared in the written language, a distinction between the two letters didn't yet exist and they were interchangeable; however, the *Oxford English Dictionary* says that the theory doesn't fit the facts. Another theory is based on a medieval form *lueftenant* that's known in French dialect; this matches a Scots spelling of the fifteenth century and it may be that English speakers picked up this variant way of saying the word. A further idea is that they may have heard the glided sound at the end of *lieu* when it appeared in compounds as a *v* or an *f*.

Early spellings like *leef-*, *lyff-* and *leif-* show writers were trying to record a pronunciation rather like the now-standard British one; others like *lyeu-* and *lew-* suggest that the other form was also around, most probably modelled on the common French way of saying the word. The spelling settled on *lieutenant* only in the seventeenth century.

The change to the American version might be the result of a speak-as-you-spell movement but, if that is the case, we have to explain why it happened in the US and not in the UK. It actually shifted through the influence of Noah Webster, a prominent advocate of spelling and pronunciation reform. In his famous dictionary of 1828, he said the word should be said as 'lutenant', though he continued to spell it *lieutenant*.

Others also felt that the usual pronunciation of the word should be deplored as a corruption and ought to be corrected. John Walker wrote in his *Critical Pronouncing Dictionary* of 1791, 'the regular sound, as if written Lewtenant, seems not so remote from the corruption as to make us lose all hope that it will in time be the actual pronunciation'. Despite Webster, it was only slowly adopted in the US, though by 1893 *Funk's Standard Dictionary* in the US was able to note that the *lieu* pronunciation was 'almost confined to the retired list of the navy', indicating that Walker and Webster had triumphed.

Life of Riley

Q. I'd like to *live the life of Riley*, have a really good time without any cares, but if I ever achieve it, who is this Riley person whom I shall be emulating?

A. Oh, dear. The experts have been struggling with this one for decades but can't agree on who Riley might have been or how he managed to achieve his enviable existence of comfort and ease. He (that much is assumed) was certainly fictional, but competing theories argue that he might have been either American or British. They can't even agree whether he was Riley or Reilly (or even sometimes O'Reilly). However, the finger of suspicion points most clearly to popular music.

William and Mary Morris suggested in the *Morris Dictionary of Word and Phrase Origin* that the origin lies in a once-famous American comic song:

> **Is that Mister Reilly, can anyone tell?**
> **Is that Mister Reilly that owns the hotel?**
> **Well, if that's Mister Reilly they speak of so highly,**
> **Upon me soul, Riley, you're doing quite well.**

Written in 1883 by Pat Rooney, a well-known vaudeville comedian, singer and Irish impersonator. The hero, an innkeeper, describes what he will do when he strikes it rich: 'New York will be swimming in wine' and 'A hundred a day will be very small pay / when the White House and Capitol are mine.' The indications are that it became popular very quickly. The lyric was quoted in *The New York Times* on 29 January 1884 as a sarcastic comment about how difficult it was to find out the extent to which the city registrar, John Reilly, had profited from his office. In December the same year the *Philadelphia Record* used it in referring to a New York police captain, also of the same surname, who was supposedly (and surprisingly) untouched by a city financial scandal.

Other musical compositions have been suggested. It has been said that there was one of 1890 performed by the well-known burlesque performers Edward Harrigan and

Tony Hart. I've only been able to trace their play of that year, *Reilly and the Four Hundred*, and the supposed link is probably a mistake based on the title. Another version put forward (by H. L. Mencken) is 'The Best in the House is None Too Good for Reilly', by Charles E. Lawlor and James W. Blake. I don't have its date, but it was certainly written after their first and most famous song, 'The Sidewalks of New York', whose words Blake knocked out in an hour on the counter of the hat shop where he was working as a clerk in 1894.

Pat Rooney's song was revived during the First World War:

> **The song heard just now wherever the Tommies are gathered together is nothing else than our old favorite, 'Is This Mr. Reilly They Speak of So Highly. Is This Mr. Reilly That Keeps the Hotel?' Several months ago it became a craze with the English soldiers.**
>
> *The Star And Sentinel*, Gettysburg, 1 October 1915. The newspaper said that the song had quite displaced 'It's a Long Way to Tipperary' as the soldiers' favourite. British publishers in search of the rights, it reported, were surprised to discover that it was actually American. How it got into the trenches of northern France one can only guess.

A problem is that the expression *living the life of Reilly* doesn't appear in either the Rooney or the Lawlor–Blake lyric. However, they certainly put the idea in people's heads of a link between the surname and the leisured lifestyle of a very rich man.

The first known examples of the phrase are American and strongly suggest that it started life in the US Army around the time America entered the First World War in 1917. Small-town newspapers frequently published letters sent home by soldiers from training camps in the US and from active service in France. Many of them remarked on this strange expression they'd never heard before:

> **Besides the Polish troops there are a few quartermaster's corps men and two companies of regulars here for guard duty. In**

addition there are about 43 medical men and we live like princes or, as they say here, 'the life of Riley.' We get wonderful 'eats' and have the best pass privileges of any men at the post.

Lowell Sun, Massachusetts, 16 January 1918. This is an extract from a letter home by Private Robert D. Ward, who was on the medical staff at Fort Niagara, New York state.

The best time we had was the morning after when we occupied cities formerly held by the Huns. They must have led the life of Reilly as we caught them all asleep in beds and it was quite a sight to see our boys chasing them around in their pajamas – the German officers' pajamas, not our boys'.

Bridgeport Telegram, Connecticut, 22 October 1918.

In Britain, it is often claimed that the expression is of Anglo-Irish origins, based on a music-hall song of the immediate post-war period, though the lyric is using the phrase in a way that suggests the audience was expected to recognize it:

**Faith and my name is Kelly, Michael Kelly,
But I'm living the life of Reilly just the same.**

'My Name is Kelly', written by Harry Pease in 1919.

Putting all this together, the most likely sequence is that at some point around the time of America's entry into the First World War the expression was either created among troops in the US Army or was a previously locally known expression that was spread and popularized by contacts within army camps. Either way it echoed Rooney's vaudeville song. It was then taken to France, was picked up by British soldiers who had been exposed to Rooney's song earlier in the war, who took it into civvy street, where Harry Pease picked it up.

Lipograms

Q. I'm sure I have seen a short story (maybe it was very short) that was written without the use of the letter *e*. Have you ever come across such an item?

A. There are a very few such works, usually created more as a demonstration of the writer's technical flair than as a contribution to literature:

> **Now, any author, from history's dawn, always had that most important aid to writing: an ability to call upon any word in his dictionary in building up his story. That is, our strict laws as to word construction did not block his path. But in my story that mighty obstruction will constantly stand in my path; for many an important, common word I cannot adopt, owing to its orthography.**

> From the first chapter of *Gadsby*, a 50,000-word novel written by Ernest Vincent Wright in 1939 entirely without the letter *e*; it was described rather sniffily by one critic as 'artistically unpretentious'. In his introduction, Wright said, 'The entire manuscript of this story was written with the E type-bar of the typewriter tied down; thus making it impossible for that letter to be printed. This was done so that none of that vowel might slip in, accidentally; and many did try to do so!' He even had to stop the printer heading each section with the word 'chapter'. If the title reminds you of F. Scott Fitzgerald's *The Great Gatsby*, you're on the mark, as Wright's work was in part a response to what he saw as a 'negative' novel.

Such works are called *lipograms*, from the Greek *lipogrammatos*, 'missing a letter'. Usually *e* is left out, no doubt because that's the most frequent letter in most European languages and so presents lipogrammatists with their greatest challenge – for example, they can't use such common words as *the*, *we* or *are*. It is no accident that the word for such a work was coined in Greek, since there are examples known from classical times of exactly this kind of wordplay; the Greek poet Pindar is reputed to have written verse without the letter sigma, because he didn't like the hissing sound it made.

Another writer, Tryphiodorus, rewrote the *Odyssey* without an alpha in the first book, a beta in the second, and so on through the alphabet (conveniently, the *Odyssey* has twenty-four books, the same as the number of letters in the Greek alphabet; or did that give him the idea?).

There have been numerous other such works down the centuries. Another famous modern example is George Perec's French-language novel *La Disparition* of 1969, also written without the letter *e*. Remarkably, this was translated into English by Gilbert Adair in 1994 as *A Void* under the same constraint, for which he won the 1995 Scott Moncrieff Prize for French–English translation.

James Thurber wrote a story, *The Wonderful O*, about pirates who banned the use of the letter *o*, which is about the problem of leaving out a letter rather than an example of a lipogram.

Living daylights

Q. We had a rousing discussion over our second bottle of Merlot last night about just what it means to have the *living daylights* scared out of one. I'm hoping you can tell me what *living daylights* are, and where the expression comes from.

A. You're not alone. Though the phrase *living daylights* is common in several fixed phrases, hardly anyone now knows what one's *daylights* actually are.

> **Cruella De Vil terrified the living daylights out of children: the leering queen of furs, plotting to skin Dalmatian puppies to make a coat, was a surprisingly prescient lesson in the horrors of the fur trade and the importance of family.**
>
> *The Times*, 13 June 2008.

Daylights was used in the eighteenth century to mean one's eyes, as a metaphoric extension from the function of the eyes, to see daylight.

> **I don't use to be so treated. If the lady says such another word to me, d—n me, I will darken her daylights.**
>
> *Amelia*, by Henry Fielding, 1751. To *darken one's daylights* meant to close up the eyes with blows, to half-blind a person through giving them black eyes.

It extended its meaning rather later to mean any vital part of the body, not just the eyes. So a sentence like 'they had the daylights beaten out of them' would be taken to mean the persons concerned suffered severe injury. There are many examples in the nineteenth century of expressions like 'knock the daylights out of him' or 'scare the daylights out of him'.

In the later nineteenth century, the original term was expanded to *living daylights*. Perhaps *daylights* by then had become less clear in meaning, so that an extra word had to be added to restore its full force. It was unnecessary repetition, since one's daylights were always alive, but logic has never been a powerful influence on the creators of words and phrases, or we wouldn't have expressions like *free gift*.

The earliest example I've come across is this:

> **'Jehosaphat!' said the sportsman. 'I'm not going to be insulted by a miserable rabbit,' and he started to club the living daylights out of the beast with his gun.**
>
> *The Bangor Daily Whig And Courier*, Maine, 8 September 1890. This is from a brief tale about one Col. W. W. Foote, who 'overcame a contumacious rabbit' on the slopes of Mount Shasta in California, 'where winter snows grow quite tall'. After shooting it and clubbing it without the animal's moving, he found it had earlier frozen to death.

Lobbyist

Q. A story on US television news about Washington's ban on smoking in restaurants and bars and how it ended the era of politics in smoke-filled rooms mentioned the origin of *lobbyist*. It was said it originated with President Ulysses S. Grant, who liked to get out of the White House and often went to Washington's Willard Hotel for brandy and cigars. Anyone who wanted access to the president to make their mark on politics would know to find him in the lobby there and President Grant was the first to refer to these power brokers as *lobbyists*. I hadn't previously heard this. Is it correct?

A. No, not in the least. This tale has become so embedded in the subconscious of the US nation that it sometimes appears in quite reputable reference works. But it isn't true; even perfunctory enquiries about the history of the word shows it can't be.

You only have to look at the entry in the *Oxford English Dictionary*. The first example of *lobbyist* is listed as appearing in the *Cornhill Magazine* in January 1863. Ulysses S. Grant was president from 1869 to 1877, so the word was in use before he took office. A further nail in the coffin of the tale might be that the *Cornhill Magazine* was British, not American. But using electronic archives and casting my net wide for your delectation, I've been able to find examples of it in US newspapers rather earlier, including this:

> **This interest and this feeling were taken advantage of and subjected to a constant stimulation by a score of indefatigable lobbyists, who kept up an untiring attack upon the members, and especially upon the committee who had the subject in charge.**
>
> *New Hampshire Gazette*, 31 July 1849.

It would not be surprising to find still earlier examples. The job of the lobbyist had by then existed, unnamed, for many years (though *third house*, a humorous collective term for them, is known in the US from the 1840s). The *Oxford English Dictionary*'s first example of the collective term *lobby* for 'persons who frequent the lobby of the house of legislature for the purpose of influencing its members in their official action' is dated 1808. *Lobbyism*, the system of lobbying, dates from 1825. Both are recorded first in the US.

The original lobby was the one attached to the chamber of the British House of Commons, in which members could meet and talk to outsiders. This sense (and function) is recorded from the middle of the seventeenth century and was adopted in Congress when it was established more than a century later.

Loblolly boy

Q. After spending half an hour, I have been unable to locate the term *loblolly boy*, and would therefore appreciate your explaining its meaning, if you can. It is a term used in Patrick O'Brian's marvellous book *Master and Commander*.

A. Patrick O'Brian uses the term many times in his sequence of novels about the British Navy in Napoleonic times, but here's one from the book you mention, in which the ship's surgeon Dr Stephen Maturin is talking to Captain Jack Aubrey:

> 'I must go,' he said, getting up at the sound of the bell, the still-feeble bell, that his new loblolly boy rang to signify that the sick might now assemble. 'I dare not trust that fellow alone with the drugs.'
>
> *Master and Commander*, by Patrick O'Brian, 1970.

Let's start with *loblolly* itself. This was a medicinal food, a thick oatmeal gruel or porridge, perhaps with a bit of meat or some vegetables in it; other names for it were *burgoo* or *spoon-meat*. It was given to seamen recovering from sickness or injury, and so it belonged in the same category as that other supposedly restorative foodstuff, *portable soup*, which Patrick O'Brian frequently has Dr Maturin mention; this was soup that had been concentrated into a solid state ('glass-hard', O'Brian describes it at one point) to preserve it and make it easy to transport, usually in wooden cases.

The word may come from the dialectal *lob*, to bubble while boiling, and *lolly*, for broth, soup, or other food boiled in a pot, both recorded in the *English Dialect Dictionary* at the end of the nineteenth century. It's almost certainly connected to *lobscouse*, originally a sailor's dish of meat stewed with vegetables and ship's biscuit. Abbreviated to *scouse*, it became attached to the English port city of Liverpool and to its dialect and inhabitants.

The *loblolly boy* was a lay assistant to the ship's surgeon, often an assistant to the surgeon's assistants, if he had any. One of his jobs was to feed the patients, hence his name, though he often had other duties as well, which sometimes led to him being referred to as the ship's errand boy. *Loblolly* had another sense, a figurative dialect one of a rustic bumpkin, which reveals the loblolly boy's position in the hierarchy of the ship – somewhere between the cabin boy and a ship's rat. The term *loblolly boy* was often one of derision among the seamen. As John Masefield had a character say in *Martin Hyde*, 'What's a lad with good friends doing as loblolly boy?'

Long arm of the law

Q. I was in a shop recently when the girl behind the counter dropped something between the display cabinets. There was a police officer waiting in line and she said, 'Do you think the *long arm of the law* can get this out for me?' This has me wondering. Do you know the origin of the phrase?

A. These days it's a dreadfully overworked cliché by which to describe the local police force, one that's found in every English-speaking country; it's often intentionally humorous, but sometimes otherwise:

> The man was in a 55-mph zone and didn't have a motorcycle operator's license, and the long arm of the law was overhead in a Washington State Patrol airplane.
>
> *Seattle Post-Intelligencer*, 28 June 2008. A very long arm indeed!

It seems to have appeared around the middle of the nineteenth century:

> *'Taking a drop too much.'* – A Mr Neville, of western New York, has married a Miss Amanda Drop, while having another wife. The long arm of the law dropped down on him, and walked him off to prison for bigamy.
>
> *Milwaukie Commercial Herald*, Wisconsin, 8 July 1844. The newspaper's title is correct: it's using an old spelling of *Milwaukee*.

In the same period there was also *make a long arm*, to reach out to a great distance; later in the century another phrase appeared, *the long arm of coincidence*. Our expression clearly belongs with this set, all of them being based on *long arm*, a phrase that often appeared by itself and which meant the extent of one's reach.

There was also *strong arm of the law*, which is older:

> There are some print shops, and those in the most frequented streets of this metropolis, which occasionally shock all sense of

decency by their exhibitions. Such public nuisances we should
be glad to see removed by the strong arm of the law.

The Times, 16 September 1814.

So far as I can tell, *strong arm of the law* was used more widely
in the US than the UK during the nineteenth century and
always with serious intent (at least in the examples I've
looked at). It, too, seems to have become a journalistic
cliché. Might it be that *long arm of the law* was created as an
alternative based on the near rhyme in its first word?

Both versions appear together here:

The gamblers ... pursued their course with varying success, until
the failure of a spirited enterprise in the way of their profession,
dispersed them in various directions, and caused their career to
receive a sudden check from the long and strong arm of the law.

The Old Curiosity Shop, by Charles Dickens, 1841. Dickens reused the phrase in
Master Humphrey's Clock in 1847.

Dickens is here putting together the two forms of the
phrase, so suggesting both were already widely known by
this date. But I can't find an earlier example of *long arm of the
law*, so it's just possible that Dickens invented it, though its
presence only three years later in the US newspaper quoted
above suggests not. Whatever the truth of the matter, *the
long and strong arm of the law*, though less popular than the
others, became well known in the nineteenth century and
has survived to the present day.

Loo

Q. Having just returned home to the US, you seem to be the
right person to turn to for information on a strange little
word we heard while we were visiting in your country: *loo*,
meaning a bathroom or restroom. Where could this possibly
come from?

A. There are many theories about this word but few firm facts and its origin is one of the more celebrated puzzles in word history. The one thing almost everybody agrees on is that it's French in origin, or at least has French connections, though opinions differ on what these might be.

A lot of the theories can be disposed of by checking the known first dates of use. The *Oxford English Dictionary*'s first firm entry is dated as recently as 1940:

> I suppose it is unreal because we have been expecting it for so long now, and have known that it must be got over before we can go on with our lives. Like in the night when you want to go to the loo and it is miles away down a freezing cold passage and yet you know you have to go down that passage before you can be happy and sleep again.
>
> *Pigeon Pie*, by Nancy Mitford, 1940. The thing that must be got over is the Second World War, which, alas, caused the book to fall dead from the press.

However, the *Oxford English Dictionary* cites earlier examples, one from a letter of 1936 that refers to 'a lu-lu', which might from context be a toilet, and another from a previous work by Nancy Mitford:

> His correct and slightly pompous manner combined with the absence in his speech of such expressions as 'O.K. loo', 'I couldn't be more amused', 'We'll call it a day', 'lousy', 'It was a riot', 'My sweetie-boo', and 'What a poodle-pie' to indicate the barrier of half a generation between himself, Paul and Bobby; a barrier which more than any other often precludes understanding, if not friendship, between young and youngish people.
>
> *Christmas Pudding*, by Nancy Mitford, 1932, a high-spirited story of love and larks among the young and fashionable. Like the book's modern readers, the *Oxford English Dictionary*'s editors can only guess at the meaning of *loo* here.

The comparatively recent eruption of the expression requires us to dismiss entirely the old story that it comes from the habit of the more caring and thoughtful Scottish housewives, in the days before plumbing, of warning passers-by on the street below with the cry *Gardy loo!* before chucking the contents of their chamber pots out of upstairs windows. (It's said to be a corrupted form of the French *gardez l'eau!* or 'watch out for the water!') And equally the late date refutes the suggestion that it comes from the French *bordalou*, a portable commode resembling a sauce boat carried by eighteenth-century ladies in their muffs. Some writers have suggested a connection with *Waterloo*, neither the London railway station nor the battle site but supposedly a trade name in the early twentieth century for cast-iron lavatory cisterns, a joke or play on the older standard term *water closet*; this idea is principally based on its enigmatic appearance in James Joyce's *Ulysses* of 1922: 'O yes, *mon loup*. How much cost? Waterloo. Watercloset.' One proposed non-French origin is that *loo* was a modified form of *lee*, for the side of a ship away from the wind (largely on the grounds that *leeward* was often said as *looward*), supposedly the side used to relieve oneself in the happy expectation that the results wouldn't make a return visit. The fact that ships had places for the purpose right at the bows, hence called *heads*, is enough to put the suggestion out of consideration.

Yet another theory, rather more plausibly, has it that it comes from the French euphemism *lieux d'aisances*, literally 'places of ease' (it's always plural), known from the beginning of the nineteenth century. This might have been picked up by British servicemen fighting in France in the First World War, who would have inevitably shortened it and pronounced *lieux* as 'loo'.

As matters stand, unless some earlier example turns up, we're all left guessing.

Lord love a duck

Q. *Lord love a duck*: is it a long-winded rhyme for an expletive that has to remain unuttered in this polite company, or is there a story behind it?

A. Not a lot, I'm afraid. It's a mild expression of surprise, once well known in Britain and dating from the early twentieth century. It has been used a lot in inoffensive situations, so I very much doubt that it's a euphemism for the F-word.

> **This remark impressed Stump as an exquisite joke. His rage yielded to a rumble of hoarse laughter. 'Lord love a duck!' he guffawed. 'If only I'd ha' knowed, I could have told my missus. It would have cheered her up for a week.'**
>
> *The Wheel O' Fortune*, by Louis Tracy, 1907. Mr Tracy was a British journalist and prolific author, who also wrote under the pen names Gordon Holmes and Robert Fraser. He was fond of the expression and used it in at least two other novels.

> **'Well, Lord love a duck!' replied the butler, who in his moments of relaxation was addicted to homely expletives of the lower London type.**
>
> *The Coming of Bill*, by P. G. Wodehouse, 1920. Wodehouse's butlers were usually ultra-dignified and intimidatingly formal, so it's good to get a rare glimpse of one with his linguistic guard down.

But why should aristocrats dally amorously with anatine animals? And why should their proclivities be turned into an exclamation? It might have been a fake Cockney version of 'Lord love us!' never uttered in real life. Or it might be a line from some music-hall sketch long gone from memory. Perhaps the whole point about it is that it doesn't make sense?

Lukewarm

Q. This question was posed on the US television programme, *The Late, Late Show with Craig Ferguson*, 'Who is Luke and why does he have his own temperature?'

A. I presume no good answer was given, which is why you're turning to me? That's the trouble with these smart lines, they're fun for a moment but leave you unsatisfied and wanting more. As it happens, *lukewarm* has an intriguing history.

The word has been spelled in all sorts of different ways down the centuries, including *lew-warm*, *loo-warm* (desirable in any house), *lewke-warm* and *luckwarm*. The first part was mainly in dialect use and transmitted orally, so the spelling only settled down to our modern version in standard English in the eighteenth century, though it hasn't entirely vanished in these other forms.

> **But the solid quantity of cookery accomplished was out of proportion with so much display; and when we desisted, after two applications of the fire, the sound egg was little more than loo-warm.**
>
> *An Inland Voyage*, by Robert Louis Stevenson, 1878. This was Stevenson's first book, in which he recounted a canoe trip in Belgium and France that he made in 1876 with a friend from university days, Sir Walter Simpson.

Luke has, of course, nothing whatever to do with the given name. It comes from an Old English adjective *hléow* that is linked to *hléo*, shelter or *lee* (a word that has frequently been spelled *lew* in British dialects), and to another Old English word meaning debilitated that developed into *lew*, weak or wan. To be *lukewarm* is to be only weakly warm, tepid.

An odd sidelight is that from the thirteenth century, *luke* by itself could mean *lukewarm*, as could *lew* (the *English Dialect Dictionary* reported a century ago that it was then still being widely used in various spellings throughout England,

Scotland and Ireland). So you could argue that *lukewarm* means 'warm warm'.

Mad as a hatter

Q. Can you enlighten me about the origins of *mad as a hatter*? Why were hatters thought to be mad? Was it through having to deal with whiny rich women all day long?

A. It's an intriguing idea, but no, nothing like that.

These days we associate *mad as a hatter* with a bit of Victorian children's whimsy:

> **'In *that* direction,' the Cat said, waving its right paw round, 'lives a Hatter: and in *that* direction,' waving the other paw, 'lives a March Hare. Visit either you like: they're both mad.'**
>
> *Alice in Wonderland*, by Lewis Carroll, 1865. Though the Cheshire Cat describes the hatter as mad, neither *mad as a hatter* nor *mad hatter* appears in the text. Carroll expected his readers to make the connection without spelling out the expression, by then well known.

The earliest example known was discovered by Stephen Goranson of Duke University in *Blackwood's Magazine* of Edinburgh; a section called *Noctes Ambrosianae* featured imaginary conversations among the local wits of the time. In the issue of June 1829 this exchange occurs: '"He's raving." "Dementit." "Mad as a hatter. Hand me a segar."' The vocabulary (*dementit* for demented; *segar* for cigar) suggests an attempt at projecting a North American vernacular.

> **Father he larfed out like any thing; I thought he would never stop – and sister Sall got right up and walked out of the room, as mad as a hatter.**
>
> *The Clockmaker; or the Sayings and Doings of Samuel Slick of Slickville*, by Thomas Chandler Haliburton, 1836. You will note that Haliburton doesn't feel the need to explain the saying. This, coupled with the language of *Blackwood's Magazine*, suggests it may indeed be of North American origin.

We were talking about it at mess, yesterday, and chaffing Derby Oaks – until he was as mad as a hatter.

Pendennis, by William Makepeace Thackeray, serialised between 1848 and 1850. Curiously, the character of Captain Shandon in this work was modelled by Thackeray on William Maginn, one of the creators of the *Noctes Ambrosianae*.

Note, by the way, that *mad* is being used in both these cases in the sense of anger rather than insanity, so these examples better fit the sense of phrases like *mad as a wet hen*, *mad as a hornet*, *mad as a cut snake*, *mad as a meat axe*, and other wonderful similes, of which the first two are American and the last two from Australia or New Zealand. But Thomas Hughes, in *Tom Brown's Schooldays*, used it the same way that Lewis Carroll was later to do: 'He's a very good fellow, but as mad as a hatter'.

Few people who use the phrase today realize that there's a story of human suffering behind it; the term derives from an early industrial occupational disease. Felt hats were once very popular in North America and Europe; an example is the top hat. The best sorts were made from beaver fur, but cheaper ones used furs such as rabbit instead.

A complicated set of processes was needed to turn the fur into a finished hat. With the cheaper sorts of fur, an early step was to brush a solution of a mercury compound – usually mercurous nitrate – on to the fur to roughen the fibres and make them mat more easily, a process called *carroting* because it made the fur turn orange. Beaver fur had natural serrated edges that made this unnecessary, one reason why it was preferred, but the cost and scarcity of beaver meant that other furs had to be used. Whatever the source of the fur, the fibres were then shaved off the skin and turned into felt, which was later immersed in a boiling acid solution to thicken and harden it. Finishing processes included steaming the hat to shape and ironing it. In all these steps, hatters working in poorly ventilated workshops would breathe in the mercury compounds and accumulate the metal in their bodies.

We now know that mercury is a cumulative poison that causes kidney and brain damage. Physical symptoms include extreme trembling of the hands (known at the time as *hatter's shakes*), loosening of teeth, loss of co-ordination, and slurred speech; mental ones include irritability, loss of memory, depression, anxiety and other personality changes. This came to be called *mad hatter syndrome*.

It's been a long time since mercury was used in making hats, and now all that remains is a relic phrase that links to a nasty period in manufacturing history. But *mad hatter syndrome* remains in the medical literature as a description of the symptoms of mercury poisoning, not least because it was later suffered by dentists filling teeth with mercury amalgam.

Man of straw

Q. A story in the *Guardian* on 15 January 2008 suggested an origin for the term *man of straw*: '[It] stems from the days when mostly private prosecutions were brought with bribed witnesses. They used to stand outside court with straws in their shoes to signify their testimony could be bought.' Why do so many explanations for English phrases seem so incredible? Why would someone stand outside a courtroom with straw in their shoes? And wouldn't the simple fact you had, itself make you an unreliable witness? I suppose what I'm asking is, is it true?

A. Not a hope. It's a popular etymology. There's no trace anywhere in legal history of straw-shod bribable false witnesses. The idea of standing with straw in your shoes outside a court to indicate you're available to take part in an illegal act for money is so funny only someone with a common-sense bypass could seriously put it forward.

Let's go back to the early days of *man of straw*, at the very end of the sixteenth century. It then was a sham or dummy, like a scarecrow stuffed with straw. It evolved quickly into the specific sense of a sham argument, an invented adverse argument put up by a debater, only to be triumphantly refuted.

> **In the first place, Mr. Choate assumes that there are certain deluded persons who affirm that all compromises in politics are wrong. Having stuffed out his man of straw, he proceeds gravely to argue with him.**
>
> *Atlantic Monthly*, August 1858. Rufus Choate was an eccentric Massachusetts lawyer, who was described in one biography as having 'a brilliant legal mind and flamboyant oratorical skills', said to be the first lawyer (and one of the few ever) to successfully argue that a client had committed his crimes while sleepwalking. He was active in politics: the writer, a Republican, was commenting on a speech Choate gave on 4 July 1858 to the Young Men's Democratic Association of Boston.

The idea of a *man of straw* being one without money is a nineteenth-century extension:

> **'But the costs, my dear Sir, the costs of all this,' reasoned the attorney, when he had recovered from his momentary surprise. 'If the defendant be a man of straw, who is to pay the costs, Sir?'**
>
> *The Pickwick Papers*, by Charles Dickens, 1837.

This is now the most common British sense, especially in legal contexts – in which it refers to a person not worth suing or otherwise pursuing for money because he has none – though the older meanings also survive.

My guess is that the *Guardian* writer was instead thinking of *straw bail*, a once-common term for a particularly notorious practice among unscrupulous lawyers. A person who had no money but who dressed and acted respectably would be engaged to swear that the accused was known to him and of good character and would then stand bail for him. The criminal would abscond; the person bailing him could not be dunned for the bail surety, as he was a *man of straw* with nothing. I've found a reference to men sticking straws in their shoes to indicate that they were available to bail a defendant, though it seems to have been a nineteenth-century version of the folk tale you quote.

Marylebone stage

Q. For years, I was curious about the line 'So I will take the Marley Bone Coach / And whistle down the wind' in the song 'Whistle Down The Wind' by Tom Waits. Later, I discovered that Marylebone was an area in central London. Is this the origin?

A. Many people have queried this line but to little useful effect. There's no slang expression *Marley Bone Coach* or *Marylebone Coach* that I can find. There was, however, *Marylebone stage*, where *stage* refers to a stagecoach. Tom Waits may have had this in mind. Your asking the question gives me the chance to expatiate on this item of utterly defunct British slang.

To go by *Marylebone stage* meant to go on foot.

> **'The cabmen are trying it on, anyhow, just now,' thought Mr Sheldon; 'but I don't think they'll try it on with me. And if they do, there's the Marylebone stage. I'm not afraid of a five-mile walk.'**
>
> *Charlotte's Inheritance*, by Mary Elizabeth Braddon, 1868. This was her twentieth book in seven years, during which she also bore three children. She became famous for her first two novels, *Lady Audley's Secret* of 1861 and *Aurora Floyd* of 1862, two early examples of what became known as sensation fiction, featuring such everyday domestic themes as adultery,

There was indeed a stagecoach by that name which ran ('idled' would be a better term – a contemporary writer said it 'dragged tediously') the four miles from Marylebone to the City of London, taking two and a half hours to get there and three hours to come back. The slow journey was partly accounted for by the extremely bad roads of the period but mainly by an unnecessarily long stop at an inn along the way. The earliest reference I can find to it is in a court case at the Old Bailey in 1822, in which a young man was found guilty of stealing two handkerchiefs from a passenger, for which he received a whipping and six months in jail.

It was quicker to walk. This may have been part of the allusion, since *Marylebone stage* was either a joke based on the dilatoriness of this literal slowcoach, or perhaps a corruption of *marrowbone stage*, a phrase known from the 1820s. *Marrowbone* was a figurative term meaning a shinbone, hence a leg. So *marrowbone stage* has the same meaning as *Shanks's pony* or *Shanks's mare*, a personification of *shank* for the lower part of the leg. The first two expressions are equated in a book by George Augustus Sala, *Twice Around the Clock*, dated 1859: 'The humbler conveyances known as "Shanks's mare", and the "Marrowbone stage" – in more refined language, walking.'

Linking *marrowbone* and *Marylebone* was made easier because *Marylebone* in earlier times had often been written as *Marrowbone* – Samuel Pepys wrote in his *Diary* on 31 July 1667: 'Then we abroad to Marrowbone, and there walked in the garden, the first time I ever was there, and a pretty place it is.'

Both forms are now vanishingly rare. The only example in modern literature I've found is this one:

> **The Horse Guards clock chimed seven o'clock, and the first of that peculiarly urban phenomenon – commuters – appeared on their way to work, conveyed by 'the Marrowbone stage'; that is, on foot.**
>
> *The Great Train Robbery*, by Michael Crichton, 1975. The usage here is historical and correct in context, since the robbery in question was set in 1855.

Mickey Finn

Q. In an American novel I was reading recently, after a guard dog was drugged to put it temporarily out of action, a Southern man commented 'Somebody slipped the dog a Mickey Finn'. The context makes the meaning obvious, but do you know the origin and derivation?

A. A *Mickey Finn* is usually taken to be knockout drops, given to render someone insensible so they can be robbed. The drug has varied – the one most commonly mentioned is chloral hydrate, though an article in *American Speech* in April 1936, *The Argot of the Underworld Narcotic Addict* by David W. Maurer, claimed that it was often cigar ashes in a carbonated drink, a surprising concoction that we can hardly believe was effective. But the drug has sometimes been said to have been a purgative or emetic, this being a quick way for staff to get an obnoxious drunk or violent patron out of a bar.

Another reason for slipping someone an emetic became a notorious case in 1918:

> **Chicago, June 22 – State's Attorney Hoyne, acting on informa-tion as to coercive measures used by waiters to compel the**

> giving of tips, arrested 100 waiters, members of Waiters' Union, Local No. 7, today. Mr. Hoyne had a report that waiters used a certain powder in the dishes of known opponents to the tipping system. The powders, according to Mr. Hoyne, produced nausea and were known as 'Mickey Finns.' It is thought that many cases of supposed ptomaine poisoning reported after meals in downtown cafes and hotels may have been caused by the 'Mickey Finns.'
>
> *Washington Post*, 23 June 1918.

The 'certain powder' was later reported to be tartar emetic. So far as we know, this scandal is the first time that a drug is mentioned in print under the name *Mickey Finn*. The case was widely reported and it seems to have been the stimulus for the term's becoming generally known.

So was there an eponymous Mickey Finn? He may have been the man of that name who ran the Lone Star Saloon and Palm Garden in Chicago from 1896 to December 1903:

> Finn was the lowliest and by far the toughest of the princes of Chicago's Whisky Row. This terrible little man – he was only five feet and five inches tall and weighed about a hundred and forty pounds – was the veritable Mickey Finn whose name became synonymous for a knockout drop.
>
> *Gem of the Prairie: An Informal History of the Chicago Underworld*, by Herbert Asbury, 1940. Mr Asbury also wrote *The Gangs of New York*, from which the Martin Scorsese film of 2002 was adapted.

The establishment seems to have been a dive of the lowest kind, in which Finn fenced stolen goods, supervised pick-pockets and ran prostitutes. He had a sideline, as Mr Asbury tells it, by which he drugged patrons with chloral hydrate, robbed them, and dumped them in an alley.

This is all rather circumstantial, not least because of the big gap between Finn's supposed activities and the first recorded use of the term in 1918, not to mention the further twenty-year gap before Mr Asbury wrote his account of events. However, Mickey Finn certainly existed and his activities were recorded in the local press at the time. The Chicago *Daily News* reported on 16 December 1903 about '"Mickey" Finn, proprietor of the Lone Star saloon', which it reported as 'the scene of blood-curdling crimes through the agency of drugged liquor' and the following day the *Inter-Ocean*, another Chicago newspaper of the period, headed a report: 'Lone Star Saloon loses its license. "Mickey" Finn's alleged "knock-out drops" ... put him out of business.'

Mr Asbury suggests that Mickey Finn, once involuntarily separated from his bar, sold the trick of making Mickey Finns to others, who continued the tradition. The Chicago locale for the 1918 waiters' scandal certainly suggests that the concept – and the term – might have been circulating in the city underworld in the intervening years.

Mickey Finn is not an uncommon Irish name. From 1885 Ernest Jarrold, a reporter on the *New York Sun*, had written stories about a naughty boy of that name. They were widely syndicated and became very popular; a book of them was published in 1899 under the title *Mickey Finn Idylls*, which was turned into a highly successful comic musical in 1903. So the name would have been in the air at the time the real Mickey Finn was running his illegal business, and the combination of the two might have caused it to stick in people's minds.

Mollycoddle

Q. A friend of mine used the word *mollycoddle* the other day and I've also come across it in sports reports about pampered England cricketers. Can you tell me where this bizarre-looking word originated?

A. Let's take its two parts separately. The second comes from the verb to *coddle*, meaning to treat somebody in an indulgent or overprotective way.

> **Growing up in the era of cater-to-kids politics, the V-Chip, and helicopter parenting, they were the most coddled generation ever, infused with their elders' belief that they possessed unique abilities.**
>
> *Business Week*, 9 January 2008. A *helicopter parent* is one who hovers over their children, rushing to prevent them suffering any harm or letting them learn from their own mistakes. The *V-chip* in US television receivers allows parents to control what their children watch according to ratings for violence, sex and language broadcast by the network.

The verb in this sense is recorded early in the nineteenth century – its first appearance is in Jane Austen's *Emma*: 'Be satisfied with doctoring and coddling yourself'. It looks very much as though it comes from an older sense of the verb that meant to boil gently, to parboil. That sense is linked to *caudle*, an old word for a warm drink of thin gruel mixed with sweetened and spiced wine or ale, which was given chiefly to sick people. Hence, by association of ideas, *coddle* took on its modern sense.

The first bit is on the face of it easy enough, since it is from the pet form of the given name *Mary* (as in Sweet Molly Malone, whom we met earlier). But *Molly* has also had a long history in several different but related senses associated with low living. It was popularized in *The Roaring Girl* of 1611, a play by the two Thomases, Middleton and Dekker, which featured a criminal called *Moll Cut-purse*.

As either *molly* or *moll*, from the early seventeenth century on it was often used to describe a prostitute, hence, much later, the American gangster's *moll*. As *molly* it was also an eighteenth-century name for a homosexual or effeminate man.

> **He behaves himself more like a Catamite, an Eunuch, or one of those Ridiculous Imitators of the Female Sex, call'd Mollies, than like a Son of Adam.**
>
> *The London Terræfilius: or, the Satyrical Reformer. Being Drolling Reflections on the Vices and Vanities of Both Sexes*, by Edward Ward, 1708. Ned Ward was a well-known satirist in prose and verse. *Terrae filius* was a Roman tag that literally meant 'son of the earth' but which actually referred to a man whose parents were unknown. At Oxford University in the seventeenth century the name was given to public orators, playing at being jesters or buffoons, who were required by statute to perform (in Latin) at the annual 'act' in July at which candidates discussed their theses and were granted their degrees. More generally, a *terrae filius* was a good-for-nothing or shady character.

It appeared a little later in the form *Miss Molly*, particularly for an effeminate young man, and a *molly house* was a meeting place for male homosexuals, as in Mark Ravenhill's play, *Mother Clap's Molly House*.

It's sometimes said that the *molly* in *mollycoddle* comes from the prostitute sense, but the usage evidence shows it was actually linked to the gay one. The noun mollycoddle, which came first, was used particularly of a man who had been over-protected in childhood and so considered to have been made effeminate or a milksop.

> **You have been bred up as a molly-coddle, Pen, and spoilt by the women.**
>
> *Pendennis*, by William Makepeace Thackeray, 1849. This is the first recorded use of the noun.

The verb came along later in the nineteenth century and was used much as we do now.

Monkey's wedding

Q. I wonder if you can shed some light on the phrase *a monkey's wedding*? When I was a child growing up in South Africa, my mother would use the saying when we had rain and sunshine at the same time. My wife tells me that she knows the saying from her family, which is mainly of Irish blood.

A. It's certainly a well-known South African expression. A related word taken from Afrikaans also exists, *jakkalstrou*, a jackal's wedding. The South African English version may be a translation word for word of the Zulu *umshado wezinkawu*, a wedding for monkeys. It's also suggested it may be from the Portuguese *casamento de rapôsa*, a vixen's wedding, with the animal changed to suit the African situation.

What is extraordinary about this expression is that there are variations on the same theme throughout the world to describe this meteorological phenomenon in cultures and languages as widely separated and diverse as can be imagined. It may be that it is the paradoxical and contradictory nature of sun occurring with rain that makes people think of a joining of opposites, sometimes with supernatural overtones.

A great many of them have animal associations, often to do with marriage – or, at least, that activity for which the word *marriage* may be considered a suitable euphemism. In Arabic, the term is *the rats are getting married*, while Bulgarians prefer to speak of bears doing so; in Hindi it becomes *the jackal's wedding*; Koreans refer to tigers likewise; an ancient Spanish saying has it that *when it rains and the sun shines, the snail mates*; in Calabria it is said that *when it rains with sun, the foxes are getting married*, for which there's a similar phrase in Japanese.

A similar expression is known in the UK:

> After a thunderstorm, when the black clouds were rolling
> away and the sun was at least peeping out from behind them,
> bathing the freshly-washed countryside in a lurid, yellow light,
> my mother would exclaim, 'Oh, look! The Fox's Wedding!' It
> was, she explained, that contrast between darkness and light,
> the blending of sunlight and shadow.

The Fox's Wedding, by Ralph Whitlock, in *The Blackmore Vale Magazine*, 1994.

A rhyming example appears in Richard Polwhele's *The History of Cornwall* of 1814: 'When clouds and sunshine are together given, the piskies dance and cuckolds go to heaven.' Here's a closely related version:

> On all things there came a fair, lovely look, as if a different air
> stood over them. It is a look that seems ready to come some-
> times on those gleamy mornings after rain, when they say, 'So
> fair the day, the cuckoo is going to heaven.'

Precious Bane, by Mary Webb, 1924. The delightful *gleamy* is now rare; it refers to weather that mixes showers with bright intervals. Which came first in the saying, I wonder, the *cuckold* or the *cuckoo*? But then, *cuckold* comes from *cuckoo*, because of the bird's habit of laying its eggs in other birds' nests.

Among other British examples, *monkey's birthday* is recorded from the south-east of England. In Jonathan Swift's *Polite Conversation* of 1738, a dialogue that satirizes the hackneyed and clichéd speech of contemporary society, appears this exchange: '*Colonel Atwit*: It rained and the sun shone at the same time. *Neverout*: Why, then the devil was beating his wife behind the door with a shoulder of mutton.'

There's a closely similar equivalent known in the American South, at least among older people: *The devil's behind his kitchen door beating his wife with a frying pan*, usually shortened just to *The devil's beating his wife*. In Quebec French-Canadians have exactly the same saying. Several other languages also invoke the devil, such as the Turkish phrase *the devils are getting married*; in Belgium there exist two versions, *it is the devil's fair* and *there's a fair going on in hell*.

Perhaps the most delightful one, though more literal than any of the others, is the American *sunshower*. I've never heard this, and it appears in few dictionaries, but it's common in the US, Canada, Australia and New Zealand, and also in parts of Britain.

> **Slate clouds rowed forward over the sun, its light dappling the hill and then the sunshower was a storm.**
>
> *Virginia Quarterly Review*, 1 October 2005.

More than one way to skin a cat

Q. Have you heard the expression *there's more than one way to skin a cat*? Is there anything interesting about it?

A. To an earnest student of language history, all phrases are interesting, it's just that some of them are more interesting than others. This one lies somewhere around the middle of the spectrum of interestingness.

The saying suggests that there's always an alternative approach to getting something done or more than one way to get what you want from somebody. There are lots of different versions.

> **There are more ways of killing a cat than choking her with cream.**
>
> *Westward Ho!*, by Charles Kingsley, 1855. There's a place in Devon with the name of the title, which was created as a watering place, a sea resort, by a commercial company that built a hotel and a golf course and named it after Kingsley's book. *Westward Ho!* is actually an ancient boatman's cry to attract potential passengers by shouting out the direction in which he will be travelling.

An earlier example in the same form is in *John Smith's Letters* of 1839. You might instead *choke your cat with butter*, which appears in Margaret Mitchell's *Gone With the Wind*, 1936. Dogs also featured, in expressions such as *there are more ways of killing a dog besides hanging him*, of which other versions were *choking him to death on fresh curds* and *choking him with pudding*.

Your version seems to be American and to date from the nineteenth century.

> **She was wise, subtle, and knew more than one way to skin a cat.**
>
> *A Connecticut Yankee in King Arthur's Court*, by Mark Twain, 1889. In an early example of the time-travel tale, Hank Morgan, a skilled mechanic, awakes to find himself transported to medieval England.

> **This is a money digging world of ours; and, as it is said, 'there are more ways than one to skin a cat,' so are there more ways than one of digging for money.**
>
> *Way down East; or, Portraitures of Yankee Life*, by the American humorist Seba Smith, 1854. The author clearly knew this as a well-known existing proverbial saying. In fact, it appears rather earlier, in the *Hagerstown Mail* of Maryland on 1 April 1836, 'At any rate, thought I, there's more than one way to skin a cat, as a butcher would say.'

The hint that the expression might have once been literal chimes with what some writers have suggested, that in the southern states of the US *more than one way to skin a cat* refers to the catfish, frequently abbreviated to *cat*, which has a tough skin and must be skinned to prepare it for cooking. From the many versions of the saying, their wide distribution and their age, this looks like a local application of a long-standing proverb.

Mortarboard

Q. The designation of *robes* for academic dress clearly comes from its origin with the clergy in the Middle Ages. But what about *mortarboards*? The best I could find was its origin in the twelfth- or thirteenth-century clergy cap, but that was not square-shaped. Does *mortarboard* refer to the guilds or is its origin more ancient?

A. The academic cap often called a *mortarboard* is indeed ancient. However, that word for it only dates from the middle of the nineteenth century and so has no link to the medieval craft guilds.

It was slang to start with, deeply deprecated by the academics who wore them, who would have identified the headgear as a *square*. Earlier generations might have called it a *corner-cap* or a *catercap* (from French *quatre*, four). An older popular term was *trencher-cap* or *trencher*, named after the flat square wooden plate on which meat was once served and cut up (hence *trencherman* for a hearty eater).

The literal mortar board is the wooden plate, usually with a handle underneath, on which bricklayers carry small amounts of mortar to work with. A similar tool is used by plasterers, but they call it a *hawk*, for unknown reasons.

The similarity in shape between the brickie's board and the academic cap led some wag to apply the name of the one to the other, as an earlier generation had with *trencher*. Our first recorded use is this:

> I will overlook your offence in assuming that portion of the academical attire, to which you gave the offensive epithet of 'mortar-board'; more especially, as you acted at the suggestion and bidding of those who ought to have known better.

> *The Further Adventures of Mr Verdant Green*, by Edward Bradley, 1854. Mr Bradley, at the time he wrote this book a curate in Huntingdonshire, used the pen name of Cuthbert Bede (from the two patron saints of Durham,

where he went to college). The book was illustrated with ninety sketches by the author, a talented artist who is also credited with creating one of the first Christmas cards, in 1847. The book recounts the adventures of Verdant Green, a sort of undergraduate Pickwick. After a slow start, the book became a huge success, selling more than 200,000 copies in the next twenty years. Whether Mr Bradley invented the slang term we may never learn, but his book certainly popularized it.

Mufti

Q. I came across the word *mufti* in one of George MacDonald Fraser's *Flashman* books. Can you tell me the origin?

A. There are two senses of *mufti* in English. One is a Muslim legal expert empowered to give *fatwas*, rulings on religious matters, the other is a member of the armed forces or some other uniformed occupation who is currently not in uniform. I'd guess it's the latter sense you have in mind because it was common in the British Army in the nineteenth century, the setting of the *Flashman* novels. It is now not so often encountered, but you can find examples from throughout the English-speaking world.

> The grizzled old fisherman looks up from his bowl at the parade of military officers in mufti and says in perfect English: Welcome to another world.
>
> *Esquire*, 1 July 2007.

In British English I'd guess this is currently the most likely way you'll encounter it:

> The money was raised through quiz nights, fetes, bazaars, mufti days and discos.
>
> *The Northants Evening Telegraph*, Kettering, 20 July 2008. A *mufti day* is one in which school pupils pay a small sum to some good cause to wear their own clothes to school.

Perhaps surprisingly, the Muslim and plain clothes senses are intimately connected. It seems to have originally been a jokey term among officers in the British Army and is first recorded early in the nineteenth century. Much later, it was explained thus:

> **A slang phrase in the army, for 'plain clothes.' ... It was perhaps originally applied to the attire of dressing-gown, smoking-cap, and slippers, which was like the Oriental dress of the Mufti who was familiar in Europe from his appearance in Molière's _Bourgeois Gentilhomme_.**
>
> _Hobson-Jobson: The Anglo-Indian Dictionary_, by Sir Henry Yule and Arthur C. Burnell, 1886.

We have to presume that army officers wore this garb while relaxing in the mess. Yule and Burnell record the Muslim sense of _mufti_, but add, 'One might safely say that it is practically unknown to any surviving member of the Indian Civil Service, and never was heard in India as a living title by any Englishman now surviving.' This suggests that the plain-clothes sense didn't originate in India but was taken there by British Army officers.

Naff

Q. Reading the _Economist_ here in the US often presents me with interesting new words, but I'm confused by its reference to the British entertainer Bruce Forsyth: 'The jokes he makes in his high-camp nasal voice are too naff for reproduction in an upmarket newspaper.' Is _naff_ an odd way to spell _naif_?

A. No, it's a word in its own right, though one with a mysterious and intriguing history. Something _naff_ is inferior and lacks taste or style. I'd not describe Brucie's jokes quite in that way myself.

Many attempts have been made to explain the origin, which are made more difficult by the adjective and verb appearing to be from different sources. The latter usually appears as the impolite instruction to *naff off!*, which *Chambers Dictionary* defines as 'a forceful expression of dismissal or contempt' and which is an obvious euphemism for *fuck off!*

The adjective famously and frequently featured in a BBC radio comedy series:

> **I couldn't be doing with a garden like this ... I mean all them horrible little naff gnomes.**
>
> A line from a sketch featuring the camp gay couple Julian and Sandy, played by Hugh Paddick and Kenneth Williams, in an edition of *Round the Horne* from 1966. The script was written by Barry Took and Marty Feldman.

The verb became famous when Princess Anne was reported to have told photographers to *naff off* when they snapped her coming off her horse and taking a ducking at the Badminton Horse Trials, though a reporter who was there at the time told me some years ago that she actually used a more forceful expletive. It's recorded some years earlier than the adjective:

> **Naff off, Stamp, for Christ sake!**
>
> *Billy Liar*, by Keith Waterhouse, 1959. This may simply be a variation on *eff off*, where *eff* is a written version of the letter *F* for *fuck*, as in the British expression to *eff and blind*, to use vulgar expletives; here *blind* refers to the imprecation *blind me!*, which became *blimey!*

Some hold that *naff* is an acronym based on some phrase, either *Not Available For Fucking* or *Normal As Fuck*, though if either ever actually existed it was a post-hoc reinterpretation. Some dictionaries, such as *Collins* and *Chambers*, suggest that it was formed as backslang from *fan*, a short form of *fanny* in the British sense of the 'front bottom' or female genitals. Another idea is that it comes from dialect, either from the northern English *naffy*, *naffhead* or *naffin* for an idiot or simpleton, or Scots *nyaff*, a puny or insignificant person. The idea that it derives from *NAAFI*, the Navy, Army, and Air Force Institutes, who provide canteens and shops for British service personnel, is a risible stretch too far.

The most plausible origin takes us back to Julian and Sandy, whose sketches were without doubt responsible for making the adjective widely known and popular. Their patois was Polari, the centuries-old showmen's cant language that had been taken up by homosexuals (both Williams and Paddick, themselves gay, used it in private life). If *naff* is indeed from Polari, where it is used in phrases like *naff omi*, a dreary man, it's most probably from the sixteenth-century Italian *gnaffa*, a despicable person.

Nick of time

Q. What is the origin of the phrase *in the nick of time*?

A. It's definitely one of the stranger idioms in the language, especially as language experts are sure that *nick* here is the same word as that for a small cut or notch.

Sometime round about the 1560s the phrase *in the nick* or *in the very nick* began to be used for the critical moment, the exact instant. The idea seems to have been that a nick was a precise marker, so that if something was in the nick it was precisely at the point it should be. Users of the expression soon found that this association of ideas needed some elaboration, so started to add *of time* to the expression, and that's the way it has stayed ever since. These days, it more usually refers to something that only just happens in time, at the last possible moment:

The 28-year-old artist was lucky to receive the award as he was late for the ceremony. Mr Binns thought the award was being announced later in the day, but after a few hurried phone calls and a quick cab ride, he arrived just in the nick of time.

Northern Star, Goonellabah, Australia, 26 June 2008.

There are a number of other expressions involving *nick*, as in a name for the devil (this time from the personal name *Nicholas* and often as *Old Nick*). There are the British slang terms for theft ('my car's been nicked!'), a police station ('the nick'), the act of being arrested ('you're nicked!') or for maintaining something in a specified condition ('you've kept the car in good nick'). There's also an American sense of defrauding a person of money by cheating or overcharging, and the Australian ideas of moving quickly or furtively or of being naked ('in the nick'). Most of these, except perhaps the last, come from senses of *nick* that may derive from an old and defunct colloquial sense of seizing an advantage or grabbing an opportunity, which isn't far from the idea of being in the nick of time.

But the history of the word is confused and complicated (there's also the animal breeders' sense of a mating that has had excellent results, for example, as well as the old gaming sense of a winning throw at dice or the sporting one of the junction between the floor and side walls in a squash court) to the extent that you'd need half a book to explain them all.

Nineteen to the dozen

Q. A dog came to visit my work today. He was very excited at being in a new place with lots of people to greet. This was evident in his bobbed tail wagging so fast it became a blur! One of our clients, a polite elderly Brit, commented, 'Oh look at its tail! It's going forty to the dozen!' She was unable to give an explanation of the meaning of that phrase. And it's certainly one that isn't used in northern Arkansas, USA. Any ideas?

A. I've never encountered *forty to the dozen* before, though the British writers J. S. Farmer and W. E. Henley recorded it in Volume 3 of *Slang and its Analogues Past and Present* in 1893. They also noted *walk off forty to the dozen*, which means to 'decamp in quick time'. This is one of the rare appearances of *forty to the dozen* in print:

> **Not only does his mind make mole-hills of grievance assume the aspect of mountains of villainy, but with his pen going forty to the dozen, he sets down in wounding words the tale of his griefs.**
>
> *Memories and Impressions*, by Ford Madox Hueffer, 1911. Though in a work by an American writer, it's generally said that this version of the expression, like the others, is mainly British. A US newspaper in 1931 included a column filler about *forty to the dozen*, asserting that this most curious expression was definitely from the UK and that it meant 'to chatter incessantly and senselessly, to gabble, to talk piffle'. Hueffer, by the way, had not then changed his surname to Ford, the one by which we know him better, which he did after the First World War.

Other counts are not uncommon. I've come across *twenty to the dozen* several times (for example, Patrick O'Brian uses it in four of his Captain Aubrey seafaring tales). *Thirteen to the dozen* appeared about 1800, perhaps growing out of a tradition of supplying an extra item in a dozen by way of good measure. It's commemorated in the phrase *baker's dozen*, though there are also records of knives and other items being sold in this way. I've also read of people being figuratively packed thirteen to the dozen in a crowded railway carriage.

Even the standard version, *nineteen to the dozen*, is a little old-fashioned, though you can find examples in newspapers and daily speech. The usual meaning, as you have gathered, is to do something at a great rate, especially talking. The idea is that when other people say merely a dozen words, the speaker gets in nineteen.

> **He was excited, almost like a kid, chattering nineteen to the dozen with the media and with the gathering at Iskcon during the launch of Appu's film.**
> *Deccan Herald*, India, 11 January 2008.

It's also sometimes used to describe rapid heartbeat in times of danger, and to refer to other fast-moving or fast-changing things, such as dogs' tails.

Yet another version, which has appeared in print in the past couple of decades, both in Australia and the UK, is *ten to the dozen*. This is a head-scratcher. Logically, one would expect something going at that rate to be slower than usual, though all the examples show that it's intended to mean exactly the same as *nineteen to the dozen*. A correspondent to *World Wide Words* told me that it's common in Lancashire: 'I was a veterinary surgeon in Colne and clients always said of their dog on the table "Ee, its heart's goin ten t'dozen." I've never dared tell any local how daft it sounds to a southerner!' It's a weird example of the way that people can use phrases without caring what the individual words actually mean.

Nobody seems to have the slightest idea why nineteen is the standard number, but it's been in that form ever since the eighteenth century. There is a story about it which associates it with the efficiency of Cornish beam engines. It is said that such engines in the Newcomen era of the eighteenth century could pump 19,000 gallons of water out of a tin mine while burning only twelve bushels of coal. This is surely a folk tale, as an origin so specific and arcane would have been unlikely to generate a popular saying. It's more likely that the figures were quoted in some treatise and were then picked up as a way to explain the origin of this puzzling phrase. But nobody can know for sure because its early history is obscure.

Nit-picking

Q. An impatient colleague in the office today accused me of *nit-picking* when I pointed out a grammatical error in what he'd written. Can you tell me where the expression comes from?

A. As a professional pedant, my view is that drawing attention to a grammatical error can never be regarded as petty or overzealous fault-finding, which is what we mean by the phrase:

> **'There must be fifty rooms in this heap.' The house was big, but fifty rooms was the sort of exaggeration that expressed Dicky's pleasure or excitement; or merely relief at not having to spend the night on the road. 'At least fifty,' I said. It was better not to correct him; Dicky called it nit-picking.**
>
> *Hope*, by Len Deighton, 1995. This novel, second in the trilogy *Faith, Hope* and *Charity* and the ninth featuring the veteran British spy Bernard Samson, is set in the closing months of the Cold War before the Berlin Wall came down.

Anybody who has had the distasteful job of removing the tiny eggs of lice (*nits*) from a child's hair will know that it's a tedious activity that requires close attention and care, as well as a *fine-tooth comb*, an implement that has given us the related figurative expression *to go through something with a fine-tooth comb*, meaning undertake a thorough investigation or scrutiny, though without the negative implications of *nit-picking*.

The word *nit*, which could also refer to the eggs of other insect parasites such as fleas, has been around in the language for as long as we have records. It appears in Old English around 825 as *hnitu*, but it has relatives in most European languages and has been traced back to an Indo-European root, so ancient has been the association of such pests with human beings.

In view of the long history of such infestations, it's remarkable that *nit-picking* and its relatives are so recent.

> **Two long-time Pentagon stand-bys are *fly-speckers* and *nit-pickers*. The first of these nouns refers to people whose sole occupation seems to be studying papers in the hope of finding flaws in the writing, rather than making any effort to improve the thought or meaning; nit-pickers are those who quarrel with trivialities of expression and meaning, but who usually end up without making concrete or justified suggestions for improvement.**
>
> *Collier's Magazine*, 24 November 1951. This is, as I write, the earliest known use of the phrase. Though *fly-speckers* has died out, *nit-picker* and its relatives have become common, taking on much of the meaning of the former.

What's even more remarkable is that there's no record of anybody ever using *nit-picking* in its literal sense, only the figurative one. Perhaps we had to wait for a time when the memory of the task was still current, but the need for it in industrialized countries had been greatly reduced through better hygiene and insecticides, for people to be able refer to it without too great a shudder of distaste. The distaste was there, though, which is why it has proved so effective as a derogatory term.

No names, no pack drill

Q. You used the phrase *no names, no pack drill* in one of your newsletters. What does this mean? I can't find it in any of my dictionaries.

A. That phrase bubbled up from my subconscious. The immediate source of the expression was my father, who served in northern France throughout the First World War. I realized at once that it might not be understood, but left it in from a mischievous desire to learn whether anybody would query it.

When it turns up today, which it doesn't all that often, it's a humorous indication that a person's name has been withheld to spare them the pain of publicity, or otherwise to avoid unfortunate consequences:

> **Well, obviously if we are a famous person we need to sign autograph books, though there is one celebrity (no names, no pack drill) who actually carries round a rubber stamp and an ink pad wherewith to stamp his name into autograph books.**
> *Independent*, 24 April 2007.

Pack drill was a common military punishment that had been introduced in the nineteenth century. Rudyard Kipling gave a description in *Soldiers Three* in 1890: 'Mulvaney was doing pack-drill – was compelled that is to say, to walk up and down in full marching order, with rifle, bayonet, ammunition, knapsack, and overcoat.' Pack drill was often done at the double, at twice the normal marching pace, which Arthur Guy Empey mentions in *Over The Top* (1917): 'Then comes "Pack Drill" or Defaulters' Parade. This consists of drilling, mostly at the double, for two hours with full equipment. Tommy hates this, because it is hard work.' You may know Kipling's poem with the lines, 'O it's pack drill for me

and a fortnight's CB / For "drunk and resisting the Guard".'
(*CB*: Confined to Barracks.)

The full expression *no names, no pack drill* seems to have
been of First World War origin, but has survived the punishment itself. The original idea was that if everybody kept
quiet about who was responsible for some infraction, then
nobody could be punished for it. The broader sense grew out
of that.

Noggin

Q. What's the origin of *noggin* for a person's head? Is
it regional slang? I do not see it in my compact *Oxford
English Dictionary* (which is the edition of 1933, I believe).
My *Webster's Dictionary* gives it only as the third definition
with no etymology.

A. The *Oxford English Dictionary*'s come on a bit since then.
The Second Edition of 1989 suggested, on the basis of the
early examples then known, that it was US slang. A revision
published online in June 2008 has taken the origin back a
century and is able to say that it started out as British sporting slang, originally from boxing.

Noggin has been in the language since the late sixteenth
century. The first sense was that of a small cup or other sort
of drinking vessel. This may well have been regional to start
with, but became established as a standard term. It's much
better known, though, as the name for a small quantity
of alcohol, usually a quarter of a pint, in which the name
of the container has been transferred to its measure and its
contents.

> 'Chancy,' he said, 'I'm going down to Sugar Camp and drink a
> noggin of whiskey with my brother Bill. Then, along about dark
> I'm going a-hunting alone.'

Farewell, I'm Bound to Leave You, by Fred Chappell, 1996, a series of linked
stories based in the Appalachian mountains in North Carolina, the area in
which Fred Chappell grew up.

It seems to have been the idea of a container that gave
rise to the fresh sense of a person's head, which came into
the language in the eighteenth century. The first known
example is this:

> Giving him a stouter on the noggin, I laid him as flat as a
> flaunder.

The Stratford Jubilee, by Francis Gentleman, 1769, a farce intended to be
performed at Foote's theatre in the Haymarket, but which seems never to
have been staged. It mocked the festival of that title which was organized
by the actor David Garrick in Stratford-upon-Avon on 6 September 1769 to
commemorate William Shakespeare (during which, by the way, the British
weather did not co-operate – it bucketed down with rain). A *stouter* is a
stout blow; *flaunder* would now be spelled *flounder*.

Noggin is a good example of that rare and memorable
phenomenon, a long-lived slang term, since it has stayed in
the language, always as slang, for two and a half centuries
and is now widely known throughout the English-speaking
world.

Not by a long chalk

Q. In an article on the BBC News website about a campaign
to kick racism out of football, the sentence 'You can see how
well it is received by the changing attitudes of people but
the job is not done by a long chalk.' How did *long chalk* end
up being usable in this kind of context?

A. This mainly British expression means 'by no means', 'not at all', so the writer is saying that the work of changing attitudes is a long way from being complete. Here's another example:

> **The wicked should be made to suffer, not only hereafter but now, and they would be. She wasn't done yet, not by a long chalk. She'd have her own back on that big gormless Irishman, if it took the last breath she breathed.**
>
> *The Lord and Mary Ann*, by Catherine Cookson, 1956.

It goes back to the days in which a count or score of almost any kind was marked up on a convenient surface using chalk. At a pub or ale house this might be a note of the amount of credit you had been given (often called *the chalk* in the early nineteenth century):

> **There was a bar at the Jolly Bargemen, with some alarmingly long chalk scores in it on the wall at the side of the door, which seemed to me to be never paid off. They had been there ever since I could remember, and had grown more than I had.**
>
> *Great Expectations*, by Charles Dickens, 1861. Young Pip is sent by his sister to fetch Joe Gargery the blacksmith from the village pub.

However, the expression almost certainly comes from a different set of chalk marks in such establishments – to note the score in a game, a habit which survives in British pubs mainly in the game of darts. A *chalk* was the name given a single mark or score:

> **Thirty-one chalks complete the game; which he who first obtains is the conqueror.**
>
> *Sports and Pastimes of the People of England*, by Joseph Strutt, 1801. He's describing a game called *half-bowl*, played indoors with a wooden ball chopped in half, with which you had to try to knock down fifteen pins. The extreme bias on the ball made the game interesting.

If your opponent had a *long chalk*, a big score, he was doing well. So *not by a long chalk* indicates a gritted-teeth intention to continue, though matters are going against you. Your opponent may have a long chalk, but you're by no means defeated.

This is the earliest example I know:

> **Might your name be Smith, said a lout to that oddest of odd fellows, I, after a rap at the door loud enough to disturb the occupants of the church-yard. Yes, it might, but it ain't by a long chalk.**
>
> *The Age*, Augusta, Maine, 11 December 1833.

That may suggest it's American, but the use of *chalk* to mean scoring goes back so much further in the language that it's more than likely *long chalk* originated in oral use in the UK and was taken across the Atlantic by settlers.

On a wing and a prayer

Q. I've come across *on a wing and a prayer* in my newspaper. What does it mean?

A. It means you're in a desperate situation and you're relying on hope to see you through.

> **There's a wing and a prayer feel to warnings that bluetongue, should it reach Cumbria, would be infinitely more devastating than foot and mouth disease ever was. It's almost as though fingers are being crossed in frail hope as farmers and Defra officials together discuss the effects of this sickness which threatens to send every business it touches to the wall.**
>
> *Cumberland News*, Carlisle, 25 February 2008.

Congratulations on getting the expression right, by the way. It's one of the more commonly mangled phrases in the language, frequently being said and written as 'on a whim and a prayer'. Believe me, there's nothing capricious about it. Anyone who can write it that way is surely too young to know the source, the Second World War US patriotic song of December 1942, 'Comin' in on a Wing and a Prayer', words by Harold Adamson and music by Jimmy McHugh. It tells the story of a plane struggling home after a bombing raid and instantly became a huge hit on both sides of the Atlantic, so much so that the phrase almost immediately entered the language:

> He did not elaborate on the five Axis planes he and fellow gunners aboard his ship knocked out of African skies, but he remembers one trip coming in 'on a wing and a prayer' with their ship shot full of holes and a buddy of his nursing a wound that 'scared us to death.'
>
> *Amarillo Daily News*, Texas, 23 April 1943.

On one's tod

Q. I used the phrase, *on one's tod*, which means to be on one's own, and then realized I didn't know its derivation. Might it be rhyming slang?

A. It is, though it also involves horse racing and British royalty. It's still in use, though less than formerly. Here's a recent example:

> In his peripheral vision he could make out a blur – yellow dress, slim body – but couldn't escape her gaze long enough to bring it into heart-aching focus. 'Here on your tod?' she asked.
>
> *One Fine Day in the Middle of the Night*, by Christopher Brookmyre, 1999.
> The former pupils of a Glasgow high school join a class reunion on a holiday resort converted from a North Sea oil rig. Events heat up when a group of

mercenaries arrive bent on blackmail, resulting in what the blurb almost said was rekindled passions meeting machine-guns.

The *tod* here is an American. He was born in 1874; his real name was James Forman Sloan, but he later let it be known that his middle name was Todhunter and so is remembered as Tod Sloan. He was an inventive and highly successful jockey who pioneered what was called the *monkey crouch* or *perching on the animal's ears* – riding with short stirrups, lying low with his head almost on the horse's neck. He was a colourful and difficult individual, who earned and squandered vast sums of money. In 1896 he crossed the Atlantic to Britain to become a rider for the then Prince of Wales, later Edward VII.

He fell disastrously from fame in 1901 when the Jockey Club, which controls British racing, denied him a licence because of some unspecified 'conduct prejudicial to the best interests of the sport' (a newspaper report in 1903 said it was because its upper-class members found his arrogance and impertinence too offensive to put up with, though others said it was because he was suspected of betting on races in which he had competed). He then lost his American and French licences.

His fall was tragically quick:

> **Tod Sloan, the former champion jockey, is reported to be working as a chauffeur at Paris for a paltry salary and to lack clothes and a place to sleep.**
>
> *Stevens Point Daily Journal*, Wisconsin, 29 October 1903.

After a chequered later career, which included attempts at film acting and running a bar in Paris, he died alone in poverty in Los Angeles of cirrhosis of the liver in 1933 – though he was well enough remembered for his death to be widely reported – and it was at about this time that the rhyming slang *to be on your Tod Sloan*, to be on your own, first appeared. Like many such phrases it became shortened and so, though the short form *on your tod* is still around, hardly anybody remembers the American jockey who inspired it.

On one's uppers

Q. Can you tell me what the expression *on your uppers* refers to? I saw it used to signify someone in dire straits. Wouldn't being *down* be more appropriate than *up*?

A. The *uppers* here are the upper parts of a boot or shoe. The implication is that the soles have worn out and that the person so described is reduced to a pair that consists mainly of the uppers – quite useless, of course – and that he or she is too poor to replace them.

The first form was *walking on one's uppers*, which gives the sense behind the saying more clearly than the later abbreviated version. It appeared in the US in the 1870s:

> **At all events, Van Horn pocketed his ill-gotten gains, and started for the Big Horn mountains, but Stevens remained, and addressing himself to faro lost his wealth, and is now walking on his uppers.**
>
> *The Butte Miner*, Montana, 10 July 1877, reporting a story about crooks in New York. *Faro* was a favourite of gamblers, a card game whose name was originally *Pharaoh*, borrowed from French, in which it was supposed to have been the nickname of the King of Hearts.

To judge from a lot of the early examples, it may have originally been actors' slang – hardly surprising, as acting is a notoriously uncertain profession, more full of people down on their luck than almost any other.

The incongruity between being *down* and being on your *uppers* must have been a large part of the inspiration for the saying and for its subsequent popularity. One early appearance makes the joke explicit:

> **If you believe in immortality of the soul, you will try a pair of our shoes, as the souls last – well almost forever. Another strong feature is that no man who is wearing our shoes can easily 'get down on his uppers'.**
>
> Sack the copywriter. An advertisement in the *Syracuse Daily Standard*, New York, 28 May 1890.

On the ball

Q. While visiting England recently I went to the Royal Observatory in Greenwich. While I was there I was told that the red ball on the observatory was raised each day. In the old days the ships' captains in the Thames would look for it in order to set their timepieces. I have no problem with that. We were then told this is the origin of the expression *on the ball*. Far be it from me to question an actor dressed as John Flamsteed, but I thought I would check with you. Can you confirm or deny this information?

A. I deny it, vehemently. It's sad that someone who works for a famous scientific institution like the Royal Observatory should go so badly wrong when it comes to a simple matter of looking up a phrase in the dictionary and checking a bit of history, but that's the way it so often is.

Details first. The red ball is what's called a *time ball*. The one at Greenwich was – still is – used to signal 1 p.m. local time. At 12.55 the ball is raised halfway up its mast and at 12.58 it is sent all the way to the top. At 1 p.m. exactly, it falls. Time balls were common in the nineteenth century before easy access to radio time signals made them redundant. They were especially important to seafarers, who

needed an accurate time reference to check their naviga-
tional chronometers.

The Greenwich time ball was first used in 1833. The first
recorded appearance of the phrase *on the ball* is from the
early years of the twentieth century. By itself, that's not
enough to disprove your costumed interpreter's thesis, but
the written evidence shows it was originally American and
that it came from sport, in particular baseball.

One early form was *to put something on the ball*, meaning
that the pitcher gave it deceptive motion or unusual speed.

> **Donlin is liable to hit any kind of a ball, and the pitcher must
> keep working with him and have 'something on' the ball all the
> time.**
>
> *Dallas Morning News*, 12 April 1908.

An example that had appeared two years earlier shows how
the expression had developed:

> **Hahn's case is no different from that of many other good pitch-
> ers. He has simply arrived at the stage which all good pitchers
> dread. Ball players do not attempt to explain why these things
> are. They say: 'He's got speed and a curve, but, there's "nothing"
> on the ball.' This vague 'nothing' is the thing. It means that the
> pitcher has lost that little 'jump', or some peculiar deceptive
> break with which he has fooled batters. If he loses that, he is
> gone.**
>
> *Washington Post*, 12 July 1906. A modern US equivalent of *nothing* here
> might be *stuff*.

By the 1930s, it had broadened its application and appeal to
mean somebody who was especially alert or capable. This
was presumably because it had been amalgamated with
an earlier expression that advised budding sportsmen to
'always keep your eye on the ball'. *On the ball* was later still
exported to Britain.

On the QT

Q. I'm trying to find out the origin of the phrase, *on the QT*, meaning off the record or in confidence.

A. In January 2007, Lewis 'Scooter' Libby, the former chief of staff to the US Vice President Dick Cheney, was on trial on charges of perjury and obstruction of justice. Ari Fleischer, the former White House press secretary, testified that Libby had said to him, 'This is hush-hush, this is on the QT, not very many people know this.' One commentator joked that Libby was 'the last person in America' to use the expression. That's not quite true, though it's hardly heard these days, either in the US or the UK. It might be that Libby was unconsciously rephrasing the publicity tagline from the 1997 film *LA Confidential*, set in the 1950s, in which Danny DeVito, playing the editor of a magazine called *Hush-Hush*, repeatedly said 'off the record, on the QT and very hush-hush'.

This is a recent British example:

> **There are even suggestions on the qt that he may soon become a permanent member of the Test Match Special team.**
> *Daily Telegraph*, 8 September 2007.

Like a lot of slang terms, its origin is lost in the mists of time and oral transmission. We're not even sure what country it comes from, with some experts arguing that it's British, while others suggest it's American. Its genesis, on the other hand, is simple enough – it's an abbreviated spelling of *quiet*, using the first and last letters only, the mild obfuscation also suggesting its meaning. Many early examples were in the form *on the strict QT*.

Its early history is confused because of a red herring dragged across the path of researchers by the slang recorders J. S. Farmer and W. E. Henley. In *Slang and Its Analogues Past and Present* in 1902, they claimed that the first written reference appeared in a British broadside ballad of 1870, which contained the line 'Whatever I tell you is on the QT'. This origin has been cited by many slang dictionaries since and quoted as fact in books on word history. Unfortunately, despite a great deal of work, nobody has been able to track that ballad down, including the researchers for the *Oxford English Dictionary* when they were revising the entry for QT recently.

Not having that, the *Oxford English Dictionary* points to this as its first example:

> **'Mr. Lennox will be here on Monday. I've just got a letter from him.' 'Oh, I'm so glad; for perhaps this time it will be possible to have one spree on the strict q.t.' Kate was thinking of exactly the same thing, but Miss Hender's crude expression took the desire out of her heart, and she remained silent.**
>
> *A Mummer's Wife*, by George Moore, 1885. Moore was an Irish writer who revolutionized the English novel with this naturalistic work; it broke away from stultifying Victorian literary conventions to deal with alcoholism and the tawdry side of the theatrical world.

It's on the basis of this example that QT is said to be a British expression. However, modern electronic databases allow us to range both more widely and more deeply into writing of all places and kinds. This turned up in a search of American newspapers:

> **My house-keeper, Mrs. Brown,**
> **Is the greatest saint in town,**
> **As tee-total as it's possible to be,**
> **It's only by her nose**
> **I know where my whiskey goes,**
> **She tipples on the strict Q. T.**
>
> *The Cambridge Jeffersonian*, 4 September 1879. This has the feel of a vaudeville song. The various verses satirize our superficially pious world, which is actually full of hypocrites who are constantly undertaking immoral actions, but always *on the strict QT*.

To have two examples so close together in time from opposite sides of the Atlantic with no other evidence is puzzling. We're left with no idea who created it or in which country.

Out of whack

Q. In one of those collections of spurious word origins that friends perennially send each other by e-mail, I found the following: 'Why do we say something is out of whack? What's a whack?' It seems a valid question. Can you supply an answer?

A. Not with a totally convincing show of certainty, no. But some pointers are possible.

Whack started life in the early eighteenth century as a verb meaning to vigorously beat or strike. It was probably an imitative noise, or perhaps derived from the older *thwack*, also imitative.

The noun developed a number of subsidiary senses. At one time, it could mean a share in a distribution, a portion of money; this was originally thieves' cant – Francis Grose, in his *Dictionary of the Vulgar Tongue* of 1785, has 'Whack, a share of a booty obtained by fraud'. British English has a couple of phrases that retain a monetary meaning. One is *pay one's whack*, to pay one's agreed contribution to shared expenses. Another is *top whack*, or *full whack*, for the maximum price or rate for something ('if you go to that shop, you'll pay top whack'). There's also the American *wacky*, for somebody or something that is odd, crazy or peculiar in a mildly funny way, which may come from *whack*, in that somebody who was crazy behaved as though he had been hit about the head.

There are some other old figurative senses, including a bargain or agreement, which evolved out of the idea of a share, and an attempt at doing something ('I'll take a whack

at that job'). These are mostly American, and it was in the
US that the sense you refer to first appeared, in the latter part
of the nineteenth century. The precursor phrase *in fine whack*,
itself puzzling, is known during that century, meaning that
something was in good condition or excellent fettle.

> **The Tycoon is in fine whack. I have rarely seen him more serene
> and busy. He is managing this war, the draft, foreign relations,
> and planning a reconstruction of the Union, all at once.**
>
> In a letter by John Hay, President Lincoln's amanuensis, dated August
> 1863. *Tycoon*, the Japanese word for a great lord or prince, was used by the
> Japanese to foreigners to refer to the shogun, the hereditary commander-
> in-chief in feudal Japan until 1868. It was first borrowed into English as
> Lincoln's nickname and only later shifted sense to mean a wealthy, powerful
> person in business or industry.

To be *out of whack* would then have meant the opposite – that
something wasn't in top form or working well. It was first
applied to people with ailments ('My back is out of whack').
In the early years of the twentieth century it started to refer
to mechanisms. It might be that the sense was influenced by
the idea that faulty mechanisms respond to a smart blow, a
technique that's sometimes called *percussive maintenance*.

Over the moon

Q. Can you tell me what the expression *over the moon* means?
I can't find it anywhere, yet it seems to be a popularly used
expression.

A. Someone who says this is delighted or extraordinarily happy.

> **Cllr Harding, who is married to Lesley and lives in Hawthorn Way,
> said he was 'over the moon' to be selected as the next mayor by
> his fellow councillors.**
>
> *Bury Free Press*, 7 March 2008.

These days in Britain it's closely linked with football and has long since become a cliché. It became very popular in the 1970s as one of a pair of opposing phrases that were often on the lips of players or managers at the end of a game. If the team had lost, the speaker was *as sick as a parrot* (in a state of deep depression, not physically ill; see the item on *sick as a dog*). If the team had won, he was *over the moon*.

But the expression is much, much older – there are examples of it that go back nearly 300 years:

> **Tis he! I know him now: I shall jump over the Moon for Joy!**
>
> *The Coquet, or the English Chevalier*, a play by Charles Molloy, which ran at a theatre at Lincoln's Inn Fields in April 1718 for three performances only.

This fuller version, common in the expression's early years, gives the clue to where it comes from, which must surely be the nursery rhyme *Hey diddle, diddle, / The Cat and the Fiddle, / The Cow jumped over the Moon*. In the *Oxford Dictionary of Nursery Rhymes* Iona and Peter Opie called it 'probably the best-known nonsense verse in the language'. The reference to it in *The Coquet* pre-dates the first recorded use of the rhyme by about half a century, since that appears in print for the first time around 1765. But, of course, it was a traditional verse that might have been in the oral culture for a very long time.

Over the yardarm

Q. Do you know the meaning and origin of the phrase *when the sun has crossed over the yardarm*? I have heard it said when it's lunch time and okay to have an alcoholic beverage.

A. That's the usual meaning among landlubbers, though I've heard of some who use it for the early evening, after-work period from about 5 pm onwards. It turns up in various forms, of which *the sun's over the yardarm* is probably the most common, but one also sees *not till the sun's over the yardarm* as an injunction, or perhaps a warning.

> **This brings me by natural progression to the great drink question. As you know, of course, the American does not drink at meals as a sensible man should. Indeed, he has no meals. He snuffs for ten minutes thrice a day. Also he has no decent notions about the sun being over the yard-arm or below the horizon. He pours his vanity into himself at unholy hours, and indeed he can hardly help it.**
>
> From *Sea to Sea*, by Rudyard Kipling, 1899, a collection of articles he wrote for an Indian newspaper, *The Pioneer* of Allahabad. This extract is from a piece he wrote in 1889 under the title *In San Francisco*. He visited that city on his way home from India to Britain (he went the long way). You might not guess from these tactless and rather snobbish remarks that Kipling liked the US and at one point came near to settling there permanently. This is the earliest known use of the expression, though as Kipling was using it expecting that his readers would understand, it must even then have been at least moderately well known.

The yardarms on a sailing ship are the horizontal timbers or spars mounted on the masts, from which the square sails are hung. (The word *yard* here is from an old Germanic word for a pointed stick, the source also of our unit of measurement.) At certain times of year it will seem from the deck that the sun has risen far enough up the sky that it is above one or other of the yardarms (I've never found out for sure whether any yardarm would do, or if it was specifically the topmost one that was meant; I presume the latter). The time it does so will obviously vary with the time of year and the ship's latitude but the consensus among mariners was that this was somewhere around noon. In the Royal Navy this was by custom and rule the time of the first rum issue of the day to officers and men. It seems that officers in sailing ships adopted a custom, even when on shore, of waiting until around this time before taking their first alcoholic drink of the day.

Though it must have been a saying of sailing-ship days, it didn't become popular among people in general until the 1930s. The days of sail are far behind us but the expression has a surprisingly wide currency still, especially in North America:

> **Jud brought him a beer from the fridge, his face still red and blotchy from crying. 'A bit early in the day,' he said, 'but the sun's over the yardarm somewhere in the world and under the circumstances ... 'Say no more,' Louis told him and opened the beer.**
>
> *Pet Sematary*, a horror story by Stephen King, 1983. This is at the point in the book at which Jud Crandall's wife has just died.

Panic button

Q. Who first hit the panic button?

A. We don't know for certain (I ought to have a rubber stamp made with that on) but the evidence points to US military pilots of the Korean War.

An early example is dated August 1950. A once famous but long-gone builder of military aircraft, the Republic Aviation Corporation of Long Island, issued a jokey guide to the slang of jet pilots in its house magazine *The Pegasus* as an 'educational aid' to civilian pilots who were retraining to fly jets. The only item of interest was *panic button*, defined as a 'state of emergency when the pilot mentally pushes buttons and switches in all directions'. Examples are known from other aviation magazines of the time, one of which referred disparagingly to some MiG pilots during the Korean War as *panic-button boys* who bailed out at the first sign of action.

What's uncertain is the exact origin. To judge by a short article in a language journal in 1956, even the flyboys weren't sure at the time. The writer suggested four possible origins, but plumped for this one:

> **The actual source seems probably to have been the bell system in the Second World War bombers (B-17, B-24) for emergency procedures such as bailout and ditching, an emergency bell system that was central in the experience of most Air Force pilots. In case of fighter or flak damage so extensive that the bomber had to be abandoned, the pilot rang a 'prepare-to-abandon' ring and then a ring meaning 'jump.' The bell system was used since the intercom was apt to be out if there was extensive damage ... The implications of the phrase seem to have come from those few times when pilots 'hit the panic button' too soon and rang for emergency procedures over minor damage, causing their crews to bail out unnecessarily.**
>
> Which Panic Button Do You Hit?, by Lt Col. James L. Jackson, in American Speech, October 1956. Col. Jackson said that to hit the panic button was used to mean that 'the person spoke or acted in unnecessary haste or near panic'.

This is supported by a quote from *The Lowell Sun* of Massachusetts, dated December 1950, that refers to US troops in Korea ('But they have a phrase to describe this senseless gossip mongering. They call it "ringing the panic button".'), by one in the *Daily Review* of Hayward, California, on 3 January 1951 ('The expression stemmed from the signal given by the pilot of a plane which is in serious trouble. He pushes a button sounding a buzzer which means everybody is to bail out.'), and by a note in *The New York Times Magazine* on 13 May 1951: 'Someone remembered the "panic button" in an airplane that is pressed when time comes to abandon ship.'

The year before Colonel Jackson's article, another reference appeared in the same journal:

> There is a switch called the 'panic button' in the cockpit of a jet
> aircraft which jettisons objects, including extra fuel tanks, in
> order to lighten the plane. Conditions under which this switch
> is used are usually quite desperate. In case of a power failure,
> for example, when all the prescribed remedial procedures fail,
> the pilot might in desperation 'push everything that's out and
> pull everything that's in,' in the hope that he might acciden-
> tally do something helpful.
>
> *A Glossary of United States Air Force Slang*, by Leo F. Engler, in *American*
> *Speech*, May 1955. This was compiled from information provided by pilots at
> the Bergstrom Air Force Base in Austin, Texas.

This fits the definition that appeared in another glossary,
in the 20 November 1950 issue of *Pacific Stars and Stripes*:
'The Panic Button automatically drops the wing tanks,
rockets, and bombs when a pilot has to jettison weight to
keep flying.'

I'm not totally convinced about Col. Jackson's dating,
despite his note that '[d]iscussion with Air Force officers and
airmen reveals that the phrase to hit the panic button was
in use during the Second World War'. There's no example
of the phrase on record before 1950, at least that I can find,
but on the other hand there are lots of them in the years
that follow, early ones all linked to the Korean War. The *Daily*
Review article also noted that 'It's a new phrase which blos-
somed in the Korean war. And now you hear it on all sides.
It's always uttered as broad humor. Whenever an outfit makes
a routine move, the big joke is that "somebody pushed the
panic button."' It may be, of course, that the phrase had been
around earlier but had been limited to the oral culture of
military pilots until it leaked out around 1950.

Whatever the precise origin, there's no doubt that the
phrase was popular among flyers in the Korean War and that
it filtered back to the US civilian population and from there
to the whole English-speaking world. It has proved a most

useful term for any button or switch that operates some device in an emergency or which raises an alarm.

Pear-shaped

Q. Somebody warned me the other day that there was a risk that a project I was working on might go *pear-shaped*, an expression new to me whose meaning wasn't at once obvious (though he did explain). What's the story behind this meaning of *pear-shaped*?

A. It's mainly a British expression that refers to an activity or project that has gone badly awry or out of control.

> **They are in chaos. The Government is paralysed, the economy is going pear-shaped and they are going to make matters even worse in the months ahead.**
> *Sunday Telegraph*, 27 July 2008.

There are plenty of things that are literally pear-shaped, of course, such as a person's outline, a particular cut of a diamond, or the shape of a bottle, anything in fact that's bulbous at one end but narrow at the other, like a pear. Singers talk about full-bodied or resonant sounds as being pear-shaped. None of this explains how your sense came about.

A common explanation, the one accepted by the *Oxford English Dictionary*, is that it comes from Royal Air Force slang. However, nobody there or anywhere else seems to know why. Some say that it may have been applied to the efforts of pilots to do aerobatics, such as loops, because it is notoriously difficult to get the manoeuvre even roughly circular, and instructors would describe the resulting distorted route of the aircraft as *pear-shaped*. I've not seen firm evidence to convince me of this explanation, which sounds a little

far-fetched. But the first recorded example certainly links
it to aerial warfare:

> **There were two bangs very close together. The whole aircraft
> shook and things went 'pear-shaped' very quickly after that.
> The controls ceased to work, the nose started to go down.**
>
> *Air War South Atlantic*, by Jeffrey Ethell and Alfred Price, 1983, an account
> of the air actions during the Falklands War between Britain and Argentina
> in 1982, in which the authors interviewed many of the servicemen involved
> and disputed several of the claims made by the government for the success
> of British surface-to-air weapons systems.

Others suggest it's a graphic description of the lower side
of a rectangle oozing downwards into the shape of a pear,
which would make it a relative of 'the bottom dropping
out'.

Sorry, that's the best I can do!

Philogynist

Q. Is there an opposite to *misogynist*?

A. I'm not entirely sure what you mean by 'opposite'. Since a
misogynist is a man who hates women, you might be wanting
the word for a lover of women.

Misogynist is from Greek. If you split it into its constituent
parts, you find there are three elements. The first is *miso-*,
hate, a prefix that turns up in English in a number of rare or
facetious words, including *misopaedia* for a hater of children
and *misocapnist* for someone who hates tobacco smoke but
most commonly in *misanthropy*, a dislike of mankind. The
second part of *misogynist* is *gyn*, woman (derived from Greek
gynē), as in *gynaecologist*. Stuck on the end is *-ist*, which
indicates an agent noun.

So we can replace the first element with *philo-*, love, to get
philogynist instead. Though rare, this is listed in most larger

dictionaries, with the abstract noun given as *philogyny*, love of women. It's rare enough that it seems to have been reinvented at need by writers down the centuries. The first citation given in the *Oxford English Dictionary* is from a work of 1651 called the *Hermeticall Banquet*.

But you could argue that another way to look at the opposite of *misogynist* is not a woman-lover, but a man-hater. The easiest way to create this is to replace the *gyn* middle part with the Greek word for a man (*anēr*, in compounds *andr-*), which is in words like *androgen*, a male sex hormone. That makes *misandrist*, though it's hardly common and appears in only a few dictionaries, with the noun for the concept being, as you'd expect, *misandry*.

The *Oxford English Dictionary* includes a quotation that points out a problem you might experience using either word:

> **Strictly speaking, neither misogynist nor misandrist specifies the gender of the person who hates: you should be able to be both female and to hate women.**
>
> *Guardian,* 3 December 1993.

So you can use either *philogynist* or *misandrist*, depending on which idea you want to convey. Or, you could just try English instead.

Pie in the sky

Q. Hi. My debating team is now in the semi-finals and we have been given the topic, 'we would rather have jam in the hand than pie in the sky.' We agree with the sentiment but are puzzled by this strange expression *pie in the sky*.

A. It refers to an unattainable prospect of future happiness:

People love the fact he's going to be competitive. But we all
realise that any idea of him winning a gold medal is pie in the
sky and even getting near the podium will be a fantastic result.

People, 20 July 2008.

It derives from the work of the IWW, the Industrial Workers
of the World, the anarchist-syndicalist labour organization
formed in the US in 1905 whose members have been called
the Wobblies. The IWW concentrated on organizing migrant
and casual workers; one of the ways in which they brought
such disparate and fragmented groups together was by song.
Every member got a book when he joined, *The Little Red Song
Book*, containing parodies of many popular songs or hymns.
One of the early ones, pre-dating the IWW, was 'Hallelujah,
I'm a Bum'.

One IWW member was Joe Hill, a Swedish-born seaman
and hobo (one of the martyrs of the union movement: he
was convicted of murder on dubious evidence and executed
in 1915; you may recall a folk song about him, sung memo-
rably by Joan Baez). He wrote several popular pro-union
parodies for them, such as *Coffee An'*, *Nearer My Job to Thee*,
The Rebel Girl and *The Preacher and the Slave*.

This last song, dating from 1911, was aimed directly at the
Salvation Army, a body anxious to save the Wobblies' souls,
while the Wobblies were more interested in filling their
bellies. The Wobblies hated the Sally Army's middle-class
Christian view that one would get one's reward in heaven
for virtue or suffering on earth. The song was a parody of
the Salvation Army hymn *In the Sweet Bye and Bye*:

> Long-haired preachers come out every night,
> Try to tell you what's wrong and what's right;
> But when asked how 'bout something to eat
> They will answer with voices so sweet:

CHORUS:
You will eat, bye and bye,
In that glorious land above the sky;
Work and pray, live on hay,
You'll get pie in the sky when you die.

By 1911, other expressions using *pie* had already been in use for some time, such as *nice as pie* and *easy as pie* and it had begun to be used for a bribe or political patronage (of rewards being distributed like slices of pie) so *pie* was already around in a figurative sense, ready to be borrowed. It certainly struck home and has been in the language ever since.

Pigs might fly

Q. I was arguing with my husband the other day about the fact that we needed a new car. He rather rudely and sarcastically responded that in our financial circumstances we would get one as soon as *pigs started to fly*. Where does this idea come from?

A. There are several variations on sayings associated with the idea of flying pigs, as examples of some event that is extremely unlikely to occur.

> **Federal Opposition Leader Kevin Rudd says he expects Labor to take a pasting in the polls over the controversy surrounding his wife's job placement business. Mr Rudd has played down a poll analysis predicting a Labor landslide at this year's federal election, saying 'pigs might fly'.**
> *The Age*, Melbourne, Australia, 28 May 2007.

We have to go back a long way to find the original of this idea. It looks like an old Scottish saying that was first written down in 1616 in an edition of John Withal's *Dictionary of*

English and Latin for children. This had an appendix of proverbs rendered into Latin, of which one was the usual form of
the saying in the sixteenth and seventeenth centuries: *pigs
fly in the air with their tails forward*. This was intended to mock
credulous people – if they could indeed fly, it seems to argue,
flying backwards would seem a small extra feat.

Another version is more famous:

> **'Thinking again?' the Duchess asked, with another dig of her
> sharp little chin. 'I've a right to think,' said Alice sharply, for she
> was beginning to feel a little worried. 'Just about as much right,'
> said the Duchess, 'as pigs have to fly.'**
>
> *Alice's Adventures in Wonderland*, by Lewis Carroll, 1865.

Other forms that have appeared at various times include
pigs could fly if they had wings, and *pigs may fly, but they are very
unlikely birds*.

Play it by ear

Q. Trying to explain the phrase *play it by ear* to my Japanese
students is difficult, especially when they ask you why the
word *ear* is used. What is the origin of this phrase?

A. The phrase *by ear* goes back a long way in a figurative
sense – the first example is in a book of 1521 which notes
that it's necessary to have a good ear when singing the
psalms.

It's a rhetorical trick called metonymy, the substitution
of an idea by another that it's closely linked with, in the
same way that we might use *Downing Street* when we really
mean the British government. It's in much the same style
as Antony's speech in Shakespeare's *Julius Caesar*: 'Friends,
Romans, countrymen, lend me your ears'. He meant this
figuratively, asking his audience to lend him the thing their

ears contained, their function – to listen to him, to hear him out.

In phrases like *by ear* the implication is one stage further removed: not merely the function of hearing but also being able to accurately reproduce a melody from memory without needing to have it written down. So we have phrases like *he has a good ear for music* and *she can play anything by ear*.

The saying has been taken yet another step further away from anything literal when people use it to mean responding in a pragmatic or extempore way to events as they arise, without planning. This is much more recent, a creation of the twentieth century.

> **The captain shook his head doubtfully. He ran his hand over the black iron filings of his crew-cut. 'This is one hell of a situation, Commander. We'll just have to play it by ear.'**
>
> *Thunderball*, by Ian Fleming, 1961, in which Commander James Bond faces the evil Ernst Stavro Blofeld, head of the terrorist organization SPECTRE.

If this is the sense in which your Japanese students encounter it, I'm not surprised they find it puzzling.

Plonk

Q. While viewing some of the entries on an encyclopaedic website, I came across the word *plonk*, a Britishism for cheap wine. Here in the good old US of A, *plonk* is a word unknown to us, save perhaps as an onomatopoeia. Where did the term originate, and how did it come to be synonymous with cheap wine?

A. *Plonk*, as a disparaging term, especially for cheap red wine, is widely known in the UK and – despite your comments – to some extent in the USA. The term is also used humorously but without the negative undertones:

> **Shrewd investors who piled money into plonk to pick the perfect portfolio have been toasting another year of soaring profits. In some cases, the money made on cases of upmarket claret has more than trebled in the past three years.**
> *Glasgow Evening Times*, 1 February 2008.

It's so fixed a part of British English that many people are surprised to hear that it was originally Australian. In that country you may at one time have encountered references to *plonk bar* and *plonk shop* for a wine bar or shop, especially a cheap and cheerful one, to *plonk-up* for a party and to *plonked-up* or *plonko* for intoxicated, though I am told these are all rather dated. There's also *plink*, which was once a joking variation, which has led some writers to guess that *plonk* is an imitative invention from the sound of a cork being pulled from a bottle.

However, the evidence indicates instead an origin in the fighting in France in the First World War, when troops from various British Empire countries who spoke only English came into contact with the French language. The result was weirdly transmogrified expressions, such as *napoo* from 'il n'y en a plus' ('there is no more'), or *san fairy ann* from 'ça ne fait rien' ('it does not matter'). *Plonk* is a tortured form of *blanc*, as in *vin blanc*, white wine.

Several humorous or mangled versions of that phrase are recorded in Australia in the decades after the end of the war, such as *vin blank*, *von blink*, *plink plonk*, *point blank*, and *plinketty plonk*. By the 1930s the word had begun to settle down into our modern form, though to judge from one newspaper report it was then referring to some sort of rotgut or moonshine, possibly a mixture of cheap wine and spirits:

> **The man who drinks illicit brews or 'plonk' (otherwise known as 'madman's soup') by the quart does it in quiet spots or at home.**
> *The Bulletin*, Sydney, 11 January 1933.

Soldiers in France certainly drank local wine. Frank Richards published a memoir of the Great War in 1933, *Old Soldiers Never Die*, which notes: 'Ving blong was very cheap ... a man could get a decent pint and a half bottle for a franc.' It's easy to see why the term didn't thrive in the UK after the First World War, since there was no tradition of wine drinking except among the upper classes or cosmopolitans. Australia produced wine at this period, nearly all of it consumed in the country, and so I would guess there was more opportunity for the term to be taken up by civilians.

Plonk started to become known in the UK only in the 1950s, partly because ordinary Brits started to drink wine, and in part because of increased exposure to Australian English, and perhaps in particular its appearance in Nevil Shute's well-known novel about Australia, *A Town Like Alice*, of 1950.

Pop one's clogs

Q. A friend and I have been trying to work this one out. *Dropping off the twig* and *kicking the bucket* are fairly obvious, but what could possibly be the origin of *popping one's clogs* as a euphemism for dying?

A. *Pop one's clogs* is mainly a British English slang expression:

> **Hurray for the man who has made a career out of comebacks. Lazarus had nothing on old Frank. When the announcement finally comes that he's popped his clogs, I for one won't be surprised if he suddenly revives during his own funeral service and starts belting out Abide With Me.**
> *Birmingham Post*, 28 January 1998.

Clogs were once standard workers' footwear in several trades in the industrial towns and cities of Britain, for women as well as men, now rarely seen but at one time an icon of midlands and northern working-class life.

> **Numerous cotton factories then abutted on this street [Oxford Road, Manchester], and I shall never forget my first experience of the one o'clock thunder caused by the clatter on the pavement of the thousands of wooden clogs, worn by men and women alike, who swept all before them.**
>
> A contributor to *Notes and Queries* in 1900 was recalling life in the 1850s.

The verb *to pop* may be the old term for pawning goods. The implication is that someone would only want to pawn his clogs when he had no further need for them, that is, when he was about to die. But it's also just possible it's linked to the idiom *to pop off*, to die, which is surprisingly old – it appears first in Samuel Foote's play of 1764, *The Patron*: 'If lady Pepperpot should happen to pop off.' Later this turned into *pop off the hooks*, which also meant to die.

The first example on record of *pop one's clogs* is from the publication *Pick of Punch* in 1970. It's used humorously in the main, frequently in connection with journalism, show business and television ('Which *Coronation Street* stalwart is due to pop his clogs?'). The written evidence suggests that it's a modern fake-archaic form, unrecorded from the times when workers did usually wear clogs to work and did pawn small items each week to tide them over cash shortages. One correspondent, however, has told me that he clearly remembers it being used in Lincolnshire fifty years ago, so it may just be a folk expression that has existed for generations without being recorded in print.

Potboiler

Q. I've been trying to find the etymology of *potboiler* ('a usually inferior work, as of art or literature, produced chiefly for profit', according to the *Merriam-Webster Dictionary*) for so long that I've forgotten what brought it to mind in the first place. I suspect it's strictly an Americanism, but can't find the answer to that, either. Can you help?

A. Those among us with an interest in archaeology will know of *potboiler* in a more literal sense. It was a stone heated in a fire and dropped into a container of water to boil it. This was a useful technique in the days when pottery wasn't available or was too fragile to be exposed directly to a fire. However, this is a comparatively modern term of science, dating only from 1872; the figurative sense you mention is actually rather older, an intriguing example of an inversion of the usual order of development.

An artistic *potboiler* served the not unrelated function of bringing in cash to keep the home fires burning and the cooking pots boiling. It was a work produced for strictly commercial reasons rather than from an artistic impulse. It often referred to one that had been rapidly executed to make a quick buck, one therefore that was likely to be poorly done. In the more elevated arenas of artistry such financial motives were considered demeaning, even though Dr Johnson had rebuked these ivory-tower attitudes with his magisterial comment that 'no man but a blockhead ever wrote, except for money'.

There seems also to have been a strong feeling that to keep one's reputation alive before the public one had to originate new works regularly, a view that's summarized in the modern academic's mantra of 'publish or perish'. One had to keep the pot figuratively boiling in order to stay in the game.

This is the earliest example of the term so far known:

> I am no stranger to the merit of the fine portrait of Mr. Abel
> at his desk, in the act of composing; of Mr. Hone, with his face
> partly shaded by his hat; of a primate walking in the country;
> and of some others which appear now and then, and in great
> measure compensate for the heaps of inconsequential trash,
> or pot-boilers (as they are called) which are obtruded upon the
> public view; this may be lamented but cannot be helped, as an
> exhibition must be made up of what the painters are employed
> about.
>
> *An Account of a Series of Pictures, in the Great Room of the Society of Arts,
> Manufactures and Commerce, at the Adelphi,* by James Barry, 1793. Barry was
> a noted painter of the eighteenth century, who had the year before been
> elected as professor of painting at the Royal Academy. Despite his waspish
> comments, the main purpose of his pamphlet was to describe the six big
> paintings he had completed for the Society in the Great Room. The *primate*
> was presumably an archbishop, not an ape.

A closely related expression exists, variously written as *to
boil the pot, to keep the pot boiling* or *to make the pot boil*, which
meant to make a living, to provide one's livelihood. Though
the *Oxford English Dictionary* traces it back as far as 1661, this
example is contemporary with Barry's usage:

> As learning, though I have the proper respect for it, won't serve
> to make the pot boil, you must needs be glad of more substan-
> tial fuel.
>
> *Camilla,* by Fanny Burney, 1796. Jane Austen was much struck with this,
> Burney's third novel, which has some finely drawn characters and sly
> satirical wit at the expense of the social limitations of marriage. Of this she
> had direct and recent knowledge, having only three years earlier married
> a penniless French emigré, Alexandre d'Arblay. The novel made enough
> money that they were able to buy a cottage, which they named after the
> book.

So the expression is definitely British, not American.

Pulling one's leg

Q. In the UK, we say someone is *pulling your leg* when they are joking. We even have *pull the other one*, as a way to acknowledge that one's leg is being pulled. But why should tugging on an extremity mean teasing or having a joke with someone?

A. Oh, dear, I wish we knew. People keep asking me this, but there's very little evidence on which to base a sensible reply.

It used to be confidently asserted that the term arose in Britain, since this was for long the first known example:

> **You can send me word by some of the boats, if you can't come yourself. I shall be very anxious until I know, then I shall be able to pull the leg of that chap Mike. He is always about here trying to do me.**
>
> *'Blackbirding' in the South Pacific, or the first White Man on the Beach*, by William Churchward, 1888. *Blackbirding* was the recruitment of South Sea islanders to work on cotton and sugar plantations in Fiji, Samoa and Australia. It was officially voluntary, but often amounted to kidnapping or enslavement.

But an earlier example has now turned up, from an American newspaper:

> **There's Colonel Goshen, the giant, you know; he got struck on little Daisy Henry, who isn't much higher than his knee. She's the freak that married General Whatman, a dwarf, who is ugly enough to sour milk. The Chinese giant once told me he had half a dozen wives at home, but I think he was pulling my leg.**
>
> *The Wellsboro Agitator*, Pennsylvania, 20 February 1883. The article, reproduced from the *Philadelphia Times* of the day before, ostensibly focused on the marriage of R. R. Moffitt, a tattooed man, and Miss Leo Hernandez, the Spanish bearded lady; however, that was an excuse that allowed prurient enquiries into people regarded as abnormal or monstrous.

Some writers suggest the expression may have had something to do with tripping a person up as a joke, or figuratively tripping him by catching him out in some error to make him seem foolish. Others prefer to link it to street thieves, who might trip their mark up to make it easier to steal from him. But why either activity should be likened to pulling a person's leg is unclear. It's often ghoulishly said that it derives from the days of public hangings, in which friends of the condemned person would pull on his legs to speed the process of asphyxiation and so ensure a quicker death; but it's hardly possible to equate that with a jape or deception, or indeed the date of the first appearance of the phrase.

None of these have any appeal except as stories. The truth is out there, but it's keeping itself well hidden.

Push the envelope

Q. I've always been puzzled by the phrase *pushing the envelope*; it's an incongruous image that doesn't seem to have any relationship to its meaning. Can you tell me where it comes from?

A. It's an excellent example of the way that a bit of specialized jargon known only to a few practitioners can move into the general language. It comes from mathematics, specifically as it is used in aeroplane design. It was popularized by a well-known book:

> One of the phrases that kept running through the conversation was 'pushing the outside of the envelope.' The envelope was a flight-test term referring to the limits of a particular aircraft's performance, how tight a turn it could make at such-and-such a speed, and so on. 'Pushing the outside,' probing the outer limits, of the envelope seemed to be the great challenge and satisfaction of flight test. At first, 'pushing the outside of the envelope'

was not a particularly terrifying phrase to hear. It sounded once more as if the boys were just talking about sports.

The Right Stuff, by Tom Wolfe, 1979. This bestselling example of the New Journalism, Wolfe's own term for journalists who adopted literary styles that incorporated fictional elements and subjective responses, told the story of the test pilots of the Mercury and Apollo space programme, focusing especially on the psychology of the pilots. The *right stuff* of the title was an elusive quality of courage and skill allied to a willingness to take risks.

In mathematics, an *envelope* is the enclosing boundary of a set or family of curves that's touched by every curve in the system. It's also used in electrical engineering for the curve that you get when you connect the successive peaks of a wave. This *envelope* curve encloses or *envelops* all the component curves. In aeronautics, the *flight envelope* is the outer boundary of all the curves that describe the safe performance of the aircraft under various conditions of engine thrust, speed, altitude, atmospheric conditions and the like. It's taken to be the known limits for the safe performance of the craft.

Test pilots have to test (or *push*) these limits to establish exactly what the plane is capable of doing, and where failure is likely to occur – to compare calculated performance limits with ones derived from experience. Tom Wolfe was using an older form of the phrase, *pushing the outside of the envelope*; it also appears as *pushing the edge of the envelope*.

Following his book and film, the phrase began to move into the wider world, in the process frequently being shortened to just *push the envelope*, which completely loses the sense; the first recorded use in the more general sense of going (or attempting to go) beyond the limits of what is known to be possible came in the mid 1980s. This is an early example:

> **We all agree that the use of chemicals and dope is an inappropriate and potentially dangerous practice; it is a practice**

that should be condemned. Yet serious athletes will continue to push the envelope to gain more efficiency, shorter times, better stamina. The will to win is fearsome.

Alton Telegraph, Illinois, 23 September 1985.

h ttp://www.worldwideweb.org

Q followed by U

Q. In English words, the letter *q* is always followed by *u* – the only such mandatory letter pair I can recall. But it is also used in words transliterated from other alphabets (such as the Arabic *qat* for narcotic leaves), where the letter *k* would presumably work just as well. How did it achieve its rather odd status?

A. It all started long before English even existed. The Phoenicians had two symbols in their alphabet for *k*, for the very best of reasons – they had two distinct *k* sounds, only one of which we have in English. (Other Semitic languages, such as Hebrew and Arabic, have three *k* sounds.) The one we don't have – a guttural sound at the back of the mouth – the Phoenicians represented by a symbol a little like our modern *q* that they called *Qōf* (their word for a monkey, perhaps because the tail of the letter reminded them of a monkey's). This was used in particular before vowels that are also sounded at the back of the mouth, especially *o* and *u*.

The Greeks took the Phoenician symbol over as *qoppa* or *koppa*. This isn't in the classical Greek alphabet – it was dropped as unnecessary around 400 BC, because Greek, from a different language group, has never had the sound it represents. However, a version of the Greek alphabet that did still contain koppa was borrowed by the Etruscans, whose language is from yet a third language group (they probably got it from Greek colonists who settled in the region of Italy now called Campania). The Etruscan alphabet had three symbols for the *k* sound – gamma was used before *e* and *i*, kappa was used before *a* and koppa before *o* and *u* (gamma was available because Etruscans had no hard g sound in their language).

In turn (you're still following my trip around the Mediterranean, I hope), the Romans took their alphabet from the Etruscans; like the Greeks, Latin had only the one *k* sound. As a result, over time kappa was dropped, koppa evolved into *q*, and gamma into *c* (these changes explain why Greek words spelled with *k* have their Latin equivalents spelled with *c*). The Romans used *q* only before *u*, to represent the *kw* sound that was common in the language. However, the combination was actually written as *qv*, since the Roman alphabet didn't have a *u* and *v* was a vowel in classical Latin.

If we move on about a thousand years, we find that Old English had the same *kw* sound, but represented it by *cw*, since *q* wasn't in their version of the alphabet (so, for example, *queen* in Old English was spelled *cwen*). French, however, continued the Latin *qv*. After the Norman Conquest, French spelling gradually took over in England, eventually replacing the Old English *cw* by Latinate *qv* and then *qu* when *u* came into the alphabet, though this change took about 300 years to complete. As many writers have since pointed out, the change was unnecessary, as we don't need *qu* in the alphabet any more than the English before the Norman Conquest did – *cw* would work as well most of the time. In those situations in which *qu* is said as *k*, as in words from French like *antique*, we could use *c* or *k* instead. It's just one example of why English spelling is such a mishmash.

After all this, the reason why versions of Arabic words written in English use *q* without a following *u* is easy to understand – it's a neat way of transcribing that guttural *k* sound (the Arabic letter *qaf*) that's faithful to the way the alphabet has evolved over several millennia.

Queer somebody's pitch

Q. I was struck by the phrase *to queer the pitch* when I used it the other day. What game? How did one queer the pitch?

A. As the phrase isn't so much used as it once was, perhaps I should explain that when you *queer someone's pitch* you spoil their chances of success, usually deliberately:

> Carl's finally managed to escape the smothering grasp of one feuding family empire but, just as he's about to become ruling head of the De Souza dynasty, along comes long-lost daughter Anna to queer his pitch.
>
> *Mirror*, 9 July 2008. Aficionados will recognize a plot summary from the ITV soap *Emmerdale*.

It came originally from the argot of nineteenth-century market and street traders.

The word *pitch* here is closely related to the other British sense you give of an area of ground marked out for a sporting purpose, such as a cricket pitch or football pitch. But it's a different meaning of the word. It was the name given – then as now – to a position in a street market or the like where a trader set his barrow or stall or a place where a busker performed. And for at least 300 years *queer* had been a slang term for anything wrong, nasty, bad or worthless. (It's thought this usage was the source of *queer* for homosexual, which, however, doesn't appear until the last decade of the nineteenth century.) It's surely closely connected with the standard English *queer* for anything strange, odd, peculiar or eccentric, but exactly how we're unsure. The verb is first recorded from 1812, but is probably rather older.

Putting them together, we have *to queer one's pitch*, which originally meant to do something to spoil the success of a market or street trader. Perhaps a nearby rival shouted louder or had better patter, or an officious policeman 'interfered' with trade by moving on an illegal trader.

Later in the century, it was taken over by theatrical people, who used it to refer to something that spoiled the performance of an actor:

> **The smoke and fumes of 'blue fire' which had been used to illuminate the fight came up through the chinks of the stage, fit to choke a dozen Macbeths, and – pardon the little bit of professional slang – poor Jamie's 'pitch' was 'queered' with a vengeance.**
>
> *Stage Reminiscences: Being Recollections, Chiefly Personal, of Celebrated Theatrical & Musical Performers during the Last Forty Years. By An Old Stager* (Matthew Mackintosh), 1866. Mackintosh was a stage carpenter and stagehand in Glasgow.

Today, this sense of *pitch* is most common in *sales pitch*, originally the spiel of a trader from his market pitch to encourage people to stop and buy.

Queer Street

Q. In your explanation of *hairy at the heels* in your newsletter you quoted from John Buchan's *Huntingtower*, 'It's quite likely he's been gettin' into Queer Street.' Surely you are going to define *Queer Street*? From context it looks like being in debt, possibly to a loan shark.

A. Glad to help. You're almost there with your definition. It's now a rather dated British and Commonwealth phrase. *Queer Street* is an imaginary place where people in difficulties, in particular financial ones, are reputed to live.

> **Salaried public officials are, of course, not the only ones who have landed in queer street. More and more people are having**

trouble settling their credit card bills. The number of bankrupts has also risen.

New Straits Times, Kuala Lumpur, 31 December 2005.

That seems not to have been its first meaning. It appeared in print initially here:

QUEER STREET. Wrong. Improper. Contrary to one's wish. It is queer street, a cant phrase, to signify that it is wrong or different to our wish.

Lexicon Balatronicum, A Dictionary of Buckish Slang, University Wit and Pickpocket Eloquence, the 1811 enlarged version of A Dictionary of the Vulgar Tongue, by Captain Francis Grose.

It was used in a different sense ten years later:

Mother Mapps dropp'd her pipe, and d–d the weed, it made her sick, she said. Limping Billy was also evidently in *queer-street*.

Real Life in London, or, the rambles and adventures of Bob Tallyho, Esq., and his cousin, the Hon Tom Dashall, through the metropolis; exhibiting a living picture of fashionable characters, manners, and amusements in high and low life, by an Amateur, 1821.

Queer Street became restricted to financial embarrassment only some decades later; as late as 1902 J. S. Farmer and W. E. Henley gave three meanings for the phrase in Volume Five of *Slang and its Analogues Past and Present*: to be in a difficulty, to be wrong, and to be short of money.

Where it comes from is open to much doubt. Despite the energetic adoption of the phrase by a few modern queer theorists, it has nothing whatever to do with homosexuality. It has often been claimed that it was a variation on or corruption of *Carey Street*, the former location of the London Bankruptcy Court, the idea being, perhaps, that one reached Carey Street by way of Queer Street. As the *Oxford English Dictionary* comments, the court was established in Carey Street only in 1840, so it couldn't have been the inspiration for *Queer Street*; the *Oxford English Dictionary* might also have noted that *Carey Street* as an allusion to bankruptcy isn't recorded until the twentieth century:

> **THE YOUNG BANKRUPT, by Sampson Waterstock. An exhaustive treatise on the right mismanagement of one's affairs, with hints on the best method of bringing about a meeting of creditors. Among the chapters are the following: 'The Way to Carey Street'...**
>
> *Punch, or the London Charivari*, 17 June 1914. There was presumably some satirical reference in the name of the purported author, but if there was, it's now lost in time.

The experts discount the suggestion in the 1894 edition of E. Cobham Brewer's *Dictionary of Phrase and Fable* that it comes from a person being marked in a tradesman's ledger with the Latin verb *quaere*, to query or question, meaning that it would be desirable to make inquiries about his solvency. However, *quaere* does appear in English use and *queer*, taken from the Latin verb, is recorded in English dialect in that sense.

All in all, a most mysterious expression.

Read the riot act

Q. Somebody in the office said he was going to *read the riot act* to another member of staff over a minor transgression. What did he mean? There was certainly no riot going on, though a couple of us did remonstrate gently.

A. These days, it's just a figurative expression meaning to give an individual or a group a severe scolding or caution, or to announce that some unruly behaviour must cease.

> **The men were read the riot act and warned about safety breaches – weeks before the £32-million nuclear submarine smashed into an underwater rock in the Red Sea.**
>
> *Sun*, London, 3 June 2008.

The naked truth is that editors will read the riot act to any Tom, Dick, and Harry that uses clichés; avoid them like the plague.

Successful Scientific Writing, by Robert W. Matthews, 2007, quoting William Safire. *Read the riot act* is indeed a cliché these days.

Originally it was a deadly serious injunction to a rioting crowd to disperse. The Riot Act was passed by the British government in 1714 and came into force in 1715. This was the period of the Catholic Jacobite riots, when mobs opposed to the new Hanoverian king, George I, were attacking the meeting houses of dissenting groups. There was a very real threat of invasion by supporters of the deposed Stuart kings – as actually happened later that year and also in 1745. The government feared uprisings, and passed a draconian law making it a felony if a group of more than twelve persons who were 'unlawfully, riotously, and tumultuously assembled together' refused to disperse within an hour after they had been told to do so.

To invoke the law, one of a long list of officers (such as a justice of the peace, sheriff, under-sheriff, high or petty constable, mayor or bailiff or anyone acting for them) had to carry out a specified set of actions:

> The justice of the peace, or other person authorized by this act to make the said proclamation, shall, among the said rioters, or as near to them as he can safely come, with a loud voice command, or cause to be commanded silence to be while proclamation is making, and after that, shall openly and with loud voice make or cause to be made proclamation in these words, or like in effect: 'Our sovereign Lord the King chargeth and commandeth all persons, being assembled, immediately to disperse themselves, and peaceably to depart to their habitations, or to their lawful business, upon the pains contained in the act made in the first year of King George, for preventing tumults and riotous assemblies. God save the King.'

From the *Act for preventing Tumults and Riotous Assemblies, and for the more speedy and effectual punishing the Rioters*, 1 Geo. 1, 1714. It must have needed more courage than local worthies often possessed to stand before the mob and do this, though the provision about not coming closer than was safe must have been reassuring. The *pains* (using the word in the original Middle English sense of suffering inflicted as punishment for an offence, from Latin *poena*, a penalty) were severe – convicted persons were automatically classed as felons and so subject to the death penalty, although this was later amended to transportation for fifteen years.

The Act remained in force for a surprisingly long time, finally being repealed only in 1973 in the UK, though it had been effectively defunct for decades, had only rarely been used and was often unsuccessful in quelling riots even when it was. Similar laws still exist in Australia, Canada, the US and other countries.

Riff-raff

Q. I was watching a program about the history of English on the History Channel last night. This segment dealt with the slang created during the westward migration before the US Civil War. The rivers were the superhighways of the period and the moderator, an English gentleman, said that the well-to-do used steamboats and the less fortunate built rafts. The steering oar for the raft was called a *riff* and hence the term *riff-raff* came about for the less well-to-do. I can't verify this, but it seems plausible.

A. It's nonsense, a sad commentary on the state of television programme-making. I can find no example of *riff* used for a steering oar. The *riff-raff* are not just people without money, they're disreputable or undesirable, typically the scum or refuse of the community, a member of the rabble, the sort of people your mother probably warned you not to associate with.

The theory was spread that these wretched beings were the result of secret systematic race-pollution by riff-raff immigrants, and that they deserved no consideration whatever. They were therefore allowed only the basest forms of employment and the harshest conditions of work.

The Star Maker, 1937, by Olaf Stapledon, who despite his Scandinavian name was a British philosopher. This is an extraordinary work in which the author attempts nothing less than the complete story of human existence over billions of years, about which one historian of SF has said 'even the most extravagant superlatives are insufficient'. In the end, the Star Maker turns out to have created many universes, of which ours is one of the less successful and is about to be discarded.

To trace this one, we have to start in medieval French. There was then a set expression *rif et raf*, everything. These words are from the verbs *rifler*, to rifle through, ransack, spoil or strip, and *raffler*, to carry off, and would seem to have referred in particular to the plundering of the bodies of the dead on a battlefield and carrying off the booty.

The French phrase moved into English in much the same meaning of everything in the forms *rif and raf* or *riffe and raffe*. It was abbreviated to *riff-raff* in the fifteenth century – it can be found in William Gregory's *Chronicle of London* of about 1470. It seems to have taken some decades longer for it to have gone even further downhill and for it to be associated in particular with the dregs of society.

We're familiar with descendants of both of the original old French words in English, by the way. *Rifler* is the origin of our *riffle* in the card-shuffling sense, amongst others, and of *rifle*, for searching hurriedly through possessions for something to steal. It also gave rise to the firearms sense, since a *rifle* takes its name from the spiral grooves cut in its barrel to spin the bullet and improve its accuracy; this comes from a different sense of the French word, meaning to graze or scratch. *Raffler* lent its name to a game played with three dice, perhaps because the victor carried off the winnings.

In English the game was called *raffle*, and the word was much later applied to another form of gambling, a lottery.

And in the early nineteenth century *raffish* appeared. This adjective originally referred to somebody who was disreputable or vulgar. Only later did it acquire the undertones it now has of a person who is attractively unconventional. This may have come from the second half of *riff-raff*, or from *raff*, which had survived by itself in dialect usage in much the same sense of the lowest class of the population.

Right as rain

Q. What is the meaning and origin of the phrase, *right as rain*? Is it an aesthetically pleasing but essentially meaningless alliteration, or is *rain* really correct in some way?

A. An interesting question. Perhaps surprisingly, there have been occasional expressions starting *right as* ... for many centuries, in the sense of something being satisfactory, safe, secure or comfortable. An early example, quoted by John Heywood in his book of proverbs as long ago as 1546, is *right as a line*. In that, *right* had a literal sense of straightness, something highly desirable in a line, but it also clearly had a figurative sense of being correct or acceptable. There's an older example still, from the *Romance of the Rose* of about 1400: *right as an adamant*, where an adamant was a lodestone or magnet; used in a compass it signified the right direction, towards north.

Lots of others have followed in the centuries since.

> **You are right, master, Right as a gun.**
>
> *Prophetess*, a play by John Fletcher, 1622. Here *right* means true or correct; the mental link with *gun* was presumably because it shot bullets straight at its target.

I saw another surrounded with a crowd of two sorts of women. Some were young, quaint, clever, neat, pretty, juicy, tight, brisk, buxom, proper, kind-hearted, and as right as my leg, to any man's thinking.

Gargantua and Pantagruel, by Rabelais, in Sir Thomas Urquhart's translation of 1664. The meaning here is somewhat obscure, though 'desirable' would fit the sense.

'I hope you are well, sir.' 'Right as a trivet, sir,' replied Bob Sawyer.

The Pickwick Papers, by Charles Dickens, 1837. A trivet was a three-legged stand for a pot, kettle or other vessel placed over a fire for cooking or heating something; it was said to be *right* because it always stood firmly on its legs without rocking.

The nineteenth century, in fact, seems to have been the heyday of such expressions. About the same time as Dickens was writing, or a little later, people were saying that things were *as right as ninepence*, *as right as a book*, *as right as nails*, or *as right as the bank*. We have to guess the idea behind some of these: why *ninepence*, for example, rather than any other sum of money?

Right as rain is a latecomer to this illustrious collection of curious similes. It appeared at the end of the nineteenth century.

Wound? Hang it – it's only a scratch, man! I've stuck a lump of wadding out of your dress coat on the place – the muscle under the arm, don't you know – and I shall be as right as rain after supper.

Out of the Jaws of Death, by Frank Barrett, 1892. Barrett was a British writer of sensational novels in the last half of the nineteenth century, though one about whom few facts survive. In a review in September 1892, *The New York Times* said of the book's principal character, 'Frank Kavanagh is a tremendous villain. He is a Russian spy, a posing Nihilist, a kidnapper, a thief, and a murderer.'

> **He looked, as himself would undoubtedly have said, 'fit as a fiddle,' or 'right as rain.' His cheeks were rosy, his eyes sparkling.**
>
> In the piece entitled *A Home-Coming*, included in *Yet Again*, a collection of humorous essays by Max Beerbohm, 1909.

Since then *right as rain* has almost completely taken over from the others. It makes no more sense than the variants it has usurped and is just a play on words (though perhaps there's a lurking residual idea that rain often comes straight down, in a *right* line, in the old sense). But the alliteration was undoubtedly why it was created and it has ensured its survival.

Rum do

Q. A *rum do* means a situation that's a bit disturbing, baffling, odd or not very nice, as far as I can tell. But please put myself and my colleagues here in France out of our misery and tell us the origin. We think it may have some naval Jack Tar type of connection, but if anyone knows, it must be you. We look forward to hearing from you.

A. The books say *rum do* is an old-fashioned bit of British slang. I would agree with that, except that nobody seems to have told the British journalist, who keeps using it:

> **It seems a rum do, however, that women must wait for a cavalry of progressive male CEOs to ride to the rescue.**
>
> *The Times*, 6 February 2008. It would be possible to quote many others. However, to be fair, it is now used mostly as a deliberately old-fashioned or mildly humorous term.

The second half is easy enough to explain. A *do* is an event or happening, a sense that dates from the early nineteenth century.

Her family has a 'do' every year on the anniversary of the day her mother's father died.

People of Ship Street, by Madeline Kerr, 1958, a story about life in a Liverpool slum. Here 'do' means an organized entertainment or function.

Ha! That was a bit of a do. That's when poor old Vince got stabbed.

Soul Music, by Terry Pratchett, 1994, a Discworld novel in which music takes on magical powers to control people. *A bit of a do* can be neutral in sense, a deprecating reference to an event or entertainment ('we're having a bit of a do next week; care to come?'), but it usually refers, as here, to some fuss or commotion.

The first half has nothing to do with the spirituous drink once quaffed in quantity by members of the Royal Navy. *Rum* began as what the *Oxford English Dictionary* describes as a canting term, slang from the criminal underworld. To start with it was positive, meaning variously good, fine, excellent or great. So *rum booze* was fine or excellent drink, a *rum file* was an expert pickpocket and a *rum dab* was a dextrous thief (*dabs* are fingers; see dab hand for more about the word).

Around 1800, for reasons not well understood, *rum* did a complete flip in sense from positive to negative and started to mean something or someone odd, strange or peculiar.

She had indeed a vague feeling that he was behaving in a very noble fashion and that she ought to admire it; but also she felt inclined to laugh at him and perhaps even to despise him a little. 'He's a rum customer,' she thought.

Of Human Bondage, by Somerset Maugham, 1915. This semi-autobiographical novel is generally regarded as the best thing he ever wrote. It's been filmed three times.

Rum customer could, as here, mean an odd or peculiar person, but it could also at one time mean a man who appeared dangerous, whom it would be best to keep away from. There were once a number of slang terms that included *rum* in this

sense of something odd, all mostly obsolete – a *rum book*, for
example, was a curious or strange one, a *rum phiz* was an odd
face (from *physiognomy*) and so on. *Rum* by itself could also
mean something strange or peculiar. There's also *rummy*,
from the same source and with much the same meaning.

The *Oxford English Dictionary* guesses that it came about
through one or other of these slang expressions being
misunderstood by those unversed in criminal slang. It may
have been *rum cove* (probably from Romany *kova*, a thing or
person), originally meaning an excellent or first-class rogue,
but in which *rum* was mistakenly taken to be derogatory.
Other expressions starting in *rum* also shifted their senses
over time: at the end of the nineteenth century the *English
Dialect Dictionary* noted that *rum duke* was 'a strange, unac-
countable person', a substantial shift in sense from the
original meaning of a handsome man.

Where it comes from is disputed. Some suggest it might
have been borrowed from *Rome*, the city of glory and
grandeur, as a term of great approval (there is some slight
evidence for this in that this sense of *rum* could in its early
days be spelled *rome*); others point to the Romany *rom*, a
man. A third group, of which the *Oxford English Dictionary*
and I are members, confess we have absolutely no idea.

Safe harbour

Q. Please comment on the over-used redundant *safe harbour*.

A. Your dislike of it, I presume, is based on the etymological
history of *harbour*, which comes from the Old English *her-
ebeorg* for a shelter or refuge. It's not unreasonable to argue
that harbours are intrinsically safe, which would make the
expression a tautology. However, as so often, matters aren't
that simple.

The earliest sense of *harbour* in English – in the twelfth century – was of shelter from the elements, which might be an inn or other lodgings. (A *cold harbour* was a wayside refuge for travellers overtaken by bad weather.) It took another century before it began to be applied to a place where ships might shelter. The verb went through much the same developments, with the sense of sheltering or concealing a fugitive coming along in the fifteenth century. The closely related word *haven* is slightly older and derives from a different Old English source. Its development is the opposite of *harbour* – the maritime sense came first and the land-based place of shelter evolved from it.

Later on, the concept of safety originally explicit in both *harbour* and *haven* became to a significant extent separated from that of the physical place in which ships could dock or lie at anchor. And, of course, you could have good harbours or poor ones. As a result, English speakers began to attach adjectives to both words to show their judgement of the value of a particular anchorage or port. By the seventeenth century *safe harbour* was being used to describe one with the needful security. The *Oxford English Dictionary* has an example from 1699 in *A Dissertation Upon the Epistles of Phalaris* by the classicist Richard Bentley: 'She must not make to the next safe Harbour; but ... bear away for the remotest.'

Both expressions soon began to be used figuratively. It's hard to be sure quite when, because some early examples aren't sufficiently clear in their meaning. Here's an early example:

> **The bill underwent a great number of alterations and amend-
> ments; which were not effected without violent contest and
> altercation. At length, however, it was floated through both
> houses on the tide of a great majority, and steered into the safe
> harbour of royal approbation.**
> *Complete History of England*, by Tobias Smollett, 1758. This serious work,

edited and partly written by Smollett, was financially successful, easing the author's money problems.

We retain the idea of a harbour or a haven being a place of safety and security. However, in the law of the sea, a *safe haven* is a port in which a ship that is damaged or threatened by the weather may take refuge no matter its nationality (the alternative *port of refuge* is now also common). In the United States *safe harbor* means a procedure in a law or regulation that affords protection from liability or penalty if followed.

Because of these specialized usages, both *safe harbour* and *safe haven* have extended senses that mean they can't be said to be tautologies, though the journalistic fashion for the latter in the 1990s and early 2000s turned it into a grating cliché. Beyond that, in general usage, the compounds *safe harbour* and *safe haven* have been used for so long that they have achieved the status of idiomatic phrases. Phrases, in fact, so firmly fixed in our minds that to rail against them is pointless.

Salt of the earth

Q. If someone is the *salt of the earth* they have admirable qualities and in particular can be relied upon. Why is this when salt added to the earth makes it sterile?

A. The expression is Biblical:

> **Ye are the salt of the earth: but if the salt have lost his savour, wherewith shall it be salted? it is thenceforth good for nothing, but to be cast out, and to be trodden under foot of men.**
>
> *King James Bible*, 1611, Matthew, 5:13.

Salt has always been one of the most prized commodities, essential both for life and for preserving food. Roman soldiers were paid an allowance to buy salt, the origin of our *salary*. A man *worth his salt* is efficient or capable. To *eat salt* with someone was to accept his hospitality and a person who did so was bound to look after his host's interests. The Bible also speaks of a covenant of salt, one of holy and perpetual obligation. Newborn children were in ancient times rubbed with salt to protect them against evil forces.

To Jesus, therefore, *salt of the earth* was a great compliment. To understand his comment fully, though, you have to know a bit about where Jews of his time got their salt. Some came from salt pans on the margins of the Dead Sea, but much was obtained from Mount Sodom (Jebel Usdum in Arabic), a ridge of limestone and rock salt at the southwest corner of the Dead Sea, where a pillar of salt is said to have given rise to the legend of Lot's wife. This rock salt was the literal salt of the earth, a valuable commodity. Because the deposit's outer layer was exposed to the elements, it became contaminated and its salt content depleted by weathering, losing its taste and value, so becoming good for nothing.

The use of salt to poison the ground is entirely separate.

Say uncle

Q. I know as kids we found ourselves from time to time in precarious positions being goaded into surrender. The magic word was not *surrender*. Rather, the bullies of the day would only let go if we said *Uncle!* So my question begins with, why *Uncle*? And while you're at it, where does the word come from anyway? By any other measure it's a funny word.

A. There's been a lot of speculation about this idiom. As a result of help from several sources, I'm able to provide a clear pointer to where it comes from.

The expression is American, from the early twentieth century:

> **This Time it is 'Martie' Graves and Don Johns who made them say 'Uncle.'**
>
> In an advertisement for Excelsior Auto-Cycles in the *Modesto News*, California, 11 May 1912. The pair had smashed a total of thirty-eight world speed records at a meeting in Los Angeles a few days before, riding Excelsior motorbikes as you might expect.

The speculations are ingenious. At least two writers have argued that it derives from Irish *anacal*, meaning mercy; another proposes that it's a childish modification of *knuckle under*. If they sound unlikely, try a theory that it goes back to a Latin expression used by Roman youngsters who got into trouble: *patrue mi patruissime* 'uncle, my best of uncles'. It may be rather more probable that it's a requirement that the person should be forced to cry for his uncle in order to be let free. But why *uncle* rather than father or mother?

The earliest examples – found by Dan Norder – are all part of a joke. This has a number of forms which appeared in various US newspapers from 1891 through to about 1907 and then reappeared in the early 1940s, often on the children's pages. This is the earliest he has found:

> A gentleman was boasting that his parrot would repeat anything he told him. For example, he told him several times, before some friends, to say 'Uncle,' but the parrot would not repeat it. In anger he seized the bird, and half-twisting his neck, said: 'Say "uncle," you beggar!' and threw him into the fowl pen, in which he had ten prize fowls. Shortly afterward, thinking he had killed the parrot, he went to the pen. To his surprise he found nine of the fowls dead on the floor with their necks

wrung, and the parrot standing on the tenth twisting his neck
and screaming: 'Say "uncle," you beggar! say "uncle."'

Iowa Citizen, 9 October 1891. Later versions make the reason for choosing
uncle as the key word clearer by starting the story 'A man whose niece
had coaxed him to buy her a parrot succeeded in getting a bird that
was warranted a good talker.'

The vital question is the same as the one about the chicken
and the egg: which came first, the joke or the children's call
to submit? The *Iowa Citizen* attributes the joke to a periodical
called *Spare Moments*, a London weekly, and a British origin
is also suggested by some of the language: 'a gentleman'
and 'you beggar' sound more British than American and are
deleted in later newspaper versions of the joke. As the idiom
say uncle is apparently strictly American, the joke cannot
be an allusion to the idiom, and so the idiom must be an
allusion to the joke.

Few matters are clear-cut in etymology and there's room
for an unexplained transfer of language between US and
British English – we might imagine somebody taking the
US expression across the Atlantic before it was first written
down, which inspired an English comedian to produce
the joke, which was then fed back the other way. But the
balance of probabilities is heavily weighted towards the
American idiom being from an English joke.

Screaming ab-dabs

Q. A friend said during a recent discussion on cinema that
horror films gave her *the screaming ab-dabs*. What are *ab-dabs*
and where do I find them?

A. To give someone the *screaming ab-dabs* (or *abdabs* or
habdabs) is a British expression for inducing an attack of

extreme anxiety or irritation in someone. It's a close relative of the *heebie-jeebies*.

> **The interiors have been preserved much as they were found, and though they may delight fans of Victoriana, their combination of the brash, the sepulchral and the twee gives me the screaming habdabs.**
> *Independent on Sunday*, 9 October 2005.

It's first recorded in print in 1946 in the spelling *hab-dabs*. It seems to have become popular in the 1960s – one earlier name for the rock group Pink Floyd in that decade was *The Screaming Abdabs*.

There are few certainties about its origin. Eric Partridge, in his *Dictionary of Slang and Unconventional English*, says that *screaming abdabs* was a late 1930s expression for an attack of delirium tremens, but he doesn't provide any evidence and that sense is otherwise unrecorded, so far as I know, though the modern British sense could well be a modification of it. He also claims that two phrases – *don't give me the old abdabs* and *don't come the old abdabs with me* – were warnings in services' slang in the Second World War not to try to fool an officer or tell a fictitious story to excuse an action (or as he puts it, 'don't tell me the tale'). The version with the added *h* on the front looks like a hypercorrection, in which users assume an uncultivated speaker must be dropping an *h*.

One possible pointer to its origin might be the disparaging American slang term, *abba-dabba*, best known in the South, which denotes a person of such limited intellectual capacity he's unable to form words properly. This is recorded in print from the 1930s.

> **It is still too good to be true and I start talking abbadabba language which is double talk with a mouthful of soup.**
> *Kingsport News*, Tennessee, 19 February 1943. In a comedy piece, supposedly

That sent me to the *Historical Dictionary of American Slang*; its compiler Jonathan Lighter doesn't mention that sense, but says it's an American slang term for dessert (Eric Partridge also mentions this as a subsidiary meaning for *abdabs*, perhaps a humorous transformation of the slangy British *afters*). Professor Lighter suggests an origin in an old ragtime song whose refrain went:

> **'Aba, daba, daba, daba, daba, daba, dab,'**
> **Said the Chimpie to the Monk,**
> **'Baba, daba, daba, daba, daba, daba, dab,'**
> **Said the Monkey to the Chimp.**

'Aba Daba Honeymoon', lyric by Arthur Fields, music by Walter Donovan, published in 1914. In my youth I vaguely remember Debbie Reynolds singing it in the film *Two Weeks with Love*, which appeared in 1950; it became a hit song in its own right later. The royalties from the film eased the last two years of Fields's life.

Though it might be a complete coincidence, the similarity between the *abba dabba* of the title and *abdabs* is too striking to be ruled out entirely as a possible source. The link between meaningless monkey chatter and the slang term for an inability to speak properly is obvious enough. Jonathon Green proposes in *Cassell's Dictionary of Slang* that *abdabs* might have referred to delirium tremens as a result of the spluttering, hesitant speech of somebody so afflicted. It's possible that *abba-dabba* was brought to the UK sometime in the 1930s or early 1940s, perhaps by US service personnel, and was transformed into our modern expression.

Scuttlebutt

Q. My friend and I have been trying to figure out the origin of the word *scuttlebutt*. Do you have any thoughts on this?

A. *Scuttlebutt* is gossip:

> **'Oh, sure, anything the Syndicate is backing turns to gold. But'**
> **– Greenbriar dropped his voice – 'I hear gossip. Maybe only**
> **scuttlebutt, of course. Even so . . .'**
>
> *The Sheep Look Up*, by John Brunner, 1972, a dystopian tale in which the
> policies of a US government controlled by big business have led to extreme
> levels of pollution in cities.

The second half is easy enough – *butt* is just the old word for a large cask (from late Latin *buttis*, a cask or wineskin). The first half appears in the language in several senses with different origins, so we have to be sure we've got the right one. It's not the flattish open container, made of wickerwork at one time, whose name survives in *coal scuttle*; that's Old English, from Latin *scutella* for a dish or platter (its first sense in English). Nor is it the one that means to move with short quick steps, perhaps like a spider; that comes from an old English dialect word.

The sense we want is the one that refers to a hole cut in a ship's timbers. That's been around since the fifteenth century, when sailors called any smallish hatchway or open-ing in the deck a scuttle, especially if it was covered with a lid of some sort; it was (and remains) the usual term for an opening to let in light or air. It's of uncertain origin, but might be from the Old French *escoutille*, a hatchway. The verb *to scuttle* dates from the mid seventeenth century, at first in the sense of sinking a ship specifically by cutting holes in it – today we use it for doing so by any means.

Sailing ships commonly had a water cask on deck so the crew had easy access to drinking water during the day. To make it easier to scoop the water out with a tin pot or dipper, the head of the cask would be removed or a hole cut in one side. It became known as the *scuttled butt* – the cask with a hole in it. Fresh water was so precious that in naval ships a guard was posted by the butt to ensure that water was taken only to drink and not, for example, to wash clothes with.

It was the one place where members of the crew on duty in various parts of the ship could meet and talk during the working day.

> **There is no part of a frigate where you will see more going and coming of strangers, and overhear more greetings and gossipings of acquaintances, than in the immediate vicinity of the scuttle-butt, just forward of the main-hatchway, on the gun-deck.**
>
> *White Jacket; or The World in a Man-of-War*, by Herman Melville, 1850. Today's office water coolers have pretty much the same ambience, though in an infinitely less arduous and brutal context. The work, based on Melville's service in the US Navy, was severely critical of every aspect of naval life; in particular, its graphic descriptions of floggings were instrumental in getting the practice banned.

Real scuttlebutts have long since passed into naval history (though the word continues to be used in the US Navy for a drinking fountain) and the word has shifted its meaning to the rumour and gossip itself rather than the place where one exchanged it.

Sea change

Q. The phrase *sea change* appears frequently in both books and newspapers, and the only definition I've been able to find for it is that it is a transformation. How did the phrase come about and why?

A. It's a quotation from Shakespeare.

> **Full fathom five thy father lies,**
> **Of his bones are coral made:**
> **Those are pearls that were his eyes:**
> **Nothing of him that doth fade,**
> **But doth suffer a sea-change**
> **Into something rich and strange.**

This is part of the song that the spirit Ariel sings in Act 1, Scene 2 of *The Tempest*, 1610. At Prospero's urging he is falsely telling Ferdinand, son of Alonso, the King of Naples, that his father is dead following the shipwreck on Prospero's island, though Prospero knows very well that Alonso is safe on the other side of the island. *Fade* here means 'decompose' and *suffer*, 'undergo'.

Shakespeare obviously meant that the transformation of the body of Alonso was made by the sea, but we have come to refer to a *sea change* as being a profound transformation caused by any agency, one that isn't easily reversed. Writers who think it has something to do with the ebb and flow of the tide and use it for a recurring shift in policy or opinion, or for a minor change, are unjustly diluting Shakespeare's vision. I wish a figurative full fathom five to such people.

The point at which it stopped being a direct quotation and turned into an idiom is hard to pin down, though it seems to have happened as late as the nineteenth century and in the US, not in Britain. The *Oxford English Dictionary* finds the first allusive use in one of Ezra Pound's poems from 1917. But examples can be found earlier than that.

> In the mean time, a great deal of the more substantial part of Eastford's prosperity, together with as much of the show of it as could not be kept up to any advantage, had passed away. Like other towns on the Atlantic coast, it had suffered – 'a sea-change'.

Eastford: or, Household Sketches, by George Lunt, 1855. The author's real name was Wesley Brooke, a poet whom Edgar Allan Poe described as being 'of much vigour of style and massiveness of thought'; he was also a Boston lawyer and at one time editor of the *Boston Daily Courier*.

Everything suffers a sea-change in the depths of Mr. Hawthorne's mind, gets rimmed with an impalpable fringe of melancholy moss, and there is a tone of sadness in this book as in the rest, but it does not leave us sad.

In a review of Nathaniel Hawthorne's last major novel, *The Marble Faun: or, The Romance of Monte Beni*, in the issue of the US magazine *Atlantic Monthly* for April 1860.

Shaggy dog story

Q. Having heard several clever *shaggy dog stories* recently, I wondered what the origin of the term is.

A. Today, *shaggy dog story* refers to a long, rambling joke, full of inconsequential detail and irrelevant asides, which ends in an anticlimax instead of the expected punchline. It's amusing only because it's absurdly pointless. Its teller often has more fun showing off his storytelling virtuosity than the audience does in hearing the result. The expected response is not a laugh, but a frustrated groan.

By now the so-called Indo-US nuclear deal has become a shaggy dog story: a prolonged bad joke that goes on and on with no end or punchline in sight.

The Times of India, 19 June 2008.

The first shaggy dog stories seem to have been variations on a tall tale that was indeed about a shaggy-haired dog. In 1953, Eric Partridge wrote a monograph, *The 'Shaggy Dog' Story, Its Origin, Development and Nature*. He wrote, 'the best explanation of the term is that it arose in a story very widely circulated only since 1942 or 1943, although it was apparently invented in the 1930's'. He was pretty much spot on with his dating, lacking only the information that the term started in the US; the earliest known use of the term, recently discovered, was in *Esquire* magazine in May 1937. All early appearances of the term are from US publications, including an obscure collection of shaggy dog stories dated 1946. However, the term soon crossed the Atlantic, as you can judge from the date of Eric Partridge's book.

There are many candidates for the original, including one that Eric Partridge quoted. A grand householder in Park Lane, London, had the great misfortune to lose a very valuable and rather shaggy dog. He advertised repeatedly in *The Times*, but without luck, and finally he gave up hope. But an American in New York saw the advertisement, was touched by the man's devotion, and took great trouble to seek out a dog that matched the specification in the advertisement and which he could bring over to London on his next business trip. In due course, he presented himself at the owner's impressive house, where he was received in the householder's absence by an even more impressive butler, who glanced at the dog, bowed, winced almost imperceptibly and exclaimed, in a horror-stricken voice, 'But not so shaggy as that, sir!'

Not everybody concurs with my definition of a shaggy dog story. And it's undoubtedly true that the genre, if we may identify it with such a grand term, has evolved down the years:

> **Perhaps because the original shaggy-dog story involved an animal, the term came to be used for animal stories generally that were by no means long and tedious and that were funny. They had to be a special kind of animal story, however, one that involved an impossibility (usually the attribution of human intelligence to an animal).**
>
> *Isaac Asimov's Treasury of Humor*, Isaac Asimov, 1991. Best remembered as one of the 'big three' SF masters, along with Arthur C. Clarke and Robert

Heinlein, he wrote more than 500 books on many themes over a long lifetime. Asimov was also a noted raconteur and this book is both a joke book and a treatise on the theory of humour.

The earliest story I've found that's introduced as being a shaggy dog story is a variation on a traditional tale about a dog that can't convince anybody he talks. In this version, a trainer of two dogs, desperate for vaudeville work, has them perform an acrobatic routine for a booking agent:

> **At the end of the act he just grunted. Trainer and dogs were so discouraged. All was silent. Finally the little dog spoke up and said, 'Well, fellow, how about giving us a break and booking our act?' The agent sprang to his feet. 'My God!' he said, 'did that little dog talk?' 'No,' said the discouraged trainer, 'the big dog is a ventriloquist.' 'Here, Spot, let's get the hell out of here, no one appreciates a trained dog act anymore.'**
>
> *The Ogden Standard-Examiner*, Utah, 23 November 1942. This fits Asimov's definition to a T. The plonking final sentence is appropriately anticlimactic.

Some writers feel that shaggy dog stories should end in an atrociously punning punchline, but SF aficionados argue that a tale of that kind is instead a *feghoot*, named after a series of such stories that were first published under the general title *Through Time and Space with Ferdinand Feghoot* in the magazine *Fantasy and Science Fiction*.

The alternative term *shaggy dog tale* is also common.

Sharpshooter

Q. I once read that the origin of the word *sharpshooter* harks back to the days of the buffalo hunters in the American west. They used the old Sharps rifle and hence became known as Sharps' shooters. Do you know if there is any truth in this?

A. It's a story that's sometimes told and you can understand why, as a connection between *sharp* and *Sharps* seems obvious. It has also been said that the term was popularized during the American Civil War of the 1860s. Wrong war, wrong country, wrong rifle. The stimulus was the Napoleonic Wars and the term is British. So the short, sharp answer is that there's no truth in it.

Doubters may like the facts. The Sharps rifle was designed by Christian Sharps in the late 1840s and made from 1850 onwards by his firm, the Sharps Rifle Manufacturing Company. But the term *sharp shooter* was in use in Britain as early as 1801. The Experimental Group of Riflemen had been set up in the British Army in 1800; this led to the creation of the 95th (Rifle) Regiment in 1802 as a specialist sharpshooting force using the Baker rifle. If you're familiar with Bernard Cornwell's books about Richard Sharpe of the 95th Rifles, then you will already know this period and milieu.

> **This Regiment has several Field Pieces, and two companies of Sharp Shooters, which are very necessary in the modern Stile of War.**
>
> *Edinburgh Advertiser*, 23 June 1801, in a report about the North British Militia. This is the earliest example I can find of the term, which quickly became common, appearing in *The Times* more than twenty times in the next three years.

> **After performing wonders by his example and coolness, Lord Nelson was wounded by a French Sharpshooter, and died in three hours after, beloved and regretted in a way not to find example.**
>
> A letter from Sir Henry Blackwood to his wife Harriet, written at 1 a.m. in the morning of 22 October 1805, the day after the Battle of Trafalgar. He began his letter by reassuring her that she was 'not a husband out of pocket'. Sir Henry was the naval officer in command of the inshore squadron, who with Captain Hardy witnessed the codicil to Nelson's will, written in the cockpit of the *Victory* while Nelson was dying, which unavailingly asked

the nation to take care of Emma Hamilton. Note he uses 'sharpshooter'
unselfconsciously as the term for the rifleman, whom we would now call a
sniper.

Bavarian and Austrian riflemen and sharpshooters are
recorded earlier. The Tirailleurs (French for sharpshooters)
were Austrians who fought on the French side early in the
Napoleonic Wars. The German term *Scharfschütze* for them
is recorded in Jacobsson's *Technologisches Wörterbuch* of 1781,
so it seems certain that *sharpshooter* was borrowed into
English from German as what linguists call a calque or loan
translation, in which each element of the word is translated
literally.

Shilling ordinary

Q. I'm doing a play set in Elizabethan times, but have come
unravelled trying to find out the meaning of the phrase
shilling ordinary. The context is 'a message was brought to me
while I was sitting in the shilling ordinary.'

A. A common historical sense of *ordinary* as a noun was of
something *ordered*, set out by rule or custom, hence usual
or ordinary in our modern sense. An early example was
the food that was served regularly in a community or that
constituted one's customary daily fare. Both are known
from the fifteenth century. A further application of the idea
was to a meal in an eating-house or tavern, a sense indeed
known from Elizabethan times in the latter part of the
sixteenth century. By extension, *ordinary* was also used for
the place where the meal was served and for the company
who frequented it.

A *shilling ordinary* therefore was a meal for that price.
Though an Elizabethan might well have described a meal
in an inn as an ordinary, he wouldn't as a matter of course

have paid a shilling for it, because that would have been an expensive meal at the time – a shilling was about a day's wages for a skilled workman. The phrase itself doesn't actually appear until the latter part of the eighteenth century, though there is one rather obscure reference to a *two-shilling ordinary* in Ben Jonson's play *Every Man Out Of His Humour* of 1598, in whose first performance, incidentally, Shakespeare is said to have played one of the parts.

The meal was of highly variable quality. Sometimes it could be excellent:

> **We took our seats in a corner, whence we could observe the company. Stow whispered in my ear that this was a shilling ordinary, and one of the best in London, as was proved by the number of guests.**
>
> *London*, by Sir Walter Besant, 1892. The meal began with roast beef with peas and buttered beans, continued with roast capons and ducks and a course of cakes and fruit – a veritable feast. Nothing is said about the cost, but it hardly seems likely it was really only a shilling, even in 1892. It would seem *shilling ordinary* had become a fixed phrase indicating a set meal irrespective of price.

In the provinces it might be a plain but filling repast, if you were lucky:

> **There is a 'shilling ordinary' – which is rural English for a cut off the joint and a boiled potato, followed by hunks of the sort of cheese which believes that it pays to advertise, and this is usually well attended.**
>
> *A Damsel in Distress*, by P. G. Wodehouse, 1919. By 'it pays to advertise', Wodehouse may have been directly satirizing a famous play of 1915 with that title by Roi Cooper Megrue, Walter Hackett and Samuel Field, which became a film in 1931. However, the phrase – still very much around – exhorting businesses to shout about their wares dates back at least to the middle of the nineteenth century and was common in newspapers in the US by the 1880s.

Often it was not just indifferent but dreadful quality. In the nineteenth century, complaints and jokes about the poor fare provided in the cheaper sort of establishment were common:

> Outside the London clubs there was only the dear hotel or inn and the cheap chop house, where the steaks and pies might be well cooked, but where the shilling 'ordinary' consisted all too often of 'parboiled ox-flesh, with sodden dumplings floating in a saline, greasy mixture, surrounded by carrots looking red with disgust and turnips pale with dismay'.
>
> *Plenty and Want*, by John Burnett, 1966, quoting *Memoirs of a Stomach* of 1853, written by 'a Minister of the Interior', now known to have been Sydney Whiting. American readers may like to know that *dear* means 'expensive'.

> *Hungry Customer* [trying to carve a joint]. Here, waiter, bring me another carving knife. I can't cut anything with this villainous thing. *Honest Waiter*. Beg pardon, Sir, but we never sharpen the knives for a Shilling Ordinary.
>
> *Punch*, 18 September 1858.

Another term for the meal was *farmer's ordinary*.

> The coffee-room has in truth fallen away from its former purposes, and is now used for a farmer's ordinary on market days, and other similar purposes.
>
> *The American Senator*, by Anthony Trollope, 1877, describing the Bush Inn in the decaying town of Dillsborough in the fictitious county of Rufford.

Shiver my timbers

Q. *Shiver my timbers* turned up in a story I was reading to my children the other night. Please could you tell us all where the phrase originated?

A. It's a nautical expression, an exclamation that alludes to a ship striking some obstacle so violently that the timbers of her hull *shiver*, or break into small pieces. It's an oath along the lines of 'May I be dashed into pieces like a ship hitting a rock!'

It is first recorded in 1835 in *Jacob Faithful*, a novel by Captain Frederick Marryat of *Coral Island* fame: 'I won't thrash you Tom. Shiver my timbers if I do'. It also appears in the same year in a short story from the other side of the Atlantic:

> 'A thousand thanks, generous man, for the kind treatment of the homeless orphan – but happy she cannot be – life is to her a burden. Oh, let me die. 'Shiver my timbers if I do!' said he bluntly. 'What should I do if you were gone to the sharks? I love you with all my soul, and if you will just look kindly on a poor sailor, you shall not be desolate, while there is a spar afloat or a shot in the locker.'
>
> *Huron Reflector*, Norwalk, Ohio, 15 September 1835.

These two appearances suggest that it might originally have reflected a genuine sailors' oath that was old enough to be known in both Britain and America, though we have no record of it other than in fiction. It often appears today in the ungrammatical form *shiver me timbers!*

Though it can only be used jokingly, it has gained a continuing place in the language, almost entirely because of its many repetitions in one book:

> Cross me, and you'll go where many a good man's gone before you, first and last, these thirty year back – some to the yard-arm, shiver my timbers, and some by the board, and all to feed the fishes. There's never a man looked me between the eyes and seen a good day a'terwards, Tom Morgan, you may lay to that.
>
> *Treasure Island*, by Robert Louis Stevenson, 1883. Long John Silver makes his views plain.

Since then, it's mainly been the preserve of the writers of second-rate seafaring yarns or humorists looking for an easy line.

> **The thing that the stage sailor most craves in this life is that somebody should shiver his timbers. 'Shiver my timbers!' is the request he makes to every one he meets. But nobody ever does it.**
>
> *Stage-land: The Curious Habits and Customs of its Inhabitants*, by Jerome K. Jerome, 1889. Better known for his *Three Men in a Boat* of the same year, Jerome had been earlier a jobbing actor in London, recent memories of which fuelled this work; though humorously intended, it's actually a good source of information about the theatre of the period.

Shoot oneself in the foot

Q. Eric Partridge says that *to shoot oneself in the foot* dates from the 1980s and means a person has made a self-defeating, counter-productive blunder. I remember the expression much earlier. In the post-Second World War days it meant to take a self-inflicted, relatively minor wound in order to avoid the possibility of death or greater peril, essentially an act of cowardice. When and how did this change to the modern meaning?

A. In the sense of a self-inflicted injury for the reasons you give, it is certainly older still. My erratic memory suggests it was a well-known tactic in the First World War, rather too well known to officers and medics even then to be easily carried off.

> **The fellow who had the bed next to mine had shot himself in the foot to avoid going into a battle. A lot of them did that, but why they picked on their own feet that way is beyond me. It's a nasty place, full of small bones.**
>
> *Death in the Woods and Other Stories*, by Sherwood Anderson, 1933.

An American is describing his experiences as an aviator in the British Army in the First World War, during which he crashed his plane and was taken to hospital. A soldier who suffered a wound, from whatever cause, that was sufficiently serious for him to be sent back to Britain was called a *Blighty Boy* and the wound was a *Blighty*.

The technique has continued into modern times. Hearings held in November 1969 into the My Lai massacre during the Vietnam War were told that one soldier had 'shot himself in the foot in order to be medivac-ed out of the area so that he would not have to participate in the slaughter.'

As a literal expression describing an accidental injury it is earlier still, from the middle of the nineteenth century. I would expect that such accidents have been happening ever since firearms became portable enough for men to be careless with them. The image that at once comes to mind here is the Wild West gunslinger who tries to be the first to draw in a gunfight but who in his haste pulls the trigger before his gun is clear of the holster, inevitably shooting himself in the foot. The first example that I can find, however, is this sad report:

> **Mr. Darriel S. Leo, Consul to Basle, accidentally shot himself through the foot, four or five days ago, in a pistol gallery at Washington, and died on Sunday of lockjaw.**
> *The Appleton Post-Crescent*, Wisconsin, 29 August 1857.

A search of US newspapers found getting on for 200 items between 1960 and 1965 reporting that a man had accidentally shot himself in the foot, usually while hunting or cleaning his gun; it's no doubt a common injury down to the present day. I'm sure the expression *shoot oneself in the foot* derives from such accidents, usually the result of incompetence, and has led to our current meaning of making an embarrassing error of judgement or inadvertently making one's own situation worse. That men have done it deliberately as a way to avoid combat is only a side meaning.

The *Oxford English Dictionary*'s first figurative example, from the US, is dated 1959. It's in an extended metaphor in William White Howells's *Mankind in the Making*: 'Many a specialist has shot himself in the foot when he thought he was only cleaning a paragraph.' The *Oxford English Dictionary*'s next example is from *Aviation Week* in 1976: 'Why we seem to insist on shooting ourself in the foot over this issue, I'll never know.'

So the conversion to the modern figurative sense was in the air in the US from the end of the 1950s (and may indeed, as I suspect, be older). But it became common from the early 1980s and by 1986 had given rise to the shortened allusive description *foot-shooting*.

Short shrift

Q. I am wondering where *short shrift* came from? What is a *shrift*, and why is it *short*?

A. The first known use of the phrase in English is this:

> **RATCLIFFE: Come, come, dispatch. The duke would be at dinner. Make a short shrift: he longs to see your head.**
>
> *Richard* III, Act 3, Scene 4, by William Shakespeare, 1597. Lord Hastings has been condemned by Richard, Duke of Gloucester, to be taken out at once and beheaded and Sir Richard Ratcliffe is understandably anxious to see the matter ended.

Shakespeare's meaning for *shrift* would have been immediately known to his audience. It's from the verb *shrive*, the act of confessing to a priest followed by penance and absolution. Hastings has just asked to see a priest; Ratcliffe was telling him to be quick about his confession because Richard wanted him dead as soon as possible.

What's odd about *short shrift* is that it then doesn't appear again until Sir Walter Scott's poetic romance *The Lord of the Isles* in 1814: 'Short were his shrift in that debate'. Scott likely extracted the phrase from Shakespeare's play – he loved using archaisms. He was so influential in the early nineteenth century that he was probably single-handedly responsible for making it popular. It soon became a standard idiom in the language with the sense first of a brief respite, then of giving a matter brief and unsympathetic attention, especially in the phrase *to give short shrift* to somebody or something:

> **With the other men on board she was politely discouraging; one or two of the Army officers whom we took aboard for short stages were disposed to be gallant, and short shrift she gave them – one, I'm sure, had her heel stamped on his instep, for I saw him follow her on to the foredeck one evening, only to return red-faced and hobbling visibly.**
>
> *Flashman and the Redskins*, by George MacDonald Fraser, 1982. One of a famous series, whose main character is borrowed from the bully in *Tom Brown's Schooldays*. In the first half of the book, Flashman takes a wagon train across America, on the way meeting Kit Carson and Geronimo, ending up marrying the daughter of an Apache chieftain; in the second part he meets Ulysses S. Grant, Wild Bill Hickok, William Tecumseh Sherman and Crazy Horse and ends up at the battle of Little Big Horn with George Custer. Never a boring moment.

Shrive is itself a strange word, since its source is the Latin *scriptum*, letters or writing, from which we get words such as *script*. The modern German verb *schreiben*, to write, comes from the same source, as do similar terms in other European languages. For some reason we don't understand, *shrive* took on a special sense in the Old English and Scandinavian languages of imposing a penalty, perhaps from the idea of making a written decree. This led to the specific religious meaning and from there to our idiom for brushing somebody's concerns aside unfeelingly. Such are the oddities of language evolution.

Sick as a dog

Q. I would appreciate it if you could help me find the origin of the expression *sick as a dog*.

A. Can do. There are several expressions of the form *sick as a [something]*, that date from the eighteenth and nineteenth centuries. *Sick as a dog* is actually the oldest of them.

> **Thou knowest he's as uncertain as the wind, and if instead of quarrelling with me, he should chance to be fond, he'd make me as sick as a dog.**
>
> *The Confederacy*, by English playwright and architect Sir John Vanbrugh. This comedy, of 'lustful husbands, extravagant and scheming wives, and dishonest young men' as the *Oxford Dictionary of National Biography* describes it, was produced in his own theatre, the Queen's in London's Haymarket, in 1705. Clarissa here is speaking ill of her husband Gripe; in the language of the play he is a *money scrivener*, a usurer.

It's probably no more than an attempt to give extra force to a strongly worded statement of physical or mental unease. It was attached to a dog, I would guess, because dogs often got the short end of the linguistic stick. They've had an incredibly bad press down the years – think of *dog tired*, *a dog's life*, *dog in the manger*, *dog eat dog*, *dog's breakfast*, *go to the dogs*, *a dog's chance* and *dog Latin*.

At various times cats, rats and horses have been also dragged into the expression, though an odd thing is that horses can't vomit (not many people know that); one nineteenth-century writer did suggest that this version was used 'when a person is exceedingly sick without vomiting'.

> **Poor Miss, she's sick as a Cushion, she wants nothing but stuffing.**
>
> Stop giggling at the back. This strangest member of the set was used by Jonathan Swift in 1731 in a book we've already met in the entry for *monkey's wedding*, whose extended title is *A Complete Collection of Genteel and Ingenious Conversation, According to the Most Polite Mode and Method Now*

Used at Court, and in the best Companies of England. The work is a series of dialogues, ostensibly as a guide to improve the reader's conversational skills, but which actually records and mocks virtually every cliché of the high society of his day, which Swift alleges in his introduction he had recorded down the years in a pocket-book. *Wants*, by the way, here means 'lacks'.

The modern variation, *sick as a parrot*, which is recorded from the 1970s – at one time overused by British sportsmen as the opposite of *over the moon*, a state of euphoria consequent upon some success – refers to a state of deep mental depression rather than physical illness; this perhaps comes from instances of parrots contracting psittacosis and passing it to their human owners, though it has been plausibly suggested it has a more famous origin, in the notorious parrot sketch from *Monty Python's Flying Circus*, broadcast by BBC Television in 1969.

Skive

Q. A friend told me that the word *skive*, to get off work, is from the leather on top of a desk where elbows would rest when no work was being done. Is this right and do you know the origin of this word?

A. Interesting. Completely wrong, but interesting.

Skive is rather dated slang for avoiding school or work by staying away or leaving early; it's often heard in the form *skive off*.

> **Not bad for a guy who skived off all his dance classes at stage school because he couldn't bear the thought of having to don a leotard and some leg warmers.**
> *Daily Mail*, 17 December 2007.

It's mainly British and Commonwealth usage. American readers have only recently been exposed to it:

> 'We want to experiment with Doxy venom for our Skiving
> Snackboxes,' George told Harry under his breath. Deftly
> spraying two Doxys at once as they soared straight for his nose,
> Harry moved closer to George and muttered out of the corner
> of his mouth, 'What are Skiving Snackboxes?' 'Range of sweets
> to make you ill,' George whispered, keeping a wary eye on Mrs
> Weasley's back. 'Not seriously ill, mind, just ill enough to get
> you out of a class when you feel like it.'
>
> *Harry Potter and the Order of the Phoenix*, by J. K. Rowling, 2003.

It seems to have been military slang from the time of the First
World War, and the common assumption is that the British
Army in France borrowed it from French *esquiver*, to slink
away. The usual caveats apply, since that origin is informed
guesswork, and there's another possibility – an English
dialect verb of obscure origin meaning to move quickly.

The reason why the story you were told is intriguing is
that another well-known meaning of *skive* has been incorporated into it – to split or cut a material such as leather
into slices or strips, or to shave or pare a material to reduce
its thickness. The word isn't that old (only recorded from
the 1820s) but almost certainly goes back to Old Norse; it's
common today in – for example – the metals and plastics
industries. A person who carries out this work is also called
a *skiver*, though unlike the slang version this is a respectable
occupation.

Sky-blue pink

Q. I heard a phrase a few years back from a former colleague.
She was telling me about a poem she wrote about a *sky-blue
pink* dress; when I asked about this, she said it was a phrase
for a magical fantasy colour that she had always known. Are
you familiar with it?

A. Yes, and it was well known to my mother in London in the 1940s and also to my wife's mother, another Londoner. British people have several elaborations of it, mostly half a century old or more. Examples include *sky-blue pink with purple dots*, *sky-blue pink with yellow spots on*, and *sky-blue pink with a heavenly border*. A form once popular in northern England was *sky-blue pink with a finny addy border*, in which *finny addy* is a corruption of *finnan haddock*, a type of cold-cured smoked fish, named after Findon in Scotland; I'd guess its yellowish colour was the reason for including it.

The expression has been variously used – by exasperated adults to children when pestered about names for colours, as a 'mind your own business' off-putting reply to an unwanted question, a sarcastic description of some over-the-top or inappropriate colour, as a hand-waving term meaning 'whatever colour you want', or a dismissive comment to the effect that colour doesn't matter:

> **The father-of-three is furious that he has been convicted of being racist towards Irish people. . . . He said the fact that they were Irish had nothing to do with the situation and it would have made no difference whether they were green Martians or coloured sky blue pink.**
>
> *BBC News*, 12 May 2004.

All this might suggest that it's British, but it turns out to be American. The earliest examples appear in US sources near the end of the nineteenth century:

> **Brilliant colors in masculine garb are beginning to appear in Paris. . . . The innovation will be a boon to some of our young men, who will find ample exercise for their faculties in determining whether pea green or sky blue pink would better suit their various complexions.**
>
> *The Haverhill Daily Bulletin*, Massachusetts, 14 July 1881.

> **'I can't tell the colour,' said Binns. 'It was like a sky blue pink, with a shade of greeny brown, or something like that.'**
>
> *Arizona Weekly Journal-Miner*, 13 September 1893.

We can only surmise where it comes from, but there are many examples of advertisements both before and after these examples in which the range of colours for some item put *sky-blue* and *pink* next to each other ('Paris cashmere shawls. Cardinal, cream, sky-blue, pink, tan, wine'). You would only have to leave out a comma to create a fictitious new colour.

The reason for its continuing popularity may be linked to a series of US children's stories about a rheumatic elderly rabbit named Uncle Wiggily:

> **He splashed around and scattered the skilligimink color all over the kitchen, and when his mamma and Susie fished him out, if he wasn't dyed the most beautiful sky-blue-pink you ever saw!**
>
> *Sammie and Susie Littletail*, by Howard R. Garis, 1910. Garis was a famous, and prolific, American children's writer of the first half of the twentieth century. He invented Uncle Wiggily while working for the *Newark News*, and over four decades wrote one story a day for the paper. He also authored more than thirty stories about the adventures of Tom Swift under the pen name of Victor Appleton (a 'house pseudonym' of the Stratemeyer Syndicate, under which other authors also wrote), and lots more under other names – Laura Lee Hope, Lester Chadwick, Roy Rockwood, Clarence Young – some 500 books in total. Don't ask me about *skilligimink*, by the way: Garis seems to have been the only person ever to use the word, and where it comes from is unknown.

Sky-blue pink appeared in other authors' children's stories in the years that followed. By the 1930s it had crossed the big pond to Britain. Since millions of copies of the Uncle Wiggily stories have been sold, and many of the books are still in print, the expression continues to be introduced to new generations.

Slush fund

Q. Several news items in the press recently have featured financial transactions carried out through a *slush fund*. How did such an unlikely term become connected with money?

A. These days, references to a *slush fund* imply some illicit purpose. In particular they refer to a source of money for bribing elected officials, but more generally they can mean any illegal or unauthorized use of funds:

> **Unfortunately, this absence of control has meant that a very large number of politicians of all parties have regarded their Commons allowance as a gigantic slush fund.**
>
> *Daily Mail*, 5 July 2008.

It was originally a naval term, a wholly legitimate one. As sequences of novels about life in the Royal Navy in earlier times have graphically described, food for the lower deck was pretty dreadful. One staple was pork or beef, preserved heavily salted in casks for long voyages. The cook boiled this up in tubs in the galley as needed. One result was a mass of semi-liquid fat, called *slush*, which was skimmed off and stored in barrels called *slush tubs*.

Some of the slush was used on board ship for greasing various bits of equipment, such as the tackle blocks. Some was supplied to members of the crew for frying ship's biscuit or fresh-caught fish. The rest of it was sold off to tallow chandlers once the ship reached port to make candles. The money received was, at least in the early days, put into a fund to pay for small luxuries for the crew. This was the original *slush fund*.

This is a very early appearance of the term:

> **Other iron hoops, greater it is believed in number, were purchased from what is called the Slush Fund, and restored to**

the ship, to replace those taken as aforesaid, and the Slush Fund was reimbursed this advance by the money received from the owners of the specie which was placed in the kegs.

Connecticut Mirror, 12 September 1825. This was part of a long report fulminating at the large numbers of courts martial in the US Navy, often on minor charges. 'The whole naval force of the country seems to be divided into two parts; those who are to be tried, and those who form the Court.' Commodore Stevens had been accused, among other matters, of stealing iron cask hoops.

By the early 1870s, the term was being used in US political circles for an unofficial source of money to be used for what the *Glasgow Herald* in 1924 explained to its readers as 'illicit commission, bribery, corruption, and graft':

The stalwart bosses spent a slush fund of several hundred dollars for purchase of votes.

The Decatur Daily Review, Illinois, 7 November 1879.

So dull you could ride to China on them

Q. When I was a child, my mother used to describe knives or scissors in need of sharpening as *so dull you could ride to China on them*. In the more than half a century since then I've only heard two other people use that expression and both of them were from my hometown of Baltimore. I'd love to know if this phrase is regional as well as getting a hook on the origin of it.

A. Nothing about this strange phrase is in any of my reference books; nor does it appear in any work of mainstream literature that I can search. That it is quite unrecorded shows that it was one of those folk sayings that never made the big time.

I asked my *World Wide Words* subscribers about it. A fascinating set of responses came in, from the USA,

Canada, Australia, New Zealand, Britain, South Africa, Germany and the Netherlands, showing that phrases like it are widespread. The only significant difference in most cases was that the destination changed to be somewhere a long way from the speaker.

Several replies were from Australia. This one, from Kevin Esposito, was typical: 'In North Queensland, the phrase was "so blunt you could ride to London on it", which was frequently used by my Irish granny. It was in common use in that area through the 1940s to 1960s'. Other Australians also recall London as the destination. Michael Grounds said: 'My mother (born in Australia about 1900), who had a very English heritage, used to say of a blunt knife that you could ride to London on it, and I was delighted to hear the same expression again just recently.'

What was especially interesting was that German, Dutch and South African subscribers also recognized it. Johan Viljoen wrote: 'In Afrikaans we say: "Die mes is so stomp dat jy op hom Kaap toe kan ry" ("The knife is so dull/blunt that you can ride to the Cape on it"). The Cape refers to Cape Town.' Ted Friethoff remarked: 'The funny thing about this expression is that here in Holland my mother used the same expression about dull knives or scissors, with this difference that she used to ride to Rome on them.' S. Windeisen commented from Germany: 'The expression reminds me of something my mother says about dull knives – in German, more precisely in our Swabian regional dialect: "You could ride to Stuttgart on this knife without getting a sore behind."'

The reference to backsides is echoed by Alistair McCaw: 'My late father-in-law, who was English, often used the phrase "you could ride bare-arsed to London on this" in reference to blunt tools or knives.' Cecil Ballantine wrote from Cheltenham to say that a Wiltshire relative of his partner used that form of the expression. Angela Shingler mentioned that her mother, from East Yorkshire, also used it (though she referred to China as the destination).

The rather more pungent version of the saying suggests that it is horse riding that is being referred to, rather than any more modern form of transport. In turn – taken with the wide distribution geographically and linguistically – this suggests the expression is very old.

Soapbox

Q. In the light of all the campaigning in this US election year, I mentioned the term *soapbox* and got a few strange looks from people who had never heard the term. I refer to politicians using a platform or box to speak or preach. Can you find any other history to the use of *soapbox* or perhaps *soapboxing*?

A. Useful things, soapboxes. In quantity, bars of soap are rather weighty and they used to be packed in stout wooden boxes or crates for transport. Once emptied, the boxes were in demand. The indigent turned them into improvised furniture; children loved to put old pram wheels on them and make them into mini-racing cars, so they could run soap-box derbies. They were also just the ticket to stand on so you could be seen more easily when haranguing an audience in the street.

The most recent literal example I can think of is the soapbox, so-called, that John Major spoke from in the 1992 British general election. My journalistic contacts say that it first appeared in Cheltenham on 30 March 1992; it was certainly a wooden box from a supermarket, but as nobody packed soap in wooden boxes even then, it was instead a more flimsy orange box (at least that's what it looks like in the news photographs, with black gaffer tape wound round it to make sure it didn't fall apart and precipitate the PM into the crowd). John Major called it a soapbox to reinforce the idea that he was conducting a traditional meet-the-people election campaign.

There's no way of knowing when public speakers first turned to the soapbox or exactly when it became the term for a strident, in-your-face public tirade or political harangue, the sort long famous at Speakers' Corner in London:

> **It is the pulpit of the reformer and the housetop of the fanatic, this soapbox. From it the voice to the city is often a pious one and almost always a raucous one.**
>
> *Gaslight Sonatas*, by Fannie Hurst, 1918. She was a noted Jewish-American writer of the period from about 1910 to 1940 and many films were made from her books. This is the third of four books that featured working girls in New York City and Jewish immigrants on the Lower East Side.

An early literal reference appeared in March 1896 in the *Fort Wayne Weekly Sentinel* of Indiana: 'Then the band divided and scattered throughout the town, distributing their pamphlets and occasionally mounting a soapbox or a barrel to make a speech.' But I suspect it goes back a lot further.

The earliest example of the term used figuratively I can find is in the report of the National Convention of the Socialist Party of America in 1904, which referred to the party's *soap-box orators*. Only three years later, Jack London wrote in *The Road*, his account of his hoboing experiences of 1894, 'I get up on a soap-box to trot out the particular economic bees that buzz in my bonnet.'

The verb is also known, as is the noun *soap-boxer* for a person who uses a soap-box, both from early in the twentieth century.

Spelling bee

Q. The American institution known as the *spelling bee* has been getting a lot of attention recently – why is this competition named after a stinging insect? Or is it?

A. It used to be assumed that the bee in this case was the insect, an allusion to its social and industrious nature. The experts now prefer to point instead to the English dialect *been* or *bean*. These were variations on *boon*, once widely used in the sense of 'voluntary help, given to a farmer by his neighbours, in time of harvest, haymaking, etc' (as the *English Dialect Dictionary* put it a century ago, reporting on a word that was even then more than a century older still).

> **Last Thursday about twenty young Ladies met at the house of Mr. L. on purpose for a Spinning Match; (or what is called in the Country a Bee).**
> *Boston Gazette*, 16 October 1769.

It's likely that the link was reinforced by the similarity in names and by the insect allusion; perhaps also because at one time *been* was the plural of *bee* in some dialects (a relic of the old English plural that survives in the standard language in a few words such as *oxen*).

Despite its English origins, *bee* is a classic North American word, which developed among farmers in rural areas as the name for various kinds of mutual support at key times of year. Several acquired fixed and standard names, such as *sewing bee*, *quilting-bee*, and *raising-bee* (for barn raisings). These start to appear in print in the US from the 1820s and are common by the middle of the century.

Informal spelling contests among neighbours or in schools had long been held for recreation or instruction or as tests. They were called *spelling matches* or *spelling-schools*, names that appear in the 1840s. The basis for many competitions was the Blue-Backed Speller or Blue Speller, Noah Webster's *Elementary Spelling Book*, a work which sold more than 80 million copies in the century after its publication in 1783.

> The blue book isn't very large, but there's a good deal in it to be spelled. It contains a host of such words as 'chalybeate', 'phylactery', 'erysipelas', 'logarithmic', 'pharmaceutical' etc., *ad infinitum*, to say nothing of orthographical monstrosities of all kinds, the whole compiled for just such occasions.
>
> *Inter-Ocean*, Chicago, 30 November 1874. This report, reprinted from the *Cleveland Herald*, appeared under the headline 'A Spelling Bee: How They Conduct It in the City of Cleveland'. Apart from the headline, throughout it was referred to as a 'spelling-school'.

In 1874, US local newspapers started to report public *spelling matches* or *spelling contests* with an admission fee, in which contestants competed for prizes. They became an enormous craze – often called *spelling fever*, with the participants described as *spellists*.

> Smith says this spelling school fever is getting to be an intolerable bore. On going home to supper in a hurry, one evening lately, he found his wife sitting in front of the parlor fire, with a spelling book in her hand, and heard an indistinct mumbling, in which he could occasionally distinguish: 'c-o-m-p-l-a-c-e-n-t, s-a-t-i-s-f-i-e-d, h-a-p-p-y,' etc. 'Is supper ready, my dear?' asked he. 'S-u-p-p e-r,' was all the answer he could hear. 'Come, come, I must go up town shortly,' he said. 'S-h-o r-t-l-y,' echoed the lady, moving toward the kitchen door, pausing in the door to take one last look at McGuffey.
>
> *The Daily Free Press* of Eau Claire, Wisconsin, 26 April 1875. The reference at the end is to another famous book, *McGuffey's First Eclectic Reader*, by William McGuffey, widely used in America to teach reading well into the twentieth century.

The term *spelling bee* appears for the first time, in Brooklyn, in July 1874. In March the next year the term is recorded for one of these public contests and the term spread quickly and widely:

> **On Thursday evening last, your correspondent attended the much talked of 'Spelling Bee' held in the Academy of Music, Philadelphia, and enjoyed it exceedingly.**
>
> *Bucks County Gazette*, Bristol, Pennsylvania, 1 April 1875.

It soon reached British shores:

> **On Monday evening an entertainment of novel, amusing, and instructive character, was given in the Temperance Hall, Dresden – a spelling match, or what the Americans call a spelling bee.**
>
> *Staffordshire Sentinel*, Stoke-on-Trent, May 1875. The following month, the US journal *Harper's New Monthly Magazine* reported that 'The spelling-bee mania has spread over all England, and attacked London with especial virulence.' It didn't survive long. In 1885, *The Dictionary of Birmingham*, by Thomas Harman and Walter Showell, noted that 'The first "Spelling Bee" held in Birmingham took place January 17th, 1876. Like many other Yankee notions, it did not thrive here.'

The popularity of the spelling bee was so great that it redefined *bee* for many Americans to mean a public contest of knowledge. During the craze, other sorts were invented, including the *historical bee* and the *geographical bee*. Reformulated as *history bee* and *geographic bee*, these are still around, with *math bee* being added in the 1950s.

The craze didn't last: as early as May 1875 the *Daily Gazette and Bulletin* of Williamsport, Pennsylvania, remarked that 'The spelling fever has almost entirely subsided, and the buzz of the bee is scarcely heard any more.' This was premature, at least for other parts of the USA, but the evidence suggests it was not a long-lived fashion; spelling bees went back to being popular in a low-key way, as they had been before the craze erupted. The modern national contest dates only from 1925.

As the fashion was subsiding, Bret Harte wrote a comic poem about a spelling bee that took place among bored gold miners in a bar at Angel's Camp, California, news of this pastime having reached them from San Francisco. It did not go well:

> When 'phthisis' came they all sprang up, and vowed the man who rung
> Another blamed Greek word on them be taken out and hung.

The Spelling Bee at Angels, by Bret Harte, 1878. Matters got much worse when they were asked to spell 'gneiss'. The poem ends, 'In me you see / The only gent that lived to tell about the Spellin' Bee!'

It's hard to think what the miners would have made of *appoggiatura*, *autochthonous*, and *guerdon* – the winning words in the US National Scripps Spelling Bee 2005–08.

Spiv

Q. I have just been discussing with my son the origin of the word *spiv*. I am well aware of the meaning of the word – my late uncle Arthur English made his living depicting a lovable spiv in the 1940s and early 1950s – but until now I have never even thought about the origin of the word. My son, who is studying early 20th century history, claims that he had seen a suggestion that it was back-slang derived from *VIPs*, but I thought that this acronym was more recent than the Second World War. In any case, I couldn't see that a spiv was necessarily the opposite of a Very Important Person; indeed, I suspect that a spiv was a VIP to many customers during the war and just afterwards.

A. A spiv was typically a flashily dressed man (velvet collars and lurid kipper ties, hence the adjective *spivvy*) who made a living by various disreputable dealings, existing by his wits rather than holding down any job, and who often supported himself by petty black-market dealings. (Another name was *wide boy*, with *wide* having the old slang sense of sharp-witted, or skilled in sharp practice.) He was small-time, living on the fringes of real criminality. He is most closely associated with the Second World War and after in Britain; he always seemed able to get those coveted luxury items such as nylons that were unobtainable during that period of austerity except on the black market. As well as Arthur English, Private Walker in the BBC television series *Dad's Army* was a typical spiv; Arthur Daly, the second-hand car dealer in *Minder*, was a lineal descendant of the breed.

Spiv has lasted well and is still around:

> **High up the list is combating obesity among primary school children – which would be much easier if councils hadn't banned competitive games in schools and sold off thousands of playing fields to supermarkets and spiv property developers.**
> *Daily Mail*, 30 June 2008.

Until recently, we have had no idea where the name comes from, which has given rise to a lot of uninformed speculation. It has indeed been said that it is *VIPs* backwards; also that it was a police acronym for *Suspected Persons and Itinerant Vagrants*. *VIP* is contemporary with *spiv*, but it would be very surprising if it were the source. Apart from the sense being wrong, inverted acronyms based on word play are uncommon. The police story is a well-meaning but inept attempt at making sense of the matter.

An early appearance in print was in Axel Bracey's *School for Scoundrels* in 1934: '*Spiv*, petty crook who will turn his hand to anything so long as it does not involve honest work'. As a result of an investigation in 2007 by a BBC television programme, *Balderdash and Piffle*, we have learned that its first known appearance in print is slightly earlier, in a book of 1929, *The Crooks of the Underworld*, written under the pseudonym of G. C. Gordon; this included a reference to 'a clique of Manchester "spives"'.

We also have a better idea of the historical background to the term. The activities of Henry Bagster, a London newspaper seller and petty criminal of the early twentieth century, were widely reported at the time. Bagster's court appearances for theft, selling counterfeit goods, assault, and loitering with intent to commit a felony were recorded in the British national press between 1903 and 1906. His nickname was 'Spiv', recorded from 1904.

We don't know why he was given that nickname, though it may indicate that the slang term was in use even then. It might have come from the dialect term *spiving*, smart, or *spiff*, a well-dressed man. The latter developed into the adjective *spiffy*, smart or spruce, recorded from the 1850s, and also into *spiffed up*, smartly dressed. In the *Chambers Slang Dictionary*, Jonathon Green suggests instead the Romany *spiv*, a sparrow, which was used by gypsies, he says, 'as a derogatory reference to those who existed by picking up the leavings of their betters, criminal or legitimate'.

Spoonerism

Q. I've been told that the man who gave rise to the term *Spoonerism* never actually said one. Can this possibly be true?

A. There is indeed much evidence to suggest that William Archibald Spooner rarely if ever uttered a Spoonerism, though the legends, mischievous inventions and simple errors that have accreted around the term and his life obscure the truth.

A classic Spoonerism is the swapping of the initial sounds of two words, as in these famous but surely apocryphal examples: 'young man, you have hissed my mystery lectures and tasted your worm and you must leave Oxford by the town drain'; 'let us raise our glasses to the queer old Dean'; 'which of us has not felt in his heart a half-warmed fish?'

Spooner spent all his adult life at New College, Oxford, joining it as a scholar in 1862 and retiring as Warden (head of college) in 1924. The term *Spoonerism* began to appear in print in Britain in the 1890s:

> **The proofs were there; they could be seen;**
> **It drove me nigh to pessimism,**
> **This fruit of lawless rights between**
> **A *Malaprop* and Spoonerism!**

Punch, 7 April 1894. A poem to the anonymous author's lost love, Angelina, is mangled in the printing as a result of her spite, so that 'lover's ills' turned into 'liver pills' and 'Cupid's pinions' changed to 'Cupid's bunions'.

> **The genial public orator (Dr. Merry), the author of many a Spoonerism, brightens things up now and again with his witticisms.**

The Windsor Magazine, January 1896. The classical scholar William Merry was a fellow of Lincoln College from 1859 onwards – he became rector (head of college) in 1884 – and the public orator of Oxford University between 1880 and 1910. So he must have known Dr Spooner well. As the public orator's pronouncements are always in Latin, the thought of classical Spoonerisms is intriguing.

However, the *Oxford English Dictionary* records that it had been known colloquially in Oxford since about 1885. It reached the US in 1902:

> There are two Spooners, our own 'Badger' Spooner of Wisconsin, and Rev. Dr. Professor William Archibald Spooner of Oxford University, and both are guilty of some famous 'Spoonerisms,' writes Victor Smith in the *New York Press*. My old friend, William Braddon, knows the professor very well, and tells some funny stories of that eccentric genius, whose fame as a ludicrous word twister has spread all over Europe.
>
> *The Montgomery Advertiser*, Alabama, 25 June 1902.

Stories about Dr Spooner's strange verbal mannerisms became good copy for syndication:

> Oxford students have lately adopted the fad of going mountaineering at midnight on the roofs of the college buildings. One of these adventurers was recently caught on the roof of the house occupied by Dr. Spooner, from whose funny mistake in speaking comes the term 'Spoonerism.' Dr. Spooner is reported to have said 'shoving leopard,' when he meant 'loving shepherd.' Already, no doubt, he is credited with rejoicing that, in the case of the student who was captured on his house, he had 'rotted him on the spoof.' Dr. Spooner once made a disastrous confusion of the names of two undergraduates, Bell and Headlam, turning these words into 'Hell' and 'Bedlam.' And it is said that he once wasted hours at Greenwich asking for the 'Dull Man' inn, when what he really wanted was the 'Green Man' at Dulwich.
>
> *The Lincoln Daily Evening News*, Nebraska, 4 April 1906.

It has to be said that virtually every example on record, including these and all the other famous ones, including the hymn he supposedly introduced in chapel as 'Kinkering Kongs Their Titles Take', is an invention by ingenious members of the university who, as one undergraduate remembers, used to spend hours making them up.

Spooner did transpose items, but not like this – his inversions were more often of whole words or of ideas rather than sounds. A reliable witness records him repeatedly referring to a friend of a Dr Child as 'Dr Friend's child'. One day he passed a woman who was dressed in black and told his companion that her late husband was a very sad case, poor man, 'eaten by missionaries'. He did things backwards sometimes. One story – well attested – recounts how he spilled some salt during a college dinner and carefully poured some claret on it to mop it up, a reversal of the usual process. He is also said to have remarked on the poor lighting of some stairs and then to have turned off the lights and tried to lead his party downstairs in the dark.

Wordplay of the type that we now call Spoonerisms was rife among Oxford undergraduates from about the middle of the nineteenth century:

> **Will you poke a smipe, Pet?' asked Mr. Bouncer, rather enigmatically.**
>
> *The Adventures of Mr Verdant Green*, by Cuthbert Bede, 1854. This is an earlier work by the author we have already met in the entry on *mortarboard*.

Spooner was well known in the small community of Oxford. He was instantly recognizable, since he was an albino, with the pale face, pink eyes, white hair, poor eyesight and small stature that is characteristic of his type. Some writers have suggested that his verbal and physical quirks may have been linked with his albinism, perhaps a form of what is now called dyspraxia. Spooner later became famous for his verbal and conceptual inversions, so it's easy to see how his name could have become linked to products of undergraduate wordplay. This seems to have been from affection rather

than malice, since Spooner, known as the Spoo to undergraduates, was kindly and well liked.

Spooner was an excellent lecturer, speaker and admin-
istrator who did much to transform New College into a
modern institution. But he was no great scholar, and it's
a cruel twist of fate that he is now only remembered for a
concept he largely had foisted upon him.

St Lubbock's day

Q. Recently, while reading an old book, I came across this:
'After a while we sauntered away into the crowd and were
delighted with its resemblance to a good-natured British
rabble on St. Lubbock's Day.' I can find no reference to any
such saint. What's going on here?

A. You might describe Lubbock as a secular saint, which
he was to the British working classes near the end of the
nineteenth century.

He was John Lubbock, later the first Baron Avebury, a
banker who in 1871 as Liberal MP for London University
drafted what became the Bank Holidays Act. This established
four public holidays, the first time any holiday beyond the
common law ones of Christmas Day and Good Friday had
been established by statute and the first in history with
pay. By our standards today, they were somewhat limited,
consisting only of Easter Monday, Whit Monday, the first
Monday in August and Boxing Day.

All of these were referred to from the 1880s on as *St
Lubbock's Day*, though the title was applied particularly to
August Bank Holiday, the only summer holiday of the four
and the one on which people might most easily get out and
have some fun. To judge from the date of this story, the

name appeared almost contemporaneously with the first year's holidays:

> There was one thing I can truly say about our office, we were never serious in it. I fancy that is the case in most offices nowadays; at all events, it was the case in ours. We were always chaffing each other, playing practical jokes, telling stupid stories, scamping our work, looking at the clock, counting the weeks to next St Lubbock's Day, counting the hours to Saturday.
>
> *The Open Door*, by Charlotte Riddell, published in her collection *Weird Stories* in 1882. She was a well-known writer of the period, best known later for her ghost stories.

Not everybody approved:

> Our Bank holidays; of which very many of our superfine classes do not at all approve, and shut themselves up in elegant, but sulky seclusion on the festivals of St. Lubbock, highly indignant in their own superfine manner because their tradespeople have shut up their shops, and they, the superior ones, have some difficulty in procuring new-laid eggs and hot rolls at breakfast.
>
> *London Up to Date*, by George Augustus Sala, 1895. Sala prided himself on his productivity, honed by a period writing 3000 words of *Daily Telegraph* leaders every day. His journalism had really taken off when he was employed by Charles Dickens to work on *Household Words*, in the process, the *Oxford Dictionary of National Biography* says, 'establishing a reputation for drunkenness, quarrelsomeness, and financial and professional unreliability, which he never completely lost'.

St Lubbock's Day was recorded in a different sense by J. Redding Ware in *Passing English of the Victorian Era* of 1909, in which he said it referred particularly to August Bank Holiday but defined it as 'an orgy, a drunken riot'. It seemed that holiday celebrations had been getting out of hand. Or was this a censorious comment by the superfine classes on the unconstrained enjoyment of the lower classes?

The term is long since defunct.

Stationary versus stationery

Q. I remember learning the difference between *stationary* (not moving) and *stationery* (letterhead, envelopes, etc.) and even figured out a mnemonic device – the *e* is for *envelope*. But is there actually any significance to the similarity of the two words – is there something stationary about stationery?

A. There is indeed. Both words come from the same source, the Latin *stationarius*, for a person who was based at a military station. In medieval times a *stationarius* was a trader who had a fixed station – a shop – rather than travelling from fair to fair, a pedlar. These were usually booksellers (whose stock was too bulky and diverse to be easily carried about) and were mostly linked to the medieval universities, which is why an elevated Latin word came to be attached to them. It became *stationer* in English, a form that's recorded from the fourteenth century.

Such traders dealt in everything to do with books, not merely selling them but copying and binding them and selling related materials such as paper, pens and ink. This was before the days of printing from movable type, remember: every book had to be copied by hand. So the materials for doing so were as important to the trade as the finished article. Inevitably, the introduction of printing caused the stationer's business to change substantially over time. By the seventeenth century the term *bookseller* had come in for the trader in finished books, leaving *stationer* for the seller of writing materials.

The obsolete meaning is preserved in the name of the Stationers' Company (these days the Stationers' and Newspaper Makers' Company), one of the ancient City of London livery companies, which has always been a trade guild of booksellers and publishers. From 1557 to 1694 it controlled the production of printed books, and even down to 1911 it supervised copyrights, which is why old British books are marked as being 'registered at Stationers' Hall'.

Stationery, as a general term for the things stationers sold, appeared in the eighteenth century. There was much confusion about spelling in the early days, since *stationary* as an adjective for things that don't move about had been in the language for about a hundred years. But by the middle of the century a clear distinction had appeared, based on the logic that what a *stationer* sold had to be stuff called *stationery*.

Steal one's thunder

Q. Could you shed any light on the origins of the mysterious term *to steal one's thunder*?

A. There's a rather splendid story about the origin of this colourful phrase that connects it with John Dennis, a critic, author and playwright of the end of the seventeenth and the beginning of the eighteenth century:

> **Mr Dennis happened once to go to the play, when a tragedy was acted, in which the machinery of thunder was introduced, a new artificial method of producing which he had formerly communicated to the managers. Incensed by this circumstance, he cried out in a transport of resentment, 'That is my thunder, by G–d; the villains will play my thunder, but not my plays.'**
>
> *The Lives of the Poets of Great Britain and Ireland, to the time of Dean Swift*, by Theophilus Cibber and others, 1753. Mr Cibber, an actor and hack writer, was the son of the much more famous actor, writer, theatre manager and poet laureate Colley Cibber. The subtitle shows it was a mishmash of tittle-tattle: 'Compiled from ample materials scattered in a variety of books, and especially from the MS. notes of the late ingenious Mr. Coxeter and others, collected for this design.' Mr Cibber probably cribbed this story from *The Life of Mr. John Dennis, the Renowned Critick*, of 1734, in which a version

of the tale was told and in which it was said in passing that stage thunder had been 'oftentime introduced, to keep the audience awake'. This book had no author listed; not only that, but a note on the title page asserted that it was 'Not written by Mr Curll', a rare example of negative anonymity; the non-author was presumably the bookseller Edmund Curll.

John Dennis had indeed invented a machine to make stage thunder, which he employed in his tragedy *Appius and Virginia*, performed at Drury Lane Theatre in London in 1709. Mr Dennis, whatever his inventive gifts, was not a good writer; his play was unsuccessful and was taken off after three nights in favour of a production of *Macbeth* by another company. Dennis went to a performance and was astonished to hear his thunder machine being used.

The *Oxford Dictionary of National Biography* article on John Dennis says that the incident is probably apocryphal, a story that the poet Alexander Pope put about to further his own derogatory image of the critic. But it doesn't actually matter whether Dennis's outburst ever happened, or even whether the infamous thunder machine existed, because the tale was so often told that it became embedded in the public's mind in later decades and provided the basis for the expression.

So far as we can tell, the earliest examples of the figurative expression appeared in the US in the middle years of the following century. This is the first example I can find:

The State Journal is afraid that the Locofocos will steal its thunder, and come out in favor of a United States Bank and high protective tariff.

The Wisconsin Democrat, Madison, Wisconsin, 8 June 1843. Locofocos was a deprecatory slang term of the time for Democrats, in reference to a radical branch of the party centred in New York. Their name derived from a brand of matches, Locofoco, after an incident at one of their meetings in 1835 at which opponents turned off the gas, leaving the audience in darkness and requiring them to light matches to see by.

Steam radio

Q. Could you enlighten me about the origins of the English expression *steam radio*?

A. It was coined in the UK no later than the early 1950s at a time when television was the coming medium.

Radio, or *sound broadcasting* as it was still called in the BBC at the time, was starting to be thought old-fashioned and out of step with the times by the pioneers of television. It was also a period in which steam locomotives were being phased out on British railways and in which steam power had gained the image of a technology that was moribund and characteristic of the previous century. The equation of *steam* with *old-fashioned* most probably occurred to several people around this time and we may never learn whose fertile mind came up with it first.

These are among its early appearances in print:

> **Today radio broadcasting is so commonplace that the TV men speak of it patronisingly as 'steam radio'.**
>
> *Recollections of the Cambridge Union: 1815–1939*, by Percy Cradock, 1953. Despite the title, the personal memories of Sir Percy Cradock CGMG, as he has since become, don't go back that far. He has spent his life in public service, being at one time the UK's ambassador to China. One stimulus for the book was that he had been President of the Cambridge Union before the Second World War.

> **The flight from 'steam-radio' to television has become an admitted rout.**
>
> *British Radio Drama 1922–1956*, by Val Gielgud, 1957. Val Gielgud, the elder brother of the actor Sir John Gielgud, had risen from answering readers' letters to the *Radio Times* to become an enthusiastic pioneer of radio drama at the BBC in the late 1920s and to run the corporation's drama department for thirty-four years.

Radio, of course, has long since shaken off this defeatist and depressing belief and is still a very important force in broadcasting, belying the critics who thought it would waste away in the face of the visual medium.

Until I came to research the term, I had believed that it was the writers of *The Goon Show*, Spike Milligan in particular, who had coined the term as a defensive epithet for the older medium. The show used it so often, however, from about 1954 on, frequently with sound effects, that it must have done a lot to popularize it.

Stick one's oar in

Q. Having moved from the UK to the US, I'm often entertained by the different use of words. I've used a British term here in the US that gets blank looks: *to stick one's oar in*. Could you expose its history?

A. Certainly. Somebody who is *sticking their oar in* is interfering or meddling in some matter that doesn't concern them. It's a close relative of *sticking one's nose into* something.

> **In a bid to add a little pzazz, Cherie allowed her friend and lifestyle guru Carole Caplin to stick her oar in – with disastrous consequences when it came to a property scandal, but to little effect in terms of her husband's wardrobe.**
>
> *Scotland on Sunday*, 13 May 2007. Note the idiosyncratic spelling of pizzazz; writers are often uncertain about the number of zs, but leaving out a vowel is less usual.

Americans have told me that it is indeed known in the US, though it may be of regional distribution or used by only certain age groups. Its meaning is transparent enough even if one comes across it for the first time.

> 'Well, now, that was surely meant to apply to Urrastf, not
> Anarresti,' said an old adviser, Ferdaz, who liked to stick his
> oar in even when it steered the boat off the course he wanted.
>
> *The Dispossessed*, Ursula K. Le Guin, 1974. She is an American SF and fantasy
> writer, based in Oregon. This richly textured novel contrasting socialist and
> capitalist worlds won both a Hugo and a Nebula award.

The expression dates back to the sixteenth century and
has turned up in lots of different formulations down the
centuries. The original was *to have an oar in every man's boat*,
meaning to be involved in every man's business or affairs,
whether they wanted you to be or not. Variations include
he'll have an oar in everything, *he will put in his oar*, and *don't you
put your oar in*. There never was an actual oar – the expression has always been figurative.

One reason some Americans may be familiar with it:

> And you're just as bad as he is with your cock-and-a-bull stories
> about catching his eye and his whistling an air. But that's so like
> you! You must put in your oar!
>
> *The Mikado*, by W. S. Gilbert, 1885. The Lord High Executioner of Titipu, Ko-
> Ko, is criticizing Pitti-Sing, one of his wards. The form 'cock-and-a-bull story'
> is an older version of our more usual *cock-and-bull story* (see p. 60).

Stiff upper lip

Q. A friend recently told me to *keep a stiff upper lip*. How did
that strange idiom come to mean remaining steadfast in the
face of adversity?

A. The idea behind it is that when fear or other deep emotion
threatens to overcome a person, one of the first signs is the
upper lip beginning to tremble uncontrollably. In Britain,
it is now a popular cliché linked to the once much-admired
products of the public schools, who generations ago were sent

into the Empire to battle adversity while keeping their emotions bottled up and their countenances cheerful, because it was the thing to do.

George Orwell satirized it in his essay *Inside The Whale* of 1940: 'With Maugham it is a kind of stoical resignation, the stiff upper lip of the pukka sahib somewhere east of Suez, carrying on with his job without believing in it, like an Antonine Emperor.' P. C. Wren used it in all seriousness in *Beau Geste* in 1924: 'Anyhow, I conquered the yearning to go back to her, and when the local train loafed in I got into it, with a stiff upper lip and a bleeding heart, and set out on as eventful and strange a journey as ever a man took.'

It's so characteristically English (P. G. Wodehouse wrote a novel with the title *Stiff Upper Lip, Jeeves* in 1963) that I was amazed to find that the earliest examples on record are all North American. The oldest one I've so far found is in a publication called the *Massachusetts Spy* for 14 June 1815; 'I kept a stiff upper lip, and bought [a] license to sell my goods.' It's on record throughout the nineteenth century in works such as Thomas Haliburton's *The Clockmaker* of 1837, Harriet Beecher Stowe's *Uncle Tom's Cabin* of 1852, and in books by Horatio Alger, Petroleum V. Nasby, Mark Twain, and others. It was only near the end of the century that it started to appear in British publications.

Stool pigeon

Q. What can you tell me about the historical origins of the phrase *stool pigeon*?

A. These days a *stool pigeon* is a spy or informer:

> 'Everyone in the office has noticed the way he's been dandying up on certain evenings. And his wife is always phoning asking

where he is.' 'Everyone knows that?' 'All the girls know.' 'Does
his secretary talk about it?' 'You mustn't ask me questions like
that, darling. I can't be the office stool pigeon.'

London Match, by Len Deighton, 1985. This is the concluding novel in
the *Game, Set and Match* trilogy, the first two novels in the sequence being
Berlin Game and *Mexico Set*, which was followed by two further trilogies,
Hook, Line and Sinker and *Faith, Hope and Charity*.

When the phrase first appeared – in the US in the 1830s or
thereabouts – it instead meant a person used as a decoy,
usually to entice criminals into a trap. In that sense, it's the
same as the French *agent provocateur*.

A man informed the justice that a person had applied to him
to purchase counterfeit coin. The justice taking a quantity of
counterfeit dollars and half dollars which lay in the police office,
gave them to the man to sell to the person who had applied
for them, which he did, and the moment that he had them in
his possession, he was arrested by an officer stationed for the
purpose, and was tried and convicted for having counterfeit
coin in his possession, when in fact, had he not been supplied
by a stool pigeon, with spurious coin, he might have thought
nothing more of the matter.

Pennsylvania Inquirer and Daily Courier, 27 September 1839. The report is
headed *The Stool Pigeon System* and ends, 'A base and infamous policy, as
it strikes us, and calculated in the long run, to do infinitely more harm than
good.'

Most modern dictionaries say that the phrase came from
the practice in hunting of tying or nailing a pigeon to a
stool to act as a decoy, presumably to entice birds such as
ducks into range of the hunters' guns. The idea behind the
pigeon is obvious enough: birds will come down to feed if
they see other birds in the area, their presence suggesting
that it's safe.

But why a stool? You can hardly visualize a hunter being
prepared to traipse out into the countryside while carrying

a stool to fix his pigeon decoy to. It's just conceivable that
stool really refers to a tree stump, though that meaning of
the word has never been especially common. And in any case
how often would you find a ready-made stump just where
you needed it? There's something badly amiss with the
suggestion.

The phrase starts to make sense once we delve into the
history of words for decoys, of which there are a surprising
number. The one to focus on is the archaic term *stale*, which
probably comes from the French *estale*, applied to a pigeon
used to entice a hawk into a net. *Stale* appears in English
from the early fifteenth century; by the end of the following century it was being used for a person who entrapped
another and for a person or thing used as a lure or bait to
entrap a person. Another spelling was *stall*. At the end of
the fifteenth century this began to be recorded as a bit of
thieves' jargon for a pickpocket's accomplice, who acted as
a decoy to distract the attention of the victim. The verb for
this action evolved into phrases like *stall for time*.

It seems pretty clear from all this that the Americans
who started to employ *stool* for a decoy bird were using
yet another version of this old word. The use of *stool* in
this sense is recorded a little earlier than *stool pigeon* – the
earliest reference in the *Oxford English Dictionary* is to the
town records of Huntington, New York, in 1825: 'No person
shall be permitted to gun with macheanes [machines] or
stools in said Town'. The *Oxford English Dictionary* suggests
that *stool* is a short form of *stool pigeon*, but it seems much
more probable that *stool* came first, not least because there
are no known examples of *stool pigeon* applied to decoys, only
to people.

The other half of the expression, *pigeon*, has been used in
slang since at least the sixteenth century for a person who
allows himself to be swindled, a simpleton or fool, a sucker.

It seems that this idea formed part of the genesis of *stool pigeon*, so you might explain the term as 'a fool used as a decoy', though with a nod to the literal sense of the word. By the 1840s, *stool pigeon* had shifted from being a decoy to being an informer. By the 1920s, it was abbreviated to the now-dated term *stoolie*.

Strait and narrow

Q. I'm a journalist who was just about to write a headline containing the words *strait and narrow*, which I believe is the proper usage, from the Bible. However, I am fairly sure that my US readers would be more familiar with *straight and narrow*. Faced with the choice, I chose to phrase the headline an entirely different way. Am I being too much of a stickler? Or are there convincing precedents for the correctness of both?

A. Both have been widely used down the centuries. However, the evidence is that you would have been safer, and indeed better advised, to use *straight and narrow* for both your British and your US readers. *Straight and narrow* is now by far the more common spelling, both in the UK and the US, and is the one that's given as standard in dictionaries.

The oldest sense of *strait* is of something that's restricted or confined (it derives from Latin *stringere*, to bind tightly, which is the root of our *constrain*, *strict* and *stringent*, among other words); that's why that obsolete method of restraining lunatics called the *straitjacket* is correctly spelled like that. These days we know it mainly in the sense of a narrow stretch of navigable seaway, such as the Straits of Gibraltar. Its other extant meaning refers to a situation of difficulty, distress or need, but it usually appears only in the fixed phrases *dire straits*, for a situation of great need or extreme danger (a phrase recorded from the last decades of the nineteenth century), or *straitened circumstances*, for a person who is living in poverty.

A folk-etymological confusion between *strait* and *straight* has long been widespread. Not only do we see references to *straightjackets*, to the extent that this spelling is frequently offered as an alternative in dictionaries, but it also appears in *straight-laced* to refer to someone with strict and unbending moral attitudes, a form which dictionaries also now allow. In the latter case, the original was certainly *strait-laced*, referring to stays or corsets that were tightly laced and confining, but a term that by the sixteenth century had already taken on the modern figurative moralistic sense.

As you say, the source of the expression is a quotation from the Bible:

> **Because strait is the gate, and narrow is the way which leadeth unto life, and few there be that find it.**
> The Gospel of Matthew, Chapter 7, Verse 14, in the King James Version, 1611. The text uses *narrow* and *strait* in closely related senses to reinforce each other in successive parallel phrases.

Both *strait and narrow* and *straight and narrow* appear around the same time, the second quarter of the nineteenth century. Both forms are misunderstandings of the Biblical original: *strait and narrow* is a compression of the original that contains an unnecessary repetition of two words with virtually identical senses, while *straight and narrow* confuses the words *strait* and *straight*. Both are equally wrong and there's little to choose between them.

However, the latter has triumphed, not only because *strait* is now not well known but also because *straight and narrow* seems to make more sense, since it can be said to contain the idea of a road which is constrained, direct and undeviating, the true path of virtue that leads us unswervingly to our destination without straying into byways of temptation.

Tapping the Admiral

Q. What is the origin of the phrase *tapping the Admiral*, meaning to take a small quantity of strong drink? The story I have read is preposterous, about pickling some sailor, but I can't refute it because I don't know the real background.

A. Where did you come across that, I wonder? The expression was known among British sailors in the nineteenth century, but has been pretty much defunct for more than a century except in historical references. It could refer to legitimately taking a drink, usually brandy for reasons that will become apparent. In the tropics it was used by sailors for secretly drinking from a coconut from which the milk had been drained and replaced by rum. There was also a practice under that name of illicitly boring a hole in a cask of spirits in a ship's hold and extracting the contents through a straw.

Here's an example from what one might call its heyday:

> As Fort Simpson lay within the range of the competition of the Russians of Sitka, who used spirits in their trade, we had not been able here to abolish the sale of liquor; and such was the influence of the simple fact, that several of our crew, though not a drop was either given or sold to them, yet continued to be tolerably drunk by 'tapping the Admiral'.

An Overland Journey Round the World, during the years 1841 and 1842, by Sir George Simpson, 1847. Sir George, knighted by Queen Victoria on the eve of his journey, was a governor of the Hudson's Bay Company who in the 1820s had been governor of Prince Rupert's Land, the vast area around Hudson's Bay that was in effect owned by the company. In the journey recorded in the book, he travelled westwards across British North America, being the first European to cross the Rockies to Banff through what is now called Simpson Pass. He continued via Hawaii through Siberia, Russia and Europe back to the UK. He was then aged about 55 with failing eyesight.

Readers of a sensitive disposition should skip to the next item. Various versions exist of what I take to be the tale you mention but all purport to describe what happened to the body of Admiral Nelson after his death at the battle of Trafalgar in 1805. His remains, it is said, were put in a cask of rum to preserve them on the voyage back to Britain. Sailors who would do anything for a drink bored a hole in the cask with a gimlet and drew off quantities of the rum through a straw. So many did so that when the body arrived in London the cask was found to be nearly empty.

Though Nelson's body was indeed preserved in this way, albeit in brandy not rum (replaced with wine when his ship put into Gibraltar), the story is clearly, as you say, preposterous. For a start, the tale and the expression are older than Nelson:

> **Tapping the Admiral is still a favourite practical joke with Jolly Tars – particularly on India ships – it first originated from the puncheon of rum in which the body of Admiral Lestock was transported from Jamaica to England – the sailors soon made an end of the rum, of which when the ship cast anchor, there was not literally any remains.**
>
> The Times, 24 March 1790. A most unsatisfactory item, reproduced here in its entirety, which leaves us ignorant of the details of the practical joke (though we may hazard some guesses). Admiral Richard Lestock was best known for taking part in the English defeat at the battle of Toulon in February 1744, for which he was court-martialled. He died in 1746, unfortunately for the tale, not in Jamaica but either in London or Portsmouth, according to the Oxford Dictionary of National Biography, so there could have been no post-mortem immersion in spirits and no surreptitious cask tapping.

It is clear the legend was transferred to Nelson after Trafalgar. Similar ghoulish tales have been told in many circumstances, including one of a couple who bought a house that had once been an inn and who were delighted to find that one of the old casks in the cellar still held rum.

Only after they had drunk it and cut the cask in two to make plant containers for the garden did they find the well-preserved remains of a man inside. Jan Harald Brunvand, the American academic who has made a lifelong study of urban legends, discusses several versions of the story – he calls it *The Body in the Cask* – in *The Choking Doberman*. These include a French one about finding a body in a cask of imported Algerian wine, unfortunately only after the wine had been bottled and sold. Other tales tell of containers holding similarly preserved bodies of monkeys or apes that spring a leak on their way from Africa to museums; the leaking spirits are consumed with a gusto that turns to horror when the truth of the situation emerges.

Though the story about Lord Nelson is folklore, like all good tales it's grounded in an acute understanding of the cupidity of human beings, provides a moral lesson and is based on real situations. Important persons who died at sea in centuries past did indeed have their corpses preserved in a barrel of spirits so they could be brought home for proper burial (embalming didn't arrive until the 1860s and even then wasn't available at sea).

A related expression, *suck the monkey*, was current in the London docks in the nineteenth century to describe the practice of boring a hole in a cask of spirits to steal the contents; this may have built on the tale about monkeys' bodies preserved in casks of spirits.

Tattoo

Q. I've been wondering about the term *tattoo* and why it's used both for ink drawings on the body and for military festivals. The homepage of the Edinburgh Tattoo says that the word comes from a cry announcing closing time in the

inns in the Low Countries. How did it get connected to its
two modern meanings?

A. That sounds like one of those stories people invent to
disguise their ignorance of the real origin of an expression.
But just for once it's pretty much correct.

The original was the seventeenth-century Dutch phrase,
doe den tap toe, 'put the tap to', 'close or turn off the tap',
in which *tap* is the spigot of a beer barrel. It probably derives
from the way that the Dutch police closed the pubs at night,
by making the rounds and instructing innkeepers to shut
the taps on their casks. In time this became abbreviated in
Dutch to *taptoe* and became a colloquial phrase meaning
'Shut up!'

The first sense of *tattoo* in English was the related idea
of a signal on a drum to call soldiers back from the local
drinking establishments to their quarters at night. It's first
recorded during the early stages of the English Civil War:

> **If anyone shall bee found tiplinge or drinkinge in any Taverne,
> Inne, or Alehouse after the houre of nyne of the clock at night,
> when the Tap-too beates, hee shall pay 2s. 6d.**
>
> The standing orders of the Parliamentary garrison in Nottingham, issued
> by Colonel John Hutchinson, the governor of Nottingham Castle, in 1644.
> In modern money the fine would be about £5. Hutchinson was later to be a
> regicide, one of the signatories of Charles I's death warrant.

By the following century, the usual phrase was *to beat tattoo*,
hence one of our modern meanings, a rhythmic tapping or
drumming ('He beat a tattoo with his fingers on the table-
top'). It's also related to the US Army term *taps* in the sense
of a bugle call for lights to be put out in army quarters,
which was originally also sounded on a drum. The sense
of an evening military entertainment that extends and
elaborates the tattoo dates from the early twentieth century.

The other meaning of *tattoo*, to mark the skin with

pigments, could not be more different in origin. It was brought back from the South Pacific by Captain Cook, and appears in his journal for July 1769: 'Both sexes paint their Bodys, Tattow, as it is called in their Language. This is done by inlaying the Colour of Black under their skins, in such a manner as to be indelible.' It could be from any one of several Polynesian languages, such as Tahitian, Samoan, or Tongan.

Teach your grandmother to suck eggs

Q. I wonder if you would care to explain a phrase that my parents use (they're both in their 70s) that sounds extremely odd: *teach your grandmother to suck eggs*? Why would one want to do such a thing, even assuming that one had a grandmother (and an egg) to hand?

A. It does look odd, but its warning is well understood: don't give needless assistance or presume to offer advice to an expert, or to any elder or adult if you're a child.

> **'Don't pull that bandage so tight, doctor. You want to have me running over after you in an hour to come and loosen it.' 'That's it, Mehitabel; teach your grandmother to suck eggs.'**
>
> *The Puritans*, by Arlo Bates, 1898. Bates is now not much remembered, but he wrote five novels and six books of poetry as well as several collected works of criticism.

Many similar expressions have been invented down the years, such as *Don't teach your grandmother how to milk ducks* (which is in James Joyce's *Ulysses*), and *don't teach your grandmother to steal sheep*. These have the same kind of absurd image as the version you quote, which has survived them all and is so well known that it's sometimes abbreviated to just *don't teach your grandmother*. You may be sure that grandmothers never much sucked eggs; it was just a ridiculous image with which to punch the message home that your elders know well how to do all sorts of things you can't even imagine.

This is its first appearance in something like our modern form:

> **You would have me teach my Grandame to suck Eggs.**
>
> *Quevedo's Comical Works*, 1707, in a translation by John Stevens. Francisco de Quevedo was a prominent Spanish poet and novelist of the previous century.

Another early example was whimsically inverted:

> **I remember my old schoolmaster, who was a prodigious great scholar, used often to say, *Polly matete cry town is my daskalon*. The English of which, he told us, was, That a child may sometimes teach his grandmother to suck eggs.**
>
> *Tom Jones*, by Henry Fielding, 1749. Young Jones is rebuked by the schoolmaster Mr Partridge for daring to correct his Latin grammar. 'I have lived to a fine purpose, truly, if I am to be taught my grammar at this time of day,' Partridge said.

The idea behind it is much older. There was a classical proverb, *a swine (or a sow) to teach Minerva*, she being the Roman goddess of wisdom who would certainly need no instruction. This was translated by Nicholas Udall in 1542 as *to teach our dame to spin*, something any married woman (which is what *dame* meant then) would know very well how to do. And there are other examples of sayings designed to check the tendency of young people to give unwanted advice to their elders and betters, such as this doggerel version:

> **Teach not thy parent's mother to extract**
> **The embryo juices of the bird by suction.**
> **The good old lady can that feat enact,**
> **Quite irrespective of your kind instruction.**
>
> Anon., undated.

The cat's mother

Q. Can you tell me anything about the expression *Who's she? The cat's mother?* I've heard it used in a context in which you're talking about a woman and referring to her as *she* rather than by name.

A. All I can tell you for sure is that expressions of this type are first recorded around the end of the nineteenth century. They are corrections to children who refer impersonally to a woman as *she* rather than by name. Here's a recent example:

> **'We're not defenseless,' Tony broke in. He jabbed a finger toward Arra. 'She can defend us.' 'She is the cat's mother.' 'What?' Arra draped the cloth over the oven door handle, carefully spreading it flat. 'Just something my gran used to say. If you know a person's name, use it.'**
>
> *Smoke and Shadows*, by Tanya Huff, 2004. This is the first volume in a trilogy (all fantasy writers today are required by their publisher's marketing departments to write trilogies, in a curious reprise of the Victorian three-volume novel); it's an odd mixture of fantasy, horror, romance and mystery set in a TV company producing a series about a vampire detective.

Modern examples usually refer to it as a saying of grandparents, confirming that it has now gone out of use. And it always refers to women, not men, so we never get *cat's father*.

> **'I suppose,' said Brangwen, 'you know what sort of people we are? What sort of a bringing-up she's had?' ' "She",' thought Birkin to himself, remembering his childhood's corrections, 'is the cat's mother.'**
>
> *Women in Love*, by D. H. Lawrence, 1921.

How it came into being, I can't begin to discover.

Three sheets in the wind

Q. The phrase *three sheets to the wind* came up in conversation. Any ideas as to its origin? I have always used it as a measurement of how drunk someone is, but really have no idea what it means.

A. It's a sailor's expression, from the days of sailing ships.

Ignorant landlubbers think a sheet is a sail, but it's actually a rope (always called a *line* in sailing terminology), sometimes on really big sailing ships a chain, attached to the bottom corner of a sail. *Sheet* is an ancient mariner's term – it turns up first in inventories in English exchequer accounts in the fourteenth century – and it derives from an Old English term for the corner of a sail.

Exactly what it does depends on the type of ship. The expression dates from the days of *square-rigged ships*, so called because their sails were supported on long poles or spars called *yards* that were set at right-angles ('square') to the mast. In such ships, each sail had two sheets, one at each bottom corner. These helped to keep the sail at the correct angle to the wind (the yards they were attached to were hauled around by another set of lines called *braces*). If the sheets came loose, the sail would flutter about (or *shiver*) and the ship would wallow off its course out of control.

Extend this idea to sailors on shore leave, staggering back to the ship after a good night on the town, well tanked up. The irregular and uncertain locomotion of these jolly tars must have reminded onlookers of the way a ship lurched about when the sheets were loose. There were three sheets in the expression because a square-rigged ship had three main masts and so three principal sets of sails.

He talked a great deal about propriety and steadiness, and gave good advice to the youngsters ... but seldom went up to the town without coming down 'three sheets in the wind.'

Two Years Before the Mast, by Richard Henry Dana, 1840. He based the book on a journal he kept during a voyage in 1834 from Boston around Cape Horn to California.

Hans Schuyler has not got the wheel to-night – you see he was three sheets in the wind anyhow, and the captain says, 'Hans,' says he, 'don't tech [touch] another drop this night, or we'll never see another mornin' till we are resurrected,' and so he turned into his hammock and swung himself to sleep.

Miriam Monfort, by Catherine A. Warfield, 1873, a novel largely set in Georgia in the late 1850s.

There was a graduation in degrees of drunkenness. If you were merely *one sheet in the wind* or *a sheet in the wind's eye* you were tipsy. To be *two sheets in the wind* was to be more than merely merry. To be the full *three sheets in the wind* was to be on the verge of insensibility. There was even an intermediate stage between the last two: *to be two sheets in the wind and the third shivering*.

Wolf replenished his glass at the request of Mr. Blust, who, instead of being one sheet in the wind, was likely to get three before he took his departure from the dwelling of his brother-in-law.

The Fisher's Daughter, by Catherine Ward, 1825.

The battle-ground was now nearly deserted, and to own the truth we were, all three, at least two sheets in the wind.

Ned Myers: or, A Life Before the Mast, by the American writer James Fenimore Cooper, 1843. Although supposedly a fictional biography, it was actually based on the reminiscences of a former shipmate of Cooper's during a childhood voyage he took.

The version you give, by the way, is comparatively recent, since the original form – as you can see from these examples

– was *three sheets* in *the wind*. However, online searches show your version is now much more common than that with *in*, so maybe some day soon it will take over completely. The *to* version may be gaining ground because so many people have the mistaken idea that a *sheet* is a sail.

Through the grapevine

Q. What does *heard it through the grapevine* really mean and where does it come from?

A. Are you perhaps thinking of the Marvin Gaye song of 1968? (Or possibly the version a year before by Gladys Knight and the Pips?)

To hear through the grapevine is to learn of something informally and unofficially. The usual implication is that the information was passed person to person by word of mouth, perhaps in a confidential manner among friends or colleagues.

> **D'Erquy had heard, through the grapevine, that Eliza had been buying up bad loans from petty nobles like him who had been foolish enough to lend money to the government.**
>
> *The Confusion*, by Neal Stephenson, 2004. This is the second volume in Stephenson's Baroque Cycle that features a substantial cast of characters of the seventeenth and early eighteenth centuries, including historical savants such as Newton, Leibniz, Hooke and Pepys. The author calls it science fiction, because it's fiction about science, although it is at heart a sequence of sprawling historical novels, albeit with many anachronisms. The trilogy is so vast that the *Guardian*'s reviewer began by measuring it: 'The Baroque Cycle will occupy almost 3,000 pages and weigh four kilos'. (Luckily, my paperback set weighs a mere two kilos.)

But how can you communicate through a grapevine?

There are several expressions of this type, of which a well-known couple are *bush telegraph* and *jungle telegraph*, both referring originally to the system of communication by drum in Africa. These are historically rather odd, because they were created – at least, first reached print – well after the era of the telegraph. But that's because both are imitations of the first such expression, *grapevine telegraph*, which is where our term comes from.

The phrase was invented in the USA sometime in the late 1840s or early 1850s. It provided a wry comparison between the twisted stems of a grapevine and the straight lines of the then new electric telegraph marching across America. The telegraph was the marvel of the 1840s – Samuel Morse's first line was opened between Washington and Baltimore on 24 May 1844 and rapidly expanded in the following decade – vastly improving communications between communities. In comparison, the *grapevine telegraph* was by individual to individual, often garbling the facts or reporting untruths (so reflecting the gnarled and contorted stems of the grapevine), but likewise capable of transmitting vital messages quickly over distances.

Various early references suggest that *grapevine telegraph* was associated with clandestine communication among Southern blacks, especially slaves.

> **The Colorado ladies have their compensations; their husbands complain that they can get no goods, no machinery out from the States under a year from the time of ordering – that all business, all progress must wait this long delay; yet the ladies shine in the latest fashions of millinery and dressmaking. Modes that were just budding when I left home, I find in full blossom here. How it is done I do not understand – there must be a subtle telegraph by crinoline wires; as the southern negroes have what they call a grape-vine telegraph.**
>
> *Across the Continent: a Summer's Journey to the Rocky Mountains, the Mormons, and the Pacific States*, by Samuel Bowles, 1865. He referred to

States as a separate entity because Colorado had not then joined the Union; it did so in 1876, when it became the thirty-eighth state.

Tinhorn

The term became widely known during the American Civil War period, so much so that the phrase permanently entered the standard language. Soldiers used it in the sense of gossip or unreliable rumour, as was made clear in a diary note of 1862 reproduced in Major James Connolly's *Three Years in the Army of the Cumberland*: 'We get such "news" in the army by what we call "grape vine," that is, "grape vine telegraph." It is not at all reliable.' But it was widely acknowledged that the blacks' communications network was extremely useful to the Union cause, as John G. Nicolay and John Hay reported in *Abraham Lincoln: A History* in 1888, calling it 'one of the most important and reliable sources of knowledge to the Union commanders in the various fields, which later in the war came to be jocosely designated as the "grape-vine telegraph."'

As the telegraph slowly went out of use for most purposes, superseded by the telephone, so the expression *grapevine telegraph* became shortened to just *grapevine* and then extended again in set phrases such as *hear through the grapevine*.

Tinhorn

Q. I've been watching Westerns for years and the term *tinhorn* is always used to describe people who are new to the West. Where did the term come from?

A. My guess is that either you've misunderstood the way people were using it, or you were actually thinking of *greenhorn*, originally a young ox with newly grown horns; later on it came to mean anyone young or inexperienced, a

novice. It was originally a seventeenth-century Scots term
that was taken to the US by colonists.

> **Even when not serving, Nadal had ample other ways to win
> points in his 6-3, 6-2, 6-4 victory, storming all about the court to
> produce jaw-dropping shots that screamed down near lines and
> corners. He made Murray look like some greenhorn straggler
> just wandered down from Scotland.**
>
> *Los Angeles Times*, 2 July 2008.

The usual sense of *tinhorn*, on the other hand, is of someone
contemptible, especially a person who is pretending to have
money, influence or ability:

> **One thing was certain, and it was that wherever his Star of
> Destiny led him he would remain, underneath any veneer of
> polish which experience might give him, the barroom bully, the
> mental and moral tinhorn that Nature had made him.**
>
> *The Fighting Shepherdess*, by Caroline Lockhart, 1919. Ms Lockhart, the
> daughter of a rancher, became a journalist and a writer of Western stories.
> This one was loosely based on the life of sheepherder Lucy Morrison Moore
> and was highly successful in its day.

Tinhorn has a much more interesting history than *greenhorn*.
To find its origin we must delve into the murky world of
gambling with dice. One such diversion was usually given
the name *chuck-a-luck* in North America, a cruder variation of
a nineteenth-century game called *grand hazard*, whose name,
incidentally, had nothing to do with the old French and
British dice game from which our noun *hazard* derives and
which was the origin of the game of craps.

Chuck-a-luck was played with three dice, a chute that
tumbled the dice as they fell, and a flat area, marked with
the numbers 1 to 6, on which the players placed their bets.
The only bets possible were on one, two or three appearances of a chosen number. Modern chuck-a-luck games in
casinos usually have a wire cage in which the dice are spun

and which has given it the alternative name of *birdcage*. An earlier term used in Britain and sometimes in the US was *sweat-cloth*. A version long associated with the Royal Navy is called *crown and anchor*; this is played with dice whose faces instead of numbers feature the symbols of the four card suits plus a crown and an anchor.

Chuck-a-luck was unsophisticated and easy to set up, so it was the province of small-time gamblers on river boats, on street corners, or in low gaming establishments. Though the proper chute was made of leather, those with limited resources used a cruder one made of tin.

The term *tinhorn* referred to this cheap chute, an abbreviation of the fuller phrase *tinhorn gambler*. This was a term of contempt for these small-time operators of games of chuck-a-luck, whose patrons (*tinhorn sports*) played for small stakes. It also reflected the common view that all things made of tin were poor imitations of better quality goods (an idea that survives in our derogatory adjective *tinny*) and was also a pun on the existing sense of *tin horn* for a cheaply constructed and inharmonious musical instrument. The expression led much later to the invention of *tinhorn politician* for a crooked legislator.

Tinhorn gamblers tended to make up for the poor quality of their gaming equipment by a dressy appearance and showy demeanour, from which the later sense of the word derives. In truth, they belonged with the keepers of cheap saloons and three-card trick men, down near the bottom of the social pyramid.

To a T

Q. Our mother used to say that something described us *to a T*. I'm not sure if the last bit should be spelled as *t*, *tea* or *tee*. Can you suggest where the phrase might have come from?

A. It's usually written as *to a T*, though *to a tee* also turns up on occasion. It means that something is exactly or precisely so.

> As Oliver, Barney Clark fits the description to a T: He's small, angelic and suitably cowed by all the world has to throw at him.
>
> A review of Roman Polanski's film *Oliver Twist* in the *Fresno Bee*, 30 September 2005.

Jerome K. Jerome had fun with it:

> Harris said, however, that the river would suit him to a 'T'. I don't know what a 'T' is (except a sixpenny one, which includes bread-and-butter and cake ad lib., and is cheap at the price, if you haven't had any dinner). It seems to suit everybody, however, which is greatly to its credit.
>
> *Three Men in a Boat*, Jerome K. Jerome, 1889.

It was first written down almost exactly two centuries before Jerome used it:

> All the under Villages and Towns-men come to him for Redress; which he does to a T.
>
> *The Humours and Conversations of the Town, expos'd in two dialogues. The first of the men, the second of the women*, a satire of 1693 published anonymously by the lawyer, antiquary and author James Wright, who was also at times a translator, poet, essayist and historian of the theatre.

This rules out the possibility that it's connected with *T-shirt*, which has been suggested as the origin, but which isn't recorded before about 1920. Finding out where it came from turns out to be rather difficult. There are several candidates – one suggestion is that it comes from a *tee* in golf (or just possibly from curling). Another is that it refers to a *T-square* (a term that appears at about the same date), or to the correct completion of the letter *t* by crossing it. No evidence exists that links any of these to the expression.

The origin that most experts point to, rather cautiously, involves *T* being the first letter of a word. If this is the case, then *tittle* is easily the most likely source, since *to a tittle* was in use in exactly the same sense (with minute exactness, to the smallest particular), for nearly a century before *to a T* appeared:

> **FIRST INTELLIGENCER: The duke has more ears in court than two.**
>
> **SECOND INTELLIGENCER: I'll quote him to a tittle, let him speak wisely, and plainly ... or I shall crush him.**
>
> *Woman Hater*, a play by Francis Beaumont and John Fletcher, 1607. *Quote* here is in an obsolete sense, also used by Shakespeare, of noticing, observing, or scrutinizing someone or something closely. An *intelligencer* was a man employed to obtain secret information, an informer, spy or secret agent.

We know *tittle* now mostly in the set expression *jot or tittle*, meaning some very small amount and in which both words refer to a tiny quantity. *Jot* comes via Latin from Greek *iota*, the smallest letter of the Greek alphabet, which we also continue to use to refer to some minuscule amount; *tittle* is from the same Latin word that has given us *title*, but has usually been taken to mean a small stroke or mark in writing, notably the dot over the letter *i*.

Toad-eater

Q. I have been re-reading *Framley Parsonage* by Anthony Trollope and I wonder if you can explain the derivation of the phrase *toad-eater*? I can deduce what it means but the entire process sounds horrid.

A. The word is pretty much defunct, though *toady*, its shortened form, is still around for someone who behaves obsequiously to a person of power or influence. *Toady* is also a verb with a related sense:

> In other words, cut the boys in on it, sort them out, grease and toady and tug your forelock to these jumped up little twerps that presume they operate for the good of the game.
>
> *The Times*, 2 June 2008. The writer is fulminating against FIFA and UEFA, the governing bodies of football.

The Trollope quotation you came across is presumably this one:

> Mrs. Robarts had been brought up almost under the dowager's wing, and of course she regarded her as being worthy of much talking. Do not let persons on this account suppose that Mrs. Robarts was a tuft-hunter, or a toad-eater.
>
> *Framley Parsonage*, by Anthony Trollope, 1861. *Tufthunter* meant much the same as *toad-eater*. *Tuft* was slang for a golden ornamental tassel worn on their mortarboards by titled undergraduates at the universities of Oxford and Cambridge. Their wearers became known as *tufts* and their fawning followers as *tufthunters*. By the 1850s, *tuft* had been changed into the lower-class London slang term *toff* for a person sufficiently smartly dressed to pass as a member of the nobility and – by extension – anybody who was rich and powerful.

We have to go back to market and fairground quack doctors of the seventeenth century and earlier for the origin of *toad-eater*. It was common for such men to have an assistant to do the dirty work, often somebody young or half-witted or otherwise under the boss's thumb. As part of their sales pitch, such fake medical men sometimes made their assistants eat (or pretend to eat) a toad. The quack doctor would use his nostrums to make an apparently miraculous cure on his assistant and so enhance his reputation and his sales. As a result, *toad-eater* came to be a nickname for a servile assistant to a showman.

> **Be the most scorn'd Jack-pudding in the pack,**
> **And turn toad-eater to some foreign Quack.**
>
> *Satire on an Ignorant Quack*, by Thomas Brown, c. 1704. A *Jack-pudding* was a buffoon or clown, especially an assistant to a *mountebank*, a person who sold quack remedies, whose name is from the Italian phrase *monta in banco*, to mount a bench, the bench being the platform on which the mountebank stood to attract an audience.

As a natural-history aside: the European toad *Bufo vulgaris* was regarded as poisonous, since the warty glands on its skin secrete a nasty milky fluid containing toxins when the animal is threatened. Friends who are into natural history report they've handled toads with no trouble, but then they've not actually tried eating one; a dead one isn't poisonous, or so I've been told, provided you strip the skin off first, but the experiment is not one to be recommended.

By the eighteenth century *toad-eater* had generalized into a term for a fawning flatterer or sycophant. It could at one time refer to a dependant or a friend in humble circumstances, especially a poor female companion or attendant, which might be the specific sense that Trollope meant, though its proximity to *tuft-hunter* makes that unlikely.

Tom

Q. Very often, while watching British TV crime series, one hears the word *tom* used to refer to a (female) prostitute. Why should this be? A tom-cat, after all, is male. Is it rhyming slang?

A. It seems not to be, though it has been suggested that it's rhyming slang for *Thomas More*, a *whore*. This seems unlikely; I wonder how many people would have had Henry VIII's Lord Chancellor Sir Thomas More in the back of their minds when the term first appeared?

Tom has been around since the early part of the twentieth century but has become very much more common since the 1970s because of the slangy dialogue that has become usual in many British television cop series, starting with *The Sweeney* and now *The Bill*.

> In the wake of his resignation, we've been treated to sympathetic profiles of these 'high-class' whores, many of whom are described as highly educated. Maybe we should call them 'executive sex workers', since even referring to drug-addled ten-quid toms as prostitutes is considered an affront to their dignity these days.
>
> *Mail on Sunday*, 16 March 2008, drawing away its Victorian skirts in disgust. The resignation was that of the New York governor, Eliot Spitzer.

Tom, the common short form for the given name *Thomas*, has since late Middle English been a generic name for a man, as in *tomfool*, *tomboy* (a girl who behaves more like a boy), *peeping tom*, and the phrase *Tom, Dick and Harry*. The clue that suggests how it became connected with a woman may lie in an old bit of Australian slang, *tom-tart*, recorded since 1882. This had no implication of vice at the time, being one of the many slightly dismissive terms that males have used in various periods for a girlfriend or sweetheart, such as *donah, sheila* or *dinah*. It looks as though it was formed from *Tom's tart*, a generic name for a female companion.

Though *tart* is now an insulting term for a promiscuous woman, it was originally a short form of *sweetheart* and was a compliment. John Camden Hotten defined it in his 1864 slang dictionary as 'a term of approval applied by the London lower orders to a young woman for whom some affection is felt. The expression is not generally employed by the young men, unless the female is in "her best".' Hence, the subsidiary meaning today of *tart* as being an overdressed and flashy woman; it also accounts for the British slang verb *tart up*, to dress or make oneself up in order to try to look attractive or eye-catching, or more generally to decorate or improve the look of something.

Though the only recorded examples of *tom-tart* are Australian, our best guess is that it was taken there by emigrants who had learned it in England. In time, *tom-tart* was abbreviated to just *tom*, both in Australia and in Britain, and went seriously downhill to become a deeply derogatory description.

Incidentally, Louis E. Jackson and C. R. Hellyer, in *A Vocabulary of Criminal Slang* of 1914, said that a *tommy* was a prostitute; this is often cited in support of a derivation from the male name. It may have been a temporary form – it's otherwise unrecorded – based on *tom* or *tom-tart*, although this is unlikely, since the book was compiled on the west coast of the US (Hellyer was a detective in Portland, Oregon) a long way from the places where either term is recorded.

Top dog

Q. A display at a museum I visited recently featured pit-sawing. It said that the man who stood on the top of the log hauling on one end of the saw was called the *top dog* and the one in the pit below pulling the other end was the *bottom dog*. This was claimed to be where the expressions come from. Is this right?

A. The story's quite common and you will find it in other museum displays and also online. I remember coming across it in an exhibition at the former convict settlement of Port Arthur in Tasmania. The *top dog* was said to be the senior of the team, who controlled the cutting, while the *bottom dog* just contributed muscle power in pulling and pushing the saw. He had the worse of it because he was working with his arms above his head and got showered in sawdust.

Top dog and *bottom dog* are recorded from the US in the middle of the nineteenth century. I am sceptical to the point of dismissiveness about a source in wood sawing, because I can't find any early examples that use either expression in that context. The *dogs* were said to be the metal rods that held the timber in position on the sawhorses, though how the word might have been transferred to the two sawyers is hard to imagine. Only modern writers use the terms in connection with pit-sawing. The imagery is powerful and it's a neat story, too good perhaps to pass up, but there's nothing going for it by way of evidence.

It's much more likely that it's simply an allusion to dog fights, in which the dog on top has the better of the situation and is able to impose himself on the one underneath. But even the earliest appearances of the terms are figurative:

I know that the world, that the great big world,
Will never a moment stop
To see which dog may be in the fault,
But will shout for the dog on top.
But for *me* I never shall pause to ask
Which dog may be in the right
For my heart *will* beat, when it beats at all,
For the *under* dog in the fight.
Perchance what I've said I had better not said,
Or 'twere better I had said it incog,
But with heart and with glass filled chock to the brim
Here's a health to the *bottom dog*.

The Daily State Journal, Wisconsin, 15 April 1859. The author is not given, but is known to have been David Barker, a well-known poet from Maine. His death notice in *The New York Times* in September 1874 specifically mentions this poem, which 'was extensively copied some years ago and is frequently quoted'. This is so far the earliest known appearance of both *bottom dog* and *under dog* on record. It provoked a response a couple of months later by a man who titled his poem *The Upper Dog in the Fight*. All early examples – there are a number around this time – prefer *upper dog*, with *top dog* not appearing until later.

We concluded to visit the lodgings of Sam Collyer, who proved top dog in the fight of Wednesday, and see for ourselves.

The Morning Herald of Titusville, Pennsylvania, 3 July 1866. Sam Collyer was a Baltimore prize fighter of the period, who had shortly before beaten Barney Aaron of New York in a match lasting forty-three rounds, thereby winning $2,000.

Tracklements

Q. Can you tell me if the word *tracklements* is just obsolete or a non-word?

A. It's a real word, a delightful one, and not obsolete, just not widely known.

It's used mainly in Britain. It refers to tasty condiments

served with meat, such as mustard, mint jelly or spiced honey. I first learned the word when we bought a pot of mustard many years ago from the Tracklement Company, and the word turns up most often in references to that firm or to a similar business in the US.

Even among cookery writers it seems to be only an occasional relish to enliven prose.

> **Garnishes are traditional, down to the basket of tracklements – HP sauce, Colman's English mustard and Heinz ketchup – that accompanies the rib steak and hamburger.**
> *Independent*, 22 March 2003.

The English cookery writer Dorothy Hartley claimed to have invented the word, which she used in her book *Food in England* in 1954. She said that she had borrowed it from an English dialect word meaning 'appurtenances, impedimenta'. The problem for those tracking down its antecedents is that the dialect word concerned isn't easy to identify unambiguously.

One possibility is *trankliment*, which is listed in Joseph Wright's *English Dialect Dictionary* of 1896–1906. He cites glossaries from Cumbria, Yorkshire, Cheshire and Shropshire that spell the word several ways. It variously means a trinket, ornament or knick-knack, a toy, or odds and ends. Wright also records *tanchiments* from Cheshire and Lancashire as well as *tanklements* from Yorkshire and Lancashire. John Ayto noted in *The Glutton's Glossary* in 1990 that the word might be connected to Greek *tragemata*, the sweet course.

The founder of the Tracklement Company, William Tullberg, told me some years ago that his Lincolnshire grandmother used the word *tracklement* to describe accompaniments for meat, but that for her it 'included roast potatoes, roast parsnips, Yorkshire pudding and gravy

as well as horseradish sauce'. He added, 'When I set up
Tracklements, it seemed the obvious word to me for my
collection of mustards and herb jellies.'

We've no way of knowing for sure which of these is the
word that Dorothy Hartley had in mind when she presented
her new term, but it looks plausible that it's the Yorkshire
one. But that it has survived is at least as much due to
William Tullberg's borrowing of the word from his grandmother's Lincolnshire dialect.

Trig and trim

Q. While reading a shipping report here in New Zealand
dated 1877, I came across the phrase *trig and trim*, which
referred to a ship that had arrived at Dunedin from the Old
Country in superb condition. Are you able to provide, please,
a dissertation on its origins?

A. This phrase is extremely poorly recorded in the standard
references. However, I've found it in two very different works:

> **In her iceberg-white, holily laundered crinoline nightgown,
> under virtuous polar sheets, in her spruced and scoured dust-
> defying bedroom in trig and trim Bay View, a house for paying
> guests ...**
>
> *Under Milk Wood*, by Dylan Thomas, 1954. This delightful fable about the
> people of the little Welsh seaside town of Llareggub (spell it backwards)
> first appeared as a BBC radio play, starring the young Richard Burton. The
> description here is of twice-widowed Mrs Ogmore-Pritchard.

> **Miss Browne is a trig and trim little figure on the court as she
> glides over its surface. It is no wonder that her public love her.**
>
> *The Art of Lawn Tennis*, by Bill Tilden, 1920. 'Big Bill' Tilden, born in
> Philadelphia in 1893, was a famous and successful tennis player, for example
> leading the US Davis Cup team to seven successive victories from 1920 to
> 1926. His other book, *Match Play and the Spin of the Ball*, remains a standard

Going back a bit further, Marie Corelli included a naval reference in her *Vendetta* of 1886: 'And she has been newly rigged and painted, and she is as trig and trim a craft as you can meet with in all the wide blue waters of the Mediterranean.'

All these examples confirm that it means exactly what you suggest: that something is neat and tidy, in good order, immaculate. It is yet another example of a favourite trick among English speakers of creating reduplicated compounds. In this case, it has much the same sense as another phrase of the same type, *spick and span*.

The *Oxford English Dictionary* gives a good account of *trig*, which it says is from an old Scandinavian word *tryggr*, meaning faithful or secure. *Trig* today is principally found in northern England and Scotland and can mean someone who is nimble, brisk and alert, or a person who is neatly or smartly dressed, or someone or something that is in good physical condition, strong or sound.

Though *trig and trim* isn't recorded until the nineteenth century, it seems very likely that it had existed in Scotland and northern England for centuries. One pointer to this is that there was a closely related and much older southern English form, *trick and trim*. This form of *trick*, the *Oxford English Dictionary* says, could mean trim, neat or handsome. It was in use from about 1530 to 1630 and was very common from around 1550 to 1600. It seems that southerners converted the strange word *trig* into one that they already knew, so making *trick and trim* from *trig and trim*.

A very early example of *trick and trim* appears in Roger Ascham's 1545 book on archery, *Toxophilus*, which says, in modern spelling: 'The same reason I find true in two bows I have, whereof one is quick of cast, trick and trim, both for pleasure and profit.' It is surely relevant that the first volume of Robert Chambers' *Cyclopaedia of English Literature*, published in Edinburgh in 1843, converts Ascham's sentence to *trig and trim*.

The strong Scottish presence among colonists in the South Island of New Zealand accounts for the phrase being known there in the Scots form.

Trip the light fantastic

Q. To *trip the light fantastic*. I know what it means, but why the *light fantastic* part?

A. You're probably that much ahead of some readers, so let me nod in the direction of all those who know, while telling everyone else that to *trip the light fantastic* is an extravagant way of referring to dancing, a phrase rather more common years ago than it is now.

Just for once, it is possible to point the finger at the author of a saying:

> **Sport that wrinkled Care derides,**
> **And Laughter holding both his sides,**
> **Come, and trip it, as you go,**
> **On the light fantastic toe.**
>
> *L'Allegro*, a lyric poem written by John Milton, 1645. The Italian title can be translated as 'the cheerful man', and the poem is directed to the goddess Mirth. We've lost the sense now, because *to trip* here doesn't mean to stumble, but to move lightly and nimbly, to dance. And *fantastic* (or *fantastick*, as Milton originally spelled it) has here a sense of something marked by extravagant fancy, capricious or impulsive.

Milton's lines were borrowed in abbreviated and garbled form as a humorous way to refer to dancing, first as the phrase *trip (or ply) the light fantastic toe* and more recently even more allusively:

There, on the green sward, with no other covering than the sky, do they 'trip the light fantastic toe' until the moon and stars have shrunk into invisibility before the splendours of the rising sun.

Joseph Jenkins, by James Grant, 1843. Mr Grant was a historian and peripatetic journalist, later to be the editor of the London *Morning Advertiser*, the daily trade newspaper of the Licensed Victuallers' Association. Despite his active career, he also found time to write 40 books, virtually all of them – like this one – now forgotten.

'My daughter's one of the spinsters – Granby, my name; when we've had a drink, I'll make her find you a partner – that is, if you care for the light fantastic.' 'I should like a dance or two,' said Bailey, 'though I'm getting a bit past it now, I suppose.'

The Singing Bone, by R. Austin Freeman, 1912. The five short stories in this book all feature Freeman's detective Dr John Thorndyke, whom Freeman calls a 'medical jurispractitioner', this last word not gracing the pages of the *Oxford English Dictionary*, not least because we would now call Thorndyke a forensic scientist. The tales are examples of what's sometimes called the inverted detective story, in which the identity of the criminal act is known from the beginning and the interest lies in the way in which Thorndyke unravels it.

Such contractions – together with the change in sense of *fantastic* – makes the whole saying more than a little obscure to us moderns. That it has survived so long, at least in the United States, is probably due to this:

> **Boys and Girls together,**
> **Me and Mamie O'Rourke,**
> **Tripped the light fantastic,**
> **On the sidewalks of New York.**

'The Sidewalks of New York', music by Charles E. Lawlor, lyric by James W. Blake, 1894. The song was once under consideration as a theme song for the city. It was presumably the source of the title of the 2001 film starring Ed Burns, as well as two previous ones.

Just to reinforce how mysterious the phrase now is to some people, one online site renders the relevant line as 'We dance life's fantastics'.

Twaddle

Q. On Radio 5 on 15 January 2008, Janet Street-Porter and Simon Mayo agreed that *twaddle* was (or had been) an indecent word. I've never heard this before, and have always used the word freely. Can you enlighten me on its meaning and origin?

A. It has never been indecent. But I can guess why they should think it might be.

Twaddle has always been an insult for a certain kind of writing or speech that's variously verbose, dull, commonplace, vapid or nonsensical:

> **Everyone involved here seems so determined to play tricksy theatrical games that the heart of the show is in danger of being lost amid the pretentious twaddle.**
>
> *Daily Telegraph*, 6 June 2006. Charles Spencer was reviewing *Hear and Now* at the Gate Theatre in London.

Twaddle, meaning trivial or foolish speech or writing, has been in the language since the latter part of the eighteenth century:

> **Fanny Burney has taken possession of the ear of those who found their amusement in reading her twaddle (that piece of old fashioned slang I should not have dared to write or utter, within hearing of my dear mother).**
>
> A letter written in 1782 by Mrs Mary Delany, a famous letter writer, though even better known at one time for her flower compositions under the name of Hortus Siccus. You may judge the extent of her letter writing from its

appearing in collected form in 1862 in six volumes. Mrs Delany meant that the word was considered impolite, not obscene.

It's a variant of an older word, *twattle*, mainly dialectal, which hasn't been recorded much in print. That meant to talk foolishly or idly or to chatter inanely. A *twattle-basket* was a chatterbox. It seems to have been itself a variation on *tattle*, as in *tittle-tattle*, another of those many reduplicated terms that English is so fond of, which has also been written as *twittle-twattle*. The *Oxford English Dictionary* notes that these, and other forms, are probably echoic in origin and are primarily colloquial, not often having been written down. So it's difficult to work out which came first.

My guess is that Janet Street-Porter and Simon Mayo knew about the link with *twattle* and made the unreasonable assumption that it had a direct link with *twat* for a woman's genitals, a low slang term dating from the seventeenth century, whose origin is unknown. Of such wild guesses are folk etymologies born.

Under weigh

Q. An office colleague of mine insisted on writing *a project got under weigh* rather than *a project got under way*, whenever he described the start of some task. His explanation was that the expression had a maritime beginning, along the lines of weighing anchor to get a ship moving. I rather fancied the idea at the time, but I suspect that his story is pure fiction. The next time I use the expression, should I use *weigh* or *way*?

A. According to the best current style manuals, definitely *way*. But your colleague has the ghostly support of generations of writers. In fact, at one time, *under weigh* was

regarded as an acceptable spelling, if not always the standard one.

What happened was that the Dutch, European masters of
the sea in the seventeenth century, gave the English language – among many other nautical expressions – the term
onderweg, meaning 'on the way'. This became naturalized
as *under way* and is first recorded in English around 1740,
specifically as a maritime term meaning that a ship was
moving through the water as a result of the press of wind
on its sails (its broader meanings didn't appear until the
following century).

Some over-clever individuals connected with the sea
almost at once linked it erroneously with the phrase *to weigh
anchor*. The somewhat tenuous logic seems to have been that
once a ship had *weighed anchor*, it was *under weigh*. *Weigh* here
is the same word as the one for finding out how heavy an
object is. Both senses go back to an Old English verb that
could mean 'raise up'. The link is the act of lifting an object,
say on scales, to measure its weight.

It's easy to find a myriad of examples of *under weigh* from
the best English authors in the following two centuries,
such as Lord Byron, William Makepeace Thackeray, Frederick
Marryat, Washington Irving, Thomas Carlyle, Herman
Melville, and others:

> There were the bad odours of the town, and the rain and the
> refuse in the kennels, and the faint lamps slung across the road,
> and the huge Diligence, and its mountain of luggage, and its six
> grey horses with their tails tied up, getting under weigh at the
> coach office.
>
> *Little Dorrit*, by Charles Dickens, 1857.

It was still common as recently as the 1930s, but *weigh* has
dropped off almost to nothing now. One reason is that *under
way* almost exclusively appears in non-nautical contexts

and the link with *weighing anchor* has been broken. Another change, starting around the same time, was that the two words began to be combined into a single adverb, *underway*, on the model of other words ending in *-way*, especially *anyway*. Though this is not yet standard, with many style manuals still recommending that it should be written as two words, it has helped the shift in spelling back towards *way*.

Up in Annie's room

Q. My grandfather had many weird and wonderful expressions. When something was lost and could not be found, even after a thorough and sustained search, he often said it was *up in Annie's room, behind the clock*. Could you tell me the origin of this expression?

A. I recognized this immediately from my youth, many decades ago, because it was a phrase of my father's; I've even occasionally used it, to the mystification of younger people around me because it is now almost unknown. Could your grandfather perhaps have fought in the First World War, as my father did?

I ask because the expression was British Army slang of the period. Eric Partridge says that it dates from shortly before that war, but was 'at its height during it'. He explained that *up in Annie's room* was a common dismissive reply to a sergeant or corporal who was asking where somebody was. The implication was that the person sought wasn't just elsewhere but actively didn't want to be found. Partridge suggested the phrase was coined to suggest that the person was 'a bit of a lad with the girls', which sounds like wishful thinking. The absence of women in the barracks or battlefield trenches surely meant that *he's up in Annie's room* indicated that the person was no more to be found than was Annie, or her room.

It was after the war ended when the phrase had been taken back into civvy street that *behind the clock* was added. This makes more sense than you might think – it was common practice in homes to put bills or letters behind the mantelpiece clock as an informal filing system so they could be found when needed. Another, more fancifully extended, form is *up in Annie's room, behind the wallpaper*. The expression was taken to Australia – its first appearance in print was in W. H. Downing's *Digger Dialects* of 1919. A later Australian elaboration is *up in Annie's room, resting on a pedestal*. Dart players borrowed *up in Annie's room* for the double-one.

Up to snuff

Q. *Up to snuff* has long been used to refer to meeting some standard – or rather more often, in my experience, not meeting it. I found myself saying it today and wondered about its origin. Naturally, I thought of you. Can you tell me the origination? In other words, are you *up to snuff* with the history of the word?

A. The correct sense of the word *snuff* here won't be immediately obvious to men and women today. If we know *snuff* at all it's mainly in the sense of extinguishing something (*snuff out*), though that word originally meant to stop a candle smoking by removing the burnt end of its wick (the *snuff*). We don't immediately think of the curious habit of sniffing powdered tobacco up one's nose. But that's the meaning in *up to snuff*.

Several colloquial phrases are recorded that used this meaning of *snuff*, most of which date from the early part of the nineteenth century in Britain (such as the rarely recorded *beat to snuff*, *in high snuff* and *to give somebody snuff*), when snuff-taking was still common but less fashionable than it had been fifty years before. Up to snuff is the only one which became popular and has survived.

> **He'll not be sounded: he knows well enough**
> **The game we're after: Zooks, he's up to snuff.**
>
> *Hamlet Travestie*, by John Poole, 1810. As the title shows, Poole – a theatrical wit – was parodying the Bard. His trick was to couple Shakespeare's lines with colloquial expressions from his own era to make a curious double-line doggerel verse. It went down well with his audiences but today we miss most of the humorous references, which I suspect even at the time often weren't very funny – an evening of repetitions of a one-beat joke must surely have become tiresome. *Zooks* is short for *gadzooks*, an alteration of *God's hooks*, the nails by which Christ was fastened to the cross, an archly uttered oath even then going out of fashion.

Poole was using *up to snuff* the way people used it at his time, for somebody who was sharp, not easily fooled. This may have come from the idea of snuff being itself a sharp preparation, but more probably because it was mainly taken by men of adult years and some affluence (it was expensive) who would be able to appreciate the quality of snuff and distinguish between examples of different value. The evidence isn't there to be sure about its exact origin, though an early form of the phrase was *up to snuff and a pinch above it*, which confirms it did indeed relate to tobacco.

Whatever its origin, the meaning of the phrase shifted later to imply somebody who was efficient and capable; more recently still it has come to mean that something is up to standard or is of the required quality.

> **The schools may not want your clapped-out computer – it costs**
> **them $400 or more to bring an old Windows machine up to**
> **snuff, and even more for a Macintosh.**
>
> *Economist*, 11 January 2008.

Vulgar fractions

Q. Some fractions were, maybe still are, called *vulgar* fractions. I cannot think there is anything rude about putting one number over another, so why *vulgar*?

A. This bothered me at school and I can't recall having been given a good answer at the time.

The problem lies in the changing meaning of *vulgar*. It comes from the Latin adjective *vulgaris* that derives from *vulgus*, the common people. *Vulgate*, the Latin version of the Bible, comes from the closely related *vulgata*, meaning 'for the public' (it was so, when it was written, in the fourth century AD, when Latin was still a living language). *Vulgar* turned up first in English in the fourteenth century and then referred to something that was in common or general use or something customary or done as a matter of everyday practice. There was nothing disapproving about it. That old usage was used in phrases such as *vulgar tongue*, the language spoken by ordinary people, not one full of expletives. In time, *vulgar* went down in the world. It moved from meaning 'in ordinary use', and 'relating to the ordinary people', to 'commonplace' and then 'relating to the masses'; by the seventeenth century it had begun to assume our modern senses of 'lacking sophistication or good taste' and 'making explicit and offensive reference to sex or bodily functions'.

There's nothing vulgar in the modern sense about vulgar fractions, which got their name when *vulgar* still had its old meaning of something everyday or customary. The name came into use to distinguish 'ordinary' arithmetic from those highfalutin new decimal things, at first called *decimal fractions* to distinguish them:

To extract the Cube-Root, of any Vulgar or Decimal or Mixt fraction consisting of a whole number and a Fraction.

Thesaurium Mathematicae: Or, The Treasury of the Mathematicks, by John Taylor and William Alingham, 1707. As the title page explained, it contained a 'variety of useful practices in arithmetick, geometry, trigonometry, astronomy, geography, navigation and surveying. To which is annex'd a Table of 10000 logarithms, log-sines and log-tangents.' The term *decimal arithmetic* had come into English a century earlier, in 1608, with Robert Norton's translation of a book by the Dutch writer Simon Stevin; the English title is *Disme: The art of tenths – or Decimal Arithmetike. Disme* is his word for a tenth or a tithe, a variant of *dime* and said the same way, hence the name of the American ten-cent coin.

Writers of textbooks today do not always agree on what they mean by *vulgar fraction*, when they use the term at all, which is less often than in the past (Americans also know vulgar fractions as *common fractions*; yet another term is *simple fraction*). Traditionally, fractions of value greater than one were *improper fractions*, the other sort, of course, being *proper*, though all of them were *vulgar*. As *vulgar* has changed its meaning, some writers have assumed that *vulgar* means the same as *improper* and call only those fractions of value greater than one *vulgar fractions*. This is improper usage.

Waddle

Q. What is the origin of the word *waddle*? I have recently read about the famous Confederate captain, James Waddell, who commanded the CSS *Shenandoah* and apparently had only one leg and weighed around 200lb. This made me wonder if it was a corruption of his name referring to his gait, although I doubt it.

A. It's a neat guess but you're right to doubt it as the origin. There's no connection at all and the verb *waddle* is known from about three centuries before Captain Waddell's time.

The first known user is the Bard:

> **And since that time it is eleven years, for then she could stand
> alone, nay, by th'rood, she could have run and waddled all
> about, for even the day before, she broke her brow ...**
>
> *Romeo and Juliet*, Act I, Scene 3, by William Shakespeare, 1592. In this brief
> extract from a waterfall of words, Juliet's nurse is trying to explain in an
> outpouring of muddled exposition how it is she knows that Juliet is not
> yet 14.

Waddle is most often used of ducks and geese and other
wading birds, which is appropriate, since it's an extension
of *wade* by adding the *-le* ending that indicates an action
continually or regularly taken, what grammarians call a
frequentive. It's a member of a long long list that includes
crackle, crumple, dazzle, hobble, niggle, paddle, sparkle, topple
and *wriggle*.

Waiting for the other shoe to drop

Q. I've asked this of many people – and the type of people
who generally reply to these type of questions with a clear
answer and a 'how pifflingly undemanding' sweep of the
hand, mind you – but no one appears to know the origin of
waiting for the other shoe to drop. Where on Earth did it come
from?

A. I promise not to wave my hand in any manner. To be *waiting for the other shoe to drop* is to be prepared, often in deep
apprehension, for some consequential event or complication
to occur.

> **Worse, for long stretches of *Cassandra's Dream*, nothing
> happens; the movie is about 80 percent setup, 20 percent wait-
> ing for the other shoe to drop.**
>
> *Baltimore Sun*, 20 January 2008. The film was set and directed by Woody

Allen in London and starred Ewan McGregor and Colin Farrell. Other reviews were also unkind, the film being widely regarded as a low point in Allen's directorial career, one critic calling it 'a clumsy, clichéd morality play'.

Curiously, few of my reference works include this phrase. There was a discussion about it among members of the American Dialect Society some time ago, to no very positive effect, though it turned out to be an American invention that was a lot older than anybody thought:

> If nine out of ten of us hadn't heard that 'drop that other shoe' chestnut and molded our lives accordingly for the sake of the neighbor below us, what would be the end of us?
>
> The New York Times, March 1921. The reference to its being a chestnut means it must have been old even then, but we have no earlier example of the exact figurative phrase; however, it does also appear in the same year in Julia M. Sloane's novel The Smiling Hill-Top and Other California Sketches.

Its source must surely be some variation on the following tale, which may come from vaudeville or some long-dead comedian's repertoire, though nobody has been able to tie it down more precisely:

> The hotel was crowded and the clerk said he'd let me have the room only upon condition that I'd be very quiet. 'One of our oldest patrons has the room next you,' he said. 'And he's just a bundle of nerves. If I had any other room for you, I wouldn't put you next him, but please remember to be very quiet, so as not to annoy him.' I had a lot of things on my mind, and I forgot the clerk's injunction. I took off one shoe and dropped it on the floor before I remembered. I was awfully sorry about it, so was care-ful not to add to my misdemeanor by dropping the other. I took it off with great care and disposed it noiselessly. I got into bed as still as a mouse. Ten minutes passed, when I heard the transom over the door communicating with the next room opened violently. My next door neighbor thrust his head through. He seemed to be standing on a table or something, and he was

> fairly dancing with range. 'Darn you,' he roared, 'drop that other shoe.'
>
> *Washington Post*, 15 January 1905. In later versions, the offending shoe-dropper is usually said to be in the room above, not next door.

Closely related forms are *drop the other shoe!*, meaning to say or do the next obvious thing, or *the other shoe drops*, the obvious or feared event has finally happened. Both seem to have been known for most of the twentieth century.

Whim-wham for a goose's bridle

Q. I remember hearing part of a radio discussion on the ABC local station in Queensland, Australia, some years ago on local expressions, and among those mentioned was one similar to something that I recognized from my childhood, *a wing-wong for a goose's bridle*. Do you have any comments on this expression?

A. The original form, I have learned, was *whim-wham for a goose's bridle*, a version that is still remembered by some older people in Britain. It turns out to be a well-known Australian expression (though not used as much as it once was), a way of deflecting a question from an inquisitive child. 'What are you doing, daddy?' 'I'm making a whim-wham for a goose's bridle.' In other words, 'go away', 'stop bothering me'. As *whim-wham* is only known in Australia as part of this set phrase, folk etymology has often turned it not only into your *wing-wong*, but also into *wig-wog* and *wigwam*.

Whim-wham is an old English term for a trivial or frivolous thing, such as an ornament or trinket. It is now not much known, though not entirely obsolete. Its origin is mysterious, though it's clearly a reduplicated word, like *flim-flam*, and may derive from *whimsy* in the same way that *flim-flam* is related to *flimsy*.

Other forms of your expression that have been recorded in Britain include *a whim-wham for ducks to perch on* and *a whim-wham for a treacle mill*.

> **I should drive over to the station to see if he took a ticket for London, or Sheffield, or Birmingham, or somewhere. It's just like him. He has gone to buy screws, or something, to make a whim-wham to wind up the sun.**
>
> *The Weathercock. Being the Adventures of a Boy with a Bias*, by George Manville Fenn, 1892. The boy is 16 year old George Vane Lee, whose bias is towards invention and natural history, who lives with his uncle in a small Lincolnshire village. Fenn was a noted writer of adventure stories for boys in the second half of the nineteenth century; he was also at one time editor of *Cassell's Magazine* and drama critic of *The Echo* newspaper.

There's been a long history of nonsense phrases intended to put off intrusive enquiries about what one is doing. You might say you were *making a silver new nothing to put on your shoe*, *making layovers to catch meddlers*, or *making a whipple for a dooses poke*.

> **When a knowing blade is asked what he has been doing lately, and does not choose to tell, his reply is, that he has been very busy weaving leather aprons. (From the reports of a celebrated trial for gold robbery on the South-Western Railway.) Other similar replies are, 'I have been making a trundle for a goose's eye,' or a 'whim-wham to bridle a goose.' Sometimes a man will describe himself as 'a doll's-eye weaver.'**
>
> *The Slang Dictionary*, John Camden Hotten, 1859. A *blade* was an easy-going person, a good fellow, a word that goes back to Shakespeare, perhaps from the idea of his being figuratively sharp. The Great Gold Robbery, so called at the time, actually took place on a train of the South-*Eastern* Railway between London and Folkestone in May 1855 at which £15,000 in gold and gold coins on its way to Paris was stolen, a considerable sum at the time. At a trial in November 1856, it came out that Thomas Agar and William Pierce melted down the gold in a wash-house in the back garden of the

house where Agar was living in London. Fanny Kay, Agar's common-law wife, said in evidence that she had asked what the men were doing when they came in very wet and dirty, and they said, 'leather-apron making'. Cue laughter in court.

Whip round

Q. My wife suggested to her choir director that the choir have a *whip round* to get a gift certificate for a group of kids that they were going to sing for. The director, an American, was unfamiliar with the expression, so it had to be explained. This made us wonder where the expression came from. I never had the impression that it meant being coerced by a whip to contribute, but rather that one would collectively help to come up with enough cash. Any ideas?

A. This colloquial phrase does refer to taking a collection for an informal purpose like buying somebody a present or paying for drinks. It's mainly British and Commonwealth usage, not much known in the US, hence your director's incomprehension. Its history links the hunting field, the British parliament and the officers' mess in a regiment.

The original term was *whipper-in*, a term traditional to fox hunting in Britain:

> The *whipper-in* helps the huntsman in the field by keeping the hounds on the track of their quarry and not allowing them to become distracted by other wild or domesticated animals or endangered by going onto roads.

> *The Complete Idiot's Guide to Horseback Riding*, by Jessica Jahiel, 2000.

Whipper-in is obviously enough derived from the use of a whip by the huntsman. By the 1840s at the latest, it had been abbreviated to just *whip*. The book was written before fox hunting was officially outlawed in Britain by Act of Parliament in 2004.

In Parliament, there have long been officials of each party whose job it is to make sure that MPs attend the votes. In practice their role has always been wider than this – they're the disciplinarians of the House of Commons who make sure MPs don't step out of line or do anything silly, and especially that they always vote according to their party's call. By the later part of the eighteenth century they had begun to be jokingly referred to as *whippers-in*, by analogy with the hunting term; by the 1840s they, too, were commonly called *whips* (as indeed they still are, and not only in the British parliament by any means).

> **The parliamentary vote in support of this was only won after the whips had imposed the most rigid three-line whip upon Labour MPs who, in a free vote, would almost certainly have defeated it.**
>
> *Guardian*, 13 June 2008. *Whip* is also used for the notice sent by whips to party MPs to tell them about an impending vote. It is underlined once, twice or three times to indicate how important it is. A *three-line whip* is the most urgent, indicating that disciplinary action may be taken against any MP who fails to attend and vote.

This use of *whip* became broadened to refer to an appeal for individuals to take part in some activity – as we say, to *whip up* interest or enthusiasm. A specific sense of this came out of the British Army:

> **On ordinary days, when no strangers were present, and the usual mess allowance of a pint of wine each had been [consumed] ... a second would, perhaps, be placed upon the table, and those only who chose to partake of it would remain. After this an empty wine glass was sent round, and those who wished to sit longer put in a shilling each for an additional allowance. This was called 'whipping'; the mess-waiter took the money, fresh bottles were placed upon the table, and the company closed up to the president, to enjoy a still more social chat till bed-time.**

> *The Rifleman; or, Adventures of Percy Blake*, by Captain Michael Rafter, 1855. A young Irishman becomes an ensign in the Hereford Militia, in which he suffers many pranks, indignities and dangers during campaigns in the Peninsular War and in India. When the company *closed up* to the president, they gathered closely around him.

This military usage became more widely known, and any call for money among the members of any group also became a *whip*. The first recorded use is this:

> **If they would stand a whip of ten shillings a man, they might have a new boat.**
>
> *Tom Brown at Oxford*, by Thomas Hughes, 1861. The book is the lesser-known and less interesting sequel to the author's *Tom Brown's Schooldays*.

By the 1870s, this had turned into our modern *whip round*.

Woebegone

Q. I have long been puzzled by the fact that *woebegone* is used in a sense opposite to what the word seemingly means. I grew up with the expression *woebegone face*, meaning a sad, woeful, unhappy face. But if you take the word as it's spelled, it should mean that woe has gone, so the face should be happy and cheerful. Why does the dictionary give the reverse meaning?

A. It does look as though it's from a wish or desire: 'let woe be gone'. But the story is rather more complicated, and to answer it, we have to delve into medieval English.

    Woebegone is first recorded in *The Romance of Guy of Warwick*, of about the year 1300. At that date, people might say things like *me is woe begon*, grief has beset me or grief has closed in on me. Notice the word order, with *me* as the indirect object of the sentence, but put first. The verb is *bego*, which has been obsolete for something like 400 years, except for its participle *begone*. In medieval times it had a variety of senses, such as surround, overrun or beset.

Over time, the link between *woe* and *begone*, the past participle of *bego*, became so close that they fused into a single adjective, so tightly linked that they survived shifts in language and the loss of the verb *bego*. For some centuries it retained the sense of being afflicted by grief or oppressed with sorrow, misfortune or distress. Shakespeare uses it this way:

> **Even such a man, so faint, so spiritless,**
> **So dull, so dread in look, so woe-begone,**
> **Drew Priam's curtain in the dead of night**
> **And would have told him half his Troy was burnt.**
>
> *Henry IV, Part Two*, Act 1, Scene 1, by William Shakespeare, 1597. The reference by the Duke of Northumberland was to Priam, the last king of Troy, the city which in legend was sacked and burned by the conquering Greeks, who also killed Priam. The curtain being drawn back is the one around Priam's bed in his bedchamber.

This quotation in particular was so well known that it contributed to a revival of *woebegone* in a subtly altered sense at the beginning of the nineteenth century, not meaning somebody beset by woes, but somebody whose appearance made them look as though they were.

> **His hands hung down also along the back legs of the chair,**
> **till his fingers almost touched the ground, and altogether his**
> **appearance was pendent, drooping, and woebegone.**
>
> *The Small House at Allington*, by Anthony Trollope, 1864. Mr Lupex fears that his wife has run off with Mr Cradell. Despite its popularity, Trollope considered this, the fifth in his series of Barsetshire novels, the least of his books and declared its heroine, Lily Dale, to be a prig and a prude. The book had a renewed burst of popularity in 1992 when the then prime minister, John Major, declared it his favourite book during an appearance on *Desert Island Discs*.

We're now a long way from that medieval romance, but in continuing to use the word we retain a small vestige of middle English as a linguistic fossil. Other archaic forms in *woe* have also survived, such as *woe is me* and *woe betide you* (where *betide* means 'happen', from the obsolete *tide*, 'befall'), presumably because there's a continuing need for formulaic lamentatory utterances.

Your name is mud

Q. Do you know where *your name is mud* began? I've been told that it came from the name of Dr Samuel Mudd, who set the broken leg of John Wilkes Booth, Lincoln's assassin, and was subsequently convicted as a conspirator.

A. The facts about Dr Mudd are correct but he wasn't the source for this common phrase, which means that the person addressed is in disgrace or unpopular for some sin of omission or commission.

> ### If you forget their birthdays your name is mud.
>
> *Robber Bride*, by Margaret Atwood, 1993. This extraordinary modern fairy tale, partly based on *The Robber Bridegroom* by the Brothers Grimm, features Zenia, the classmate of three Toronto women whom she betrays and destroys, even though she is dead. Company boss Nicki is here ranting to herself about the problems of working with female assistants.

Dr Mudd certainly treated Booth and was imprisoned as a conspirator in the assassination. He was released in 1869 by Lincoln's successor, Andrew Johnson, after three years in jail, as a reward for taking over from the prison doctor, who had died during an epidemic of yellow fever. The story is often told that his name prompted the expression. However, even a cursory look at the evidence shows this can't be true.

**Mud, a stupid twaddling fellow. 'And his name is mud!'
ejaculated upon the conclusion of a silly oration, or of a *leader*
in the Courier.**

A Dictionary of the Turf, by John Bee, 1823. This first example is therefore
more than four decades earlier than Lincoln's assassination. Moreover,
the book is British, written under a pen name by John Badcock, a man so
ill-recorded that even his date and place of birth and death are unknown.
It's thought he was born about 1810 and died about 1830. A short life,
but one that left us lots of writings about horses and riding.

The expression comes not from the family name *Mudd* but
from the wet sticky earth stuff. It builds on a slang sense
of *mud* recorded in the previous century. A book called
Hell Upon Earth of 1703 includes the word in the sense of
a simpleton or a fool. In turn, this probably derives from
another that's two centuries older still, in which *mud* meant
the lowest or worst part of something, the dregs.